# The Art Of Record Production

*Richard James Burgess*

Edited by Chris Charlesworth
Cover designed by Chloë Alexander

ISBN: 0.7119.5552.2
Order No: OP 47821



**Exclusive Distributors:**
Book Sales Limited,
8/9 Frith Street,
London W1V 5TZ, UK.

Music Sales Corporation,
257 Park Avenue South,
New York, NY 10010, USA.

Music Sales Pty Limited,
120 Rothschild Avenue, Rosebery,
NSW 2018, Australia.

**To the Music Trade only:**
Music Sales Limited,
8/9, Frith Street,
London W1V 5TZ, UK.

Picture credits: Cover images supplied courtesy of Key Audio Systems Ltd/ Mackie Designs™ and Stirling Audio Systems Ltd.

Printed in Great Britain by Hartnolls, Bodmin.

A catalogue record for this book is available from the British Library.

Visit Omnibus Press at http://www.musicsales.co.uk

# *Contents*

# *Acknowledgements*

Thanks to my wife Connie and sons Ace and Blaze for allowing me the space and time to write, Chris Charlesworth for making the whole project possible, for his enthusiasm and his sharp editorial eye, Chloë Alexander for the cover design, all the artists without whom the book could not have been, and the producers, engineers, managers and friends who so generously contributed their time and tales.

Comments, corrections or casual conversation to Richard James Burgess, PO Box 646, Mayo, MD 21106-0646, USA; e-mail to burgess@compuserve.com.

# Introduction

Most people I meet outside of the music business have little or no idea what a record producer actually does. Even within the business the level of understanding about what they do and exactly how they do it is quite hazy. This book is designed to open what is normally a closed studio, for a glimpse at the wide variety of production styles, the types of individuals who do the job, the situations that a record producer has to deal with and to give some insight into how to become a record producer in the first place.

A common misconception is that a record producer is like a film producer. There are similarities but a movie may have as many as three executive producers. There may also be co-executive producers, producers, co-producers, associate producers and line producers. The producer deals with the director, the cast, the agents, the money people and the casting negotiations. Film producers very often put the whole project together, either raising the money or investing their own. They also handle the administrative side of the film making process. Many more people are involved in the making of a film than a record. Some record producers do get involved in deal making (more so in the United States than in Britain) and there may be multiple producer credits but generally the record producer is a lone gun for hire. He or she may take care of the administration but the role leans more to the creative side of the process like that of the film director.

Record producers have varying degrees of creative control over the material being recorded and wildly varying degrees of control over the performance of the artist. The exact amount of that control is related to the style of the individual producer, the types of acts he or she works with and the level of expertise and status of the artist.

The record producer will very often make the decisions as to how and where the record will be recorded, who, if anyone, will help to make it, what technical equipment will be used, how the budget will be spent, what material will go on the album, and how much the artist's creative input will be supplemented. He will also be expected to take care of the administration and paperwork.

The patriarch of record producers, Sir George Martin, says that a record producer is like a film producer and director rolled into one. Certainly it's a diverse brief. Versatility is the hallmark of most successful producers.

I've always considered the record producer's role to be like that of the blank cube in Scrabble. In the game the blank can substitute for any letter in order to complete a word. Likewise the producer needs to become (or be able to supply) whatever is necessary to make a successful record. To continue the analogy, in Scrabble you ideally save your blank until you have a particularly high scoring word that's missing a letter. Likewise the producer needs to expend his energies and expertise in the most high scoring or valuable way, always remembering the objective which is to make a successful record (whatever that means in the context of the project at hand). Referring to his changing role over four highly successful Simply Red albums, Stewart Levine said, "As a producer you have to be prepared to adapt to the circumstances, it's horses for courses and every day is different. Mick [Hucknall] wanted to take a larger role on the fifth album. When you have a situation where the artist is growing, if you are wise you help him to do just that."

"A record producer is responsible for the sound 'shape' of what comes out," says George Martin. "In many ways, he's the designer – not in the sense of creating the actual work itself, but he stages the show and presents it to the world. It's his taste that makes it what it is – good or bad."

Grammy award winning André Fischer puts it like this: "I know I'm here to be in the service of others. I can stand on my own, of course, but I'm a good accompanist. The nature of what I do as a producer is accompaniment."

On projects that have gone particularly well I've felt that the production process is one of discovery more than creation, almost like an archaeological dig. The archaeologists know there is something precious there. They may not know what it is, how big it is or even what it is made of, but their job is to uncover whatever is there without damage. Excavation may start with a bulldozer or picks and shovels. As the dig gets closer to the valuable artefacts the team will switch to much more delicate techniques, carefully brushing or blowing off the centuries of dust and dirt to expose the original beauty of the object. With some projects it is as if the record already existed before you started work on it. Maybe it's in a thousand scattered pieces. Those pieces have to be fitted back together and at first they don't make sense, but when a piece has found its rightful place you know immediately. The shape of each piece defines its ultimate position. Some pieces don't fit at all and you realise that no matter how much you try to make them fit they are from another relic altogether. Other pieces may be missing but are defined by the pieces around them and can be reconstructed. Even though you may never have seen or heard anything like it before, the work has its own shape, form and life. Once you discern that form the individual pieces slot into place.

# 1

# *What Kind Of Producer Do You Want To Be?*

## a) The All-Singing-All-Dancing-King-Of-The-Heap

These guys could easily be artists in their own right. In the movies and theatre someone who sings, dances and acts is known as a triple threat. This type of producer is a triple, quadruple or quintuple threat. They will most likely write the songs, play the instruments, sing the demos and may even engineer and program the computers into the bargain.

They are blessed with a natural, diverse musical talent, a rock solid sense of direction and their songs, arrangements, orchestrations, sounds and vocal stylings are instantly recognisable even though the vocalists themselves may be unfamiliar. That's not to say their records are "samey", just that they have an identity that shines through no matter what.

They're not a good choice for a band that writes its own material and intends to play everything on the record, but they're perfect for the solo artist who either does not write, needs a co-writer or is short of hit singles. Much in demand by record companies, these producers are the answer to many an A&R man's prayers. In one fell swoop they solve the problem of having to find a song and a producer. Their names carry a huge amount of clout at radio since, in their care, an unknown artist can get exposure that would normally be available only to an established artist.

Artists who will choose the All-Singing-All-Dancing producer usually fall into one of two categories: either the all-time great singers who do not write their own singles but can deliver someone else's song with conviction and great power; or the puppets who are often not even from the music business. These may range from established soap stars to good looking young tea boys who happen to be in the right place at the right time.

These producers almost invariably end up running their own production company or label. With the ability they have it's almost insane for them to be using their abilities any other way. The only artists it is worthwhile producing for another label are the truly great singers. Once they hit their stride they tend to have an unbroken run of hits for a number of years. Their style is usually very distinctive and can become a genre or at least sub-genre in itself.

The only downside is that when they finally drop out of favour or fashion it may be impossible for them to recover. Flexibility is not the hallmark of the All-Singing-All-Dancing-King-Of-The-Heap. The consolation, when it's all over, is the money. Unless they have been on a wilful mission to financial oblivion they should be able to buy a small country to retire to.

Generally this is a category you are born into rather than aspire to. The diverse range of skills need to be developed from a fairly young age, and the genre is often populated by production teams rather than individuals. Sometimes one of the partners is the creative genius, with the other being either the sounding board, the big picture guy, or the business brains.

Les Paul pioneered the concept of overdubbing (more like sound-on-sound the way he did it) in the late Forties and early Fifties on the revolutionary "How High The Moon". On that record he played all the guitar parts and Mary Ford sang all the vocals. This apparently simple recording technique would change forever the way records were to be made. Previously, artists performed live in the studio. The aim of the engineers and producers was to capture the sonic event as accurately as possible so that the original sound field could be reproduced in the consumer's home. Just like a Cartier Bresson or Ansel Adams photograph, which is an idealised or optimised representation of reality. As artistic as these photographers may have been, their photographs were dependent on what was happening when the shutter opened. Likewise, early recordings were a representation of a single continuous event that took place in a single environment.

Suddenly, with the technique of overdubbing, it was possible to create an entirely artificial sound picture. It was possible to have multiple takes of the same musicians. Musicians and instruments that didn't play together could be recorded at different times in different sonic environments. This was more like the way Man Ray had used the photographic medium. Using his instincts as an artist he had manipulated the photographic medium directly by placing objects onto light sensitive paper and exposing it to light. There were a lot of inventions and innovations that had to happen to bring us to where we are now, but once Les Paul crossed that bridge from reality to artificiality the stage was set.

With the advent of multi-track tape machines the process became easier and more widespread. Through the early Sixties records were still made largely by recording a band live in the studio. Overdubbing was mostly confined to vocals and additional orchestration. George Martin's arrangements on The Beatles' records and Brian Wilson's elaborate vocal overdubs on classic Beach Boys' albums such as *Pet Sounds* represent the pinnacle of this era of recording. It wasn't really until the early Seventies that artists such as Stevie Wonder and Mike Oldfield made the first successful commercial records by multi-tracking all or most of the instruments themselves. At that time Tamla Motown and Virgin, respectively, had to take a huge leap of faith to allow an artist access to as much studio time as they needed to painstakingly piece those records together without even the safety net of an outside producer. This was all the more remarkable since record companies are not renowned for embracing expensive, creative or technological innovations. (Digital recording took a long time to catch on, partly because of its negative effect on the bottom line; the same with stereo in the Fifties and Sixties.)

"I like to do everything," says Walter Afanasieff, producer of Mariah Carey and Michael Bolton, writer of hits such as Kenny G's "Don't Make Me Wait For Love" and Gladys Knight's "Licensed to Kill" and keyboard player on too many records to mention. "Some producers prefer to work with full bands and leave it up to the musicians to supply the music and the arrangements," he says. "I'll create the rhythm, the drum parts, the bass lines, the keyboard parts, the string arrangements, the horn arrangements, and the vocal arrangements. Even when the guitar players are in doing their parts, I'll be in their face every minute, every second, making sure they're giving me exactly what I want them to play. I like being responsible for every note on the record, which I suppose classifies me more as a producer/arranger."

Very often the only thing All-Singing-All-Dancing requires of his artist is that they sing. Teddy Riley says of his work with Michael Jackson and Bobby Brown, "Most of the vocal tracks were completed on the first or second try. If you can't come into the studio and sing a song the way it's supposed to be sung, then you don't need to be working with me. If the singer feels the music, and you've got the melody recorded beforehand, you're going to get the vocals down cold."

In the case of Stock, Aitken and Waterman, and latterly just Stock and Aitken, the artist's singing ability has often been secondary to prior fame. They laid the foundations for an empire by writing and producing a phenomenal run of hits for previously non-singing, but well-known soap actors Kylie Minogue and Jason Donovan.

Nowadays the new inexpensive digital technology makes it much easier, and more practical, to develop impressive studio skills at an early age. The influence of artists and producers like Prince, L.A. & Babyface and Jam and Lewis will hopefully inspire more kids to become proficient writers, arrangers and multi-instrumentalists. Those who choose not to become recording artists in their own right may well develop into the next generation of this very powerful and influential breed of producer.

Working as a team helps Jam and Lewis to handle several projects simultaneously. They have a saying, "We have no slack," that helps them to come up with a solution to any musical or technical problem. If one of them is experiencing a creative block, the other one will pick up the slack. Jimmy Jam calls Terry Lewis Vocalmaster and Terry Lewis calls Jimmy Jam Trackmaster which loosely defines the roles they play in the productions.

Although L.A. & Babyface no longer produce as a team, when they were collaborating L.A. Reid said of their highly successful and long-running relationship, "One of the biggest advantages of having a producing/songwriting partner is that you always have someone to bounce ideas off. Working by yourself can sometimes get a little stale, so it's better to have a collaborator around to help keep up the inspiration level. There are always ideas out there that you may not have thought of, and that your partner has humming around inside his head. Plus you don't have to second guess yourself when working with someone whom you trust. As my partner, Babyface, says: 'By working as part of a team, one always has the benefit of a second opinion'."

The vast majority of producers congregate in either London, New York or Los Angeles. In fact, the job can involve a lot of travelling. You very often have to go to where the artist is, where the record company is or where the studio is that has been chosen for the project. One beneficial side effect of being in the All-Singing category is that the artists will come to you, wherever you are based. Jam and Lewis are based out of Minneapolis, Teddy Riley is in Virgina Beach, Walter Afanasieff operates out of the San Francisco Bay area, and L.A. & Babyface moved at least part of their operation to Atlanta, Georgia.

## b) Humble Servant

No-one ever wants to own up to this stereotype. Almost invariably credited as a co-producer, this category of producer usually gets started as an engineer, programmer, musician or co-writer. They often connect with one particular artist early in their career. If that artist goes "mega" the "Humble Servant", having become a seemingly indispensable asset, is in line for a promotion. A co-production credit is the next logical step. Continued successful co-productions with the one artist lead to full production credits with other artists.

This type of producer is not a good choice for the artist who doesn't have a strong sense of vision and direction. He is the perfect choice for the confident, independent-minded, self directed artist who needs a right-hand person and someone to bounce ideas off. He will take care of the jobs that the artist doesn't want to deal with or doesn't have the expertise to handle; in particular the administrative, engineering and technical aspects of the production process.

In the case of the musician co-producer, the attraction for the artist may be his more formal understanding of music and help with the arrangements, songwriting or organising and rehearsing the band. Mostly these relationships become long-standing, very tight and extremely lucrative, even though the producer may be on quite low royalty rates. Very often one early relationship with an artist who turns into a superstar can turn into parallel relationships with two or maybe even three superstars if the recording/touring schedules can be synchronised.

The title may sound somewhat demeaning but the position is definitely not. It is usually a very hands-on producing role which for the right personality type is ultimately satisfying. If you are a hands-on detail person this could be one of the most fulfilling ways to do what you do best and succeed in a big way.

I wouldn't dare give an example of a producer who fits this mould. Most prefer to think of themselves as collaborators, which as we shall see is another category entirely. There are distinct differences between the "Humble Servant" and the Collaborator. The Collaborator is usually more independent and has his own working methods that the artist will, to some extent, have to accommodate. He has undoubtedly worked with many different artists and didn't build his initial reputation primarily as the right-hand man of one artist. The "Humble Servant" is much more likely to fit in with the artists' style of working and become almost like an unobtrusive extension of the artists themselves.

Steve Albini had something to say about humility in an essay he posted on the *rec.audio.pro* news group on the world-wide web. "Remember that nobody ever goes into a record store shouting, 'Give me the new album on label X, produced by producer Y, whose deal memo was hammered out by A&R guy Z and lawyers A,B and C!' People like records because they like music. Music is made by artists. You're just sitting in the chair with wheels and pressing the button. Do not forget your place! You are not the star, and you must be content with that. Do your job to the absolute limits of your ability – don't be a pussy about anything – but remember whose picture is going to be on the sleeve, and remember how much of their souls they're laying out for all to see. Don't get uppity, not even at three a.m. Don't demand more money or credit or attention than you deserve. As of right now, that's probably less than you're asking for, so start by taking a step backwards."

In many respects the "Humble Servant" is the most noble of

all the categories. Engineer/producers are the guys who garner the loyalty. These are the only producers other than the Merlin types who consistently make four or five albums with the same artist. Maybe the artists say about the Collaborator (the next category), "Oh we've collaborated with him, let's collaborate with someone else now." But an artist can get addicted to a "Humble Servant": "I love his drum sound, he knows how I work, we're comfortable, he doesn't get in my way." As Andy Jackson says: "You can roll into the next album and it's like riding a bike. You pick it up where you left off and you haven't got to reinvent the wheel."

For the right kind of personality this is a fantastic role. It takes a great amount of humility, which I believe every producer should have. At the same time they need to be quite independent and have a lot of initiative. They have to be able to take the bull by the horns and do things on their own without looking like they're trying to take over the project.

### c) Collaborator

I would say that the vast majority of producers not only fall into this category but would happily characterise themselves as falling into this category. Collaborative producers often come from bands themselves; rarely an ex-lead singer, most likely a drummer or bass player. This may be because they have a history of collaboration within their own groups. They see themselves neither as, nor even desire to be, one-man bands. They have most likely always enjoyed collaborative situations and bring that band-member-mentality to their productions. Often they will fit right in, almost as an extra member of the band. They usually prefer to steer the band towards a unanimous decision and use their casting vote sparingly. The Collaborator's hallmark is flexibility and a willingness to see the value in other people's ideas. Their own ideas are thrown into the pot with everyone else's and are not necessarily given more weight than another band member's. If the Collaborator had a catch phrase it would most likely be "the whole is greater than the sum of the parts".

This relationship is ideal for the musically secure artist who nonetheless would like to have a seasoned ear on site, someone to bounce ideas off and a different, sometimes even opposing, point of view.

The producer's experience can save the artist time, money and frustration. Although there are very few "can't be done's" in record production, there are a lot of *cul de sacs* that don't need to be explored and can be spotted easily by a studio veteran. The collaborative producer will steer the band away from time wasting endeavours and recommend methods and approaches that are proven to work for the particular genre in which the band is working.

Jerry Harrison is a good example of a collaborative producer and his approach to producing was characterised in the comment, "I might experiment in the future with playing with more of the bands I produce. But these bands I work with have all been so self-contained that I didn't want to step on anyone's toes. Most of these bands have keyboard and guitar players, and I'm really trying to get their performance down. My attitude is that it's their album, and I'm the one who's facilitating making that album."

### d) Merlin The Magician

> *"The best leader is the one who has sense enough to pick good men to do what he wants done, and the self restraint to keep from meddling with them while they do it."* (Theodore Roosevelt)

Merlin is often an intangible force in the proceedings. Perhaps mysteriously, Merlin can garner great loyalty from the artist and record company even though he may spend most of his time on the tennis court, the phone, in meetings, in the car or wherever else producers go when liberated from the studio. In a way he acts like a hands-on A&R consultant, coming in with an objective/ subjective view frequently referred to as "fresh ears".

Successful Los Angeles based engineer John X (Black Grape) had the experience of working on a four-month album project with a very famous producer who managed to appear for half an hour in the entire four months. Despite this, when the band would go out at night after the session, if anyone asked what they were doing they would proudly announce that they were recording an album with XYZ (the famous absentee producer). I guess the only explanation here is that this particular producer had built such a level of kudos and the band were so impressed by his reputation and track record that just by being associated with him they felt that some of his success would rub off on them.

There are many other fantastic stories around about Merlin. One in particular relates to a band that had just delivered their album. In classic form their A&R person said "I don't hear a single". They were told to write more songs and come up with a hit single before the company would release the album. This is by no means an unfamiliar scenario. What followed was the common outcome of this kind of situation. The band holed up in a New York City hotel for about a month attempting to create the required commercial masterpiece. They were thoroughly confused. At the tail end of the month Merlin, who had nothing to do with this particular project, happened to come by the writing room with a mutual acquaintance. The band were putting the finishing touches to the N'th contender. They were playing it through as he walked into the room. When they finished playing Merlin pronounced the song a smash. They relayed their depressing tale of what was going on with the album and their state of confusion over the last minute pressure to deliver a hit song. His response was: "I believe in this song so much that I'll produce it myself." He promptly picked up the phone, called the previously worried, but suddenly surprised and delighted, A&R person in England. He told him he'd just heard a number one song and that he would produce it himself. The A&R guy could barely contain himself. Normally, neither he nor the band in question would have had access to a producer of this calibre and reputation. Terms were agreed, the contract was quickly drawn up and Securicor trucks were dispatched with Merlin's advance money. Production would commence a.s.a.p. Merlin would not be seen again for the duration of the project. The band recorded and mixed the single on their own without so much as a phone call from Merlin. It subsequently grazed the Top Ten and launched the group into a short cycle of reasonably healthy single and album sales. Not Number One admittedly, but everyone concerned was happy. Merlin took the money and the credit and moved on to even bigger and better things.

So what actually happened here? Was Merlin's power so great that his pronouncement that the song would be a hit was sufficient to lift it straight into the charts? Was it his depth of experience that enabled him to walk into a room and immediately recognise a hit that might have been passed over by a lesser mortal? Was it his enthusiasm for the song that inspired the record company to market and promote the single effectively? Was it the mere presence of his hallowed name on the label copy that carried the record through to radio? Could he have walked in on any day in that month of writing, made the same pronouncement about any other song and achieved the same result? Who knows, but it sure is a nice way to make a living.

If Merlin does decide to spend some time in the studio the direction he gives can range from the very specific, subjective and detailed to the vague, general and philosophical. Sometimes it can be quite obscure. Brian Eno rejects the idea that there are "correct" ways to do things and thinks that we should "earn and enjoy from all the different ways we *can* do things." In keeping with his philosophy, in 1975 he developed his "Oblique Strategy" cards. They featured over one hundred possibilities to help alleviate uncertainty and stasis in the studio. Tony Visconti first showed them to me after he had worked with Eno on a David Bowie album. The cards work on a similar principle to the I-Ching. If you arrive at a point where you are unsure or there is some disagreement about what to do next, choose a card. The advice ranges from "consider a different fading system" to "look closely at the most embarrassing details and amplify them". If all else fails you might get lucky and pick the one that says "go outside and shut the door".

Eno himself says. "Normally I don't stay with the project for the whole time. I deliberately keep out so I can come back in and hear things with fresh ears. Some things will seem completely obvious to me straight away. Like "that doesn't work, that works brilliantly, this is confused". I can very quickly, within an hour's listening, set up an agenda which says, "This we must talk about philosophically, we have to look at that structurally, we have to look at this in terms of whether it's going anyway like the direction of the rest of the record". I set agendas like that, to the extent that I will say that I want to take control of this song for, say, half a day. For half a day I'll say what to do and we'll see if it works. Sometimes it doesn't. And of course any other participant can take the same role. It's very good to be in a working relationship with people and you can say, 'OK, I tried it and it doesn't work', and they say 'Yep, fine'. Fortunately most of the relationships I am in are like that. You have to have the respect for people who say 'look you're grown up, you can take an option and not pretend that it's interesting when it isn't'."

David Bowie once said about working with Eno, "It was a bit like being four-years-old again and having a rather fun uncle who could produce coins out of his ear." Flood (producer of P.J.Harvey, U2, Depeche Mode and Nine Inch Nails) who worked with Eno on the U2 project said of him, "His psychological approach is something that very much influenced me – the way that people can be encouraged, and how to judge a situation and discover what's happening, why it's happening and what its possible outcomes could be. U2's Bono said, 'With him we discovered the spirit of our music and a new confidence in ourselves'."

Talented and successful artists are not renowned for casually praising producers. As mysterious and obscure as Merlin can be, to be able to inspire these kinds of responses from major artists is a significant achievement.

Talking about his overall attitude to producing, Rick Rubin (Beastie Boys, Run DMC, Red Hot Chili Peppers and co-founder of Def Jam and Def American Records) said, "I look at producing in a very different way from most other producers. I think of it as being more like the director of a film or a play. By that, I mean that for the technical side of it, I hire engineers who I think are competent, much like a director hiring a cinematographer, and I let them do their gig. That doesn't mean I don't have very strong ideas about what I want to hear, but I don't technically know all the bells and whistles to make it sound that way."

Chili Peppers bassist Flea says, "Rick Rubin is an incredibly great producer. He keeps a balance between work and relaxing, maintains complete clarity and focus. He keeps his objectivity while we are completely caught up and so emotional. It might not be great for all bands, but we don't need that emotional push. We're just exploding and coming up with all kinds of stuff, and he helps us harness our energy. And he helps musically, making sure that every song is well-crafted. He's had a great track record with hit songs, but you can't really compare any other situation with this one." Singer Anthony Kiedis puts it most succinctly, "Rick has encompassed all the things we need in a producer."

"And he knows when to lie back on the couch and not say a word," adds guitarist John Frusciante. "As a result of his coolness, we've found the accurate, well-rounded colours of music that represent what this band is all about." Flea continues, "Some producers look at little things as they're going on, as opposed to getting the big picture of a song, or an album. Rick's suggestions don't interfere with the emotional feel. The most important thing is the energy and the soul of the music."

There's a certain point at which a producer can simply put his name on a record, get paid and just not show up. This is more common in America than in Europe. Ros Earls says, "I'm not sure whether the Americans are more honest about it. It happens sometimes that Flood is asked to mix something and before he's even done it they're saying 'you're great, you're great'. Flood is really adamant that he won't lend his name to something. He gets really angry about the way a name becomes public property, the way a name can help get a record on the radio. They're not really listening to [the work]. The kind of people I represent are very hands-on and involved. That's not to say I disapprove [of the more managerial approach]."

Merlin is undoubtedly the hardest producer-type to aspire to. Mostly we are the kind of producers we are because of our basic personality types. Age and experience are obviously modifying factors. It would be unusual for Merlin to be directly responsible for a great deal of the specific musical and technical content of the record. This is a high concept role, more to do with the overall direction and energy of the album, and the other intangibles that drive an artist's career forward. Merlin has to be able to identify talent and harness it. He is usually charismatic, powerful and extremely successful. A natural leader with an ability to see the "big picture", and not get bogged down in the details.

Merlin's occasional forays into the studio and casually dropped pearls of wisdom can earn him the same place in rock'n'roll immortality, and on the "five hundred richest" lists as weeks, months or maybe even years of arduous labour by a more conventional hands-on producer. For the producer who spends his waking hours head down over a hot console, the mere suggestion of the existence of these mystical free-spirits can be alternately frustrating, infuriating and awe inspiring.

# 2

# *How Do You Get Started?*

*"Nothing in the world can take the place of persistence. Talent will not; nothing is more common than unsuccessful men with talent. Genius will not; unrewarded genius is almost a proverb. Education will not; the world is full of educated derelicts. Persistence and determination alone are omnipotent."* Calvin Coolidge.

## What Are The Ways In?

There are seven routes, or launching pads, from which most successful record producers choose to get started:

1) The musician or artist
2) The audio engineer
3) The songwriter
4) The DJ
5) The home studio hobbyist
6) The finding a new act route
7) The who-the-hell-knows-how-they-got-started route.

Eventually, like most British motorways, this seven-lane freeway narrows down to one classic, catch-22, bottle-neck – you have to prove that you can actually produce a record before anyone will pay you money to do it or at least be a fast enough talker to convince them to let you have a go. The fastest talkers usually come from the seventh category, but we'll take them all in turn . . .

## 1) As A Musician Or Artist?

You could get your break if you have an impeccable musical reputation, possibly as an arranger or musical director, but it's more likely that you will have to produce your own very high quality demos or maybe co-produce your band's first few recordings. The latter is an excellent way to get started, largely because you have the benefit of learning at the feet of a master (one hopes) before you are thrown in the deep end.

Producing your own demos is a tried and tested route but there are several distinct disadvantages: you will be working in a vacuum; you usually need some capital to get started; and you will need to either hire a commercial studio or set up your own place – often in your bedroom, which is guaranteed to make you popular with your soul-mate! Even in these times of incredibly inexpensive digital recording equipment, a decent home set-up capable of moving you into the big league will be damaging to your financial health (unless you have a trust fund you can raid).

Certain techniques that are common currency amongst the pro's may take on the mysteries of the most arcane forms of alchemy when you are locked in your bedroom with your so-far disappointing demo and very big ambitions.

I'm biased, for sure, but I do think there are two major advantages in coming to producing from a music background: you speak the same language as the musicians and artists, and you know how it feels on the other side of the glass.

I can never forget the frustration of standing in the studio after having given my all on the last take and watching the producer, through the glass, either chatting on the phone, or having a discussion with someone in the control room. It's a very simple thing to push the talkback button and let the artist or musicians know what is going on, but it may not occur to someone who has never been a studio performer. A musician also instinctively understands how much more enjoyable the session is when the engineer has done his preparation.

Albhy Galuten who produced hits with The Bee Gees, Andy Gibb, Samantha Sang, Barbra Streisand, Kenny Rogers, Diana Ross and Dionne Warwick developed his career from his beginnings as a guitarist and keyboard player through string arranging, songwriting and eventually producing. His studio experience began at the legendary Ardent Studios in Memphis. He landed a job assisting Tom Dowd at Criteria in Miami by hanging out with friends who had been hired as part of the Atlantic rhythm section in Miami. During this time he learned his craft on records such as Eric Clapton's *Layla* and The Allman Brothers' *Eat A Peach.* The assisting job eventually led to a staff producer position with Atlantic. His musical training began with piano lessons through high school, a couple of years at Berklee in Boston and playing in several bands. He says, "There are two levels of learning: theory, notes, understanding what's going on, the technique. But there is also the development of the ears. I discovered that in the studio with Tommy Dowd and Jerry Wexler."

Another successful producer who got his start through arranging is Tony Visconti. He eventually worked with Procol Harum, The Move, T. Rex, Joe Cocker, David Bowie, Badfinger, Gentle Giant, Thin Lizzy, Boomtown Rats, The Stranglers, The Alarm and U2. In 1967 he left America to settle in Britain. "In American studios at that time, it was still the old régime where you had to make an album in three days. You'd take six to twelve hours for recording, three hours to mix it. I was being trained as a record producer in New York by my publishing company. They'd tell me what budgets were available. And I was doing a little talent scouting. I was a rejected songwriter, so in one fell swoop I was fired as a songwriter and hired as a record producer because my demos were good. Anyway, it seemed like all the records I was buying were British records, and then I would read articles about how The Beatles took one week per song to make *Revolver* – like thirteen weeks on an album – and I thought, just give me two weeks and I'll make a great album!

"Then, through very lucky circumstances, I met Denny Cordell who was the producer of Procol Harum and Joe Cocker and The Move and Georgie Fame. He had come to New York to make a record with Georgie Fame called 'Because I Love You' and he was hiring all these good players like Clark Terry to play on it, but he didn't have a chart. He thought he was just going to play them the demo, and then they'd write their own charts. So I said, 'That's going to cost you a fortune in New York City'. So I wrote a quick arrangement and copied out the trumpet line from the demo, and then the session went very well, and he hired me to be his assistant in London. I worked for Denny Cordell for two years, and through him I made a lot of contacts. I met both David Bowie and Marc Bolan during those two years. I met Bowie through his publisher, and Marc Bolan I found on my own – I went talent scouting and found him playing in a club one night. Then having hits with those two guys, people came to me."

Jerry Harrison of Talking Heads says that his co-production role on *Remain In Light* with the rest of the band and Brian Eno helped get him started as a producer. "By the time we did that album, the barriers between musicians and producer were being broken down 'cause we were writing the songs in the studio. So there were times when Brian was playing parts and we would be saying, 'Well, Brian, that's not right. Try something else'. So there was a lot of back and forth at that point. I think it was those experiences making the albums with Brian that kind of gave me the knowledge, you might say, to go on to start working with other people as a producer."

Walter Afanasieff started as a musician and worked for Bay area producer Narada Michael Walden. Eventually he stepped into the production role himself. Speaking about their working relationship in 1991 he said: "I've learned a great deal from Narada, but now it's time to leave the nest and set up my own shop. I will always draw upon what I've learned from him. However, I've been anxious to be doing things on my own for a while, and now's a great time for me to move on. We'll always be great friends, and now we'll be working neighbours. He's a great guy and incredibly talented."

Danny Saber has risen to prominence with his mid-Nineties productions for Black Grape. When I first met him in 1989 he worked in a tuxedo store in Hollywood. He was playing in a band with unsigned artist Issa Joone and making eight-track demos in her garage. He started out wanting to be a musician, Jimi Hendrix was a big influence. As a teenager he would play rhythm guitar on one tape recorder, play that tape back and record a solo over it onto another machine. He says: "When I was 15 I would go in the studio and tell the stoned-out engineer from the Sixties that I wanted to double my guitar. He would look at me and think who's this punk. Then I would nail it. With recording, it was the one thing in life that I always seemed to get right, even before I knew what I was doing. So that all led to the producing thing. At first I would do tracks with little rap bands."

Around this time he signed a publishing deal with EMI. That led to writing opportunities with a number of artists in the US and UK. His first real break was when he produced Proper Ground, Madonna's first signing for her own Maverick Records. The record was not a hit but opened the door for more work. "Even when I first met you I always wanted to produce but I had a long way to go," he told me. "I've known for a long time even since I was working with bands. I was always the one who said 'do this do that'."

Unfortunately, simply having the desire to be a record producer is not usually enough. The known universe is loaded with would-be record producers. Clearly there is a groove in the time/space continuum because an inordinate number of these aspirants seem to have slipped into the greater Los Angeles area. Most of these characters will regale you with stories about how they just didn't get the breaks or the opportunities did not open up for them. They're frequently only one (very expensive) piece of equipment away from completing their home studio to the level that they can finally deliver the killer tracks.

To be sure, everyone needs a break. No matter how talented an individual may be, multiple unknown factors have to align themselves before raw talent translates into industry success. When it comes to opportunity I believe you have to create, finagle, prepare for and at the very least develop an eagle eye for identifying what will most likely be a fleeting opportunity; a brief, fast-moving window in time that opens up before you. If you are ready, you dive through. If you are not, maybe it'll come around again and maybe it won't.

I once played with a lounge band as a substitute drummer whenever the regular drummer wanted a night off. This was a pretty good band. They played all the old jazz standards and one of the guys had actually played with Charlie Parker. Some of the musicians were full-time and some of them had day jobs. I was very young at the time but I must have had an invisible sign hanging round my neck saying that I was going somewhere in the business. At every break one of the regular players would buttonhole me and tell me how much he hated his day job and that if he just got the right breaks he would "go pro". I probably played this gig once every two or three weeks over a period of about six months. This guy's favourite band (this was the

Seventies) was The Carpenters. It gradually became apparent what he thought would constitute a lucky break. In this scenario The Carpenters would happen upon this establishment one evening having just lost their guitarist. In the middle of their fine dining experience they would gradually realise that the answer to their personnel problems was performing before their very eyes. Of course the happy end to this fairy tale is that they would whisk him away on a whirlwind agenda of tours, recording and personal appearances.

Now I may have stretched this story slightly but the basic elements are not only true but applicable in a wider sense to the actions of a lot of individuals supposedly wishing to break into the big time of the music business.

I've worked with musicians, engineers and even some record company executives who also seem to operate on the basis that a giant hand is going to reach down, pluck them from obscurity and thrust them into the forefront of the international record production arena.

I would never underplay the importance of luck, divine providence, good fortune or whatever you want to call it. However, without exception the success stories that I have encountered have been attached to individuals who not only exhibited raw talent but also persistence, determination and a willingness to take risks.

## 2) As An Audio Engineer . . .

. . . you will generally start at the bottom of the pile, making tea and coffee for the stars, the assistant stars and probably the demi-friend of the assistant to the assistant stars. Short of an engineer dying on the job this can go on for several years. In my experience most tea-boy/tape ops/assistants don't take the best advantage of these weeks/months/years. Many assistants sit at the back of the room reading magazines, talking on the phone or just looking bored. This is the only time in your life that world-class engineers and producers are going to let you look over their shoulders, study their techniques and even write down their eq's and favourite reverb settings. The assistant also participates in the most intimate studio moments and has the opportunity to learn the unteachable secret of the record producer – how to handle the artist. The best assistants, the ones who go on to bigger and better things, don't regard the job as beneath them. They instinctively recognise that they are the lubricant that keeps the session from squeaking.

Flood got his nickname when he was assisting at Morgan Studios because he was so on the ball with tea making. Flood said, "The first four years or so of my career were very important. In some respects, I think that what a lot of people are suffering from, certainly over in this country, is lack of grounding in learning a craft. From when I first started to when I first went freelance was almost six years, and I think that a lot of the time people don't have that luxury anymore, to get that experience in different situations."

"When Flood was head engineer, the tape op to assistant to engineer process was very strict," says his manager, Ros Earls. "You'd be looking for the sort of people that would turn into engineers and then producers. People like Steve Osborne (engineering partner with dance supremo Paul Okenfold), I employed him as a tea boy, it's a difficult thing to do. You're wondering whether they're going to be easy people to have around. They're going to have intelligence, musical taste, personal creative ambition. And they're not necessarily the same sort of people you want to have making your tea and filling your papers in."

Ros thinks that there's an unhealthy pressure to move up through the ranks now. She says, "It used to be that people went through a strict training and it would be like getting your 'O' levels and 'A' levels via a studio. Up to the mid-Eighties people would do their apprenticeship in a studio and then, at some point, they would realise that they were capable of doing more than engineering. Engineers have always been regarded [in England] as 'just' an engineer which they aren't in America. People there may be engineers for forty years and they are formidable talents. What's happened recently is that people are looking for a manager earlier. Studios are taking on less permanent staff. There's a lot more competition at an earlier stage now, so some people will only have a year's experience in a studio and they'll be looking for a freelance manager."

Andy Jackson came up through the ranks at Utopia Studios in London. He subsequently engineered several Pink Floyd and

Roger Waters albums. He says, "I was quite lucky when I came in. It was Utopia and it was quite new when I started. The place expanded very quickly. I got opportunities to engineer demos and jingles within a year. That was good discipline because you had to work very quickly. A lot of studios I would've had to wait two or three years before I got to engineer something." Although it is generally a slower way to get started, Andy feels that a period of assisting in a major studio is incredibly valuable. He says, "I was seeing good practice. Good sound stuff. Classic techniques. I didn't get to work with that many bad engineers. It's very easy to spot them and it just reinforces the good techniques you have learnt." And it's not just the engineering tricks that you can pick up on, but the way the producer handles the session in general. Andy says, "Everybody has a different approach. You just pick up bits and pieces. Not just in terms of techniques but attitudes to the actual fulfilment of getting a record made and ways of handling people. Bob Ezrin (who worked with Pink Floyd) has been a good example. I may not agree with everything he does but he's a 'get things done' person. Some of that's been really useful practice to have picked up. He has a little saying which is 'do anything even if it's wrong'. What he's getting at is 'let's do *something* rather than sit around scratching our heads not knowing *what* to do. Let's do something and react to it.' You can say 'this isn't right and I can see why this isn't right so it gives me an insight into what would work.'

"Some projects I've worked on have been horrendously slow. People usually assume that's because the artist is being meticulous, but a lot of it is because the artist is being lazy and doesn't show up, or they'll show up and get two hours' work done in a day. One producer I work with takes the attitude that if the artist is not there then he'll get on and make the record and the artist will have to do something about it. The producer will sit down and compile the guitar solos and if the guitarist doesn't like it, then he'll have to come in and re-do it himself. It forces his hand. It's a fine line. It's the artist's record but that's why they hire a producer. In this particular situation the producer will get it done and he will stand up to the artist. He is not overawed by the fact that this is a multi-million selling artist. He won't be a 'yes' man to them and that is one of the big reasons why he is involved. At the same time he can be quite mercenary about it. He's not there because of the art of it. If by taking a stand it forces the artist to make a decision that moves things forward, then he's happy with that outcome. He'll argue his case but the artist will have the last word."

Smashing Pumpkins' producer Alan Moulder started as an assistant engineer at the world famous Trident Studios in London. He describes how he moved from engineering to producing. "I worked with bands and you end up getting a bit of a relationship with them. Then they decide to bypass their producer to do some B-sides so you get to do some tracks on your own with them." He adds, "It's mainly from co-production – where bands want to do the record and have a big input themselves. Most of them have a pretty good idea of what they want or how they want to sound and they have a lot of ideas in their head. I'll collaborate with them to try to get that and if we come across problems I'll act like a referee or be the one to point out that something's not working. I try to make things run as smoothly as possible, as quickly as possible, and I'll come up with ideas if they're needed. Maybe with the structure of a song or if the parts aren't working. So I'll act as an extra opinion."

I believe that, to some extent, you can predict an assistant's future in the business from the first time you work with them. Among other things it's characterised in the way they deal with the lunch order. The assistants that I worked with who consistently got it wrong didn't translate into successful producers. The assistants I've worked with, including Tim Palmer (mixed Pearl Jam's first album *Ten*) when he first started at Utopia, Alan Moulder at Trident (produced Smashing Pumpkins), Pete Walsh at Utopia (produced Simple Minds) and Flood at Morgan Studios, were always right there when you needed them. They seemed to have an ability to read the "vibe" in the room. Teas and coffees would arrive at precisely the right moment. They are extremely intelligent but they don't mind doing mundane tasks. They fit in very well without being too chummy.

Chris Lord-Alge spoke about getting started as an engineer. "Find the best studio in town and fight your way in. Get a job, whether you're pushing a broom or cleaning the toilets, and work your way up from there. Don't be scared to take a chance on anything. The only way you are going to learn is by watching the best at what they do."

Don Gehman (producer of Hootie and The Blowfish's 14+ million-selling début album) said, "When I was coming up as an engineer we were always told that we were supposed to guess what the next move was, and be set up for it, before we went there. Sometimes that means doing two or three things at once, but that's the mark of a good assistant."

Engineer to producer is a very natural route. As Mitchell Froom (who started as a musician) says, "Good engineers contribute a lot to the production. People need titles, but every record has production suggestions from other people."

One problem that engineers can face when trying to make the move to production is that record companies would sooner keep paying them as an engineer, knowing that in reality they are doing a lot if not all of the production work.

Jack Douglas's track record includes six Aerosmith records, three with Cheap Trick, John Lennon's *Double Fantasy* and Alice Cooper's anthem "School's Out". Douglas started out in bands but while recording at A&R Recording found that the other side of the glass held more fascination for him. An engineer at New York's A&R Studio told him about a new studio opening up where everyone was going – Shelley Yakus, Roy Cicala, Jay Messina – The Record Plant. Douglas started out cleaning toilets and moving Hendrix tapes around in the period they were recording the *Woodstock* soundtrack there. Gradually he worked his way up to tape librarian and eventually assistant engineer. His leap to engineering was sudden and dramatic. "There was an engineer there, Jack Adams. He was doing The Who sessions for what would be *Who's Next.* He did the R&B that came into the place and didn't like rock, no matter who the artist was. So we get the room set up and he says to me, 'I hate this rock shit, I don't care about any of it'.

"Now Jack lived on a houseboat on the 79th Street boat basin. So he tells me to go into the other room and tells me to call him on the phone and say his houseboat is on fire. He was like a method actor – he needed motivation to lie. So I'm twelve feet away and telling him his houseboat's on fire, and I can hear him screaming, telling Kit Lambert (the producer) and Pete Townshend that his boat's on fire. It's sinking in the boat basin. He tells them that I'm not the assistant but the other engineer on the session and that I'll be doing the sessions. Up till then, I had only done some jingle dates and one record session with Patty LaBelle during which I had set the old Datamix console on fire by knocking someone's beer onto the transformers. So I was a little nervous. Everything was all set up. The first song was 'Won't Get Fooled Again'."

This is a particularly dramatic story but it seems a lot of engineers and producers who go on to be highly successful get thrown in the deep end early on in their careers.

Douglas made the move into production. "There were a few famous producers I was working with who had a habit of not showing up and calling to see how things were going. Bob Ezrin (Pink Floyd) made me aware that I was already producing because of that. He got me to do some Canadian records, like Crowbar, to get me to, in a sense, open out of town, so I wouldn't fall on my butt in New York. He was priming me for the next Alice Cooper album, *Muscle Of Love.*"

Greg Ladanyi also made the move from engineer to producer. He was a Grammy Award winning engineer (*Toto IV*) and was nominated as producer of the year with Don Henley on *Building The Perfect Beast.* Talking about making the move from engineering to producing he said, "I was working during a time in the record industry where artists became more involved. Engineers became more and more valuable, and I was lucky to be around. We became valuable because we could sit with the artist and help them as co-producers. That led me into co-producing, and later to producing because I got better at it, better at listening and capturing performances. And I learned about arranging songs from people like Jackson Browne and Don Henley."

The transition from engineer to producer is less painful if your engineering history encompasses mega-acts like The Beatles and Pink Floyd. Alan Parsons turned a glittering engineering career into an equally glittering production track record. "I think that producing was a fairly natural progression. I was in touch with a lot of people from EMI records, a lot of the A&R people. The first things I did were for Pilot and Cockney Rebel, both EMI projects. I think it evolved as a result of getting a reputation from the Pink Floyd album and just doing bits and pieces in a production capacity with other producers. The word just got out that I was capable of doing it. But I never actually went up to record companies and said, 'Will you let me produce this act?' They actually gave them to me, which is rather nice."

There is a story told about an engineer who was the only one from the production team in the studio throughout a particular project. He was the only one who had any day-to-day relationship with the artist and he took the brunt and the whole responsibility of the production. There were several other producers with huge names who would just dip in and out for a week and then disappear. One producer would come in and listen to a couple of tracks, give the band pointers on the mixes and take a substantial royalty. The engineer felt that he was holding the project together for not a lot of recognition. This production methodology had been set up by the artist who was already extremely successful. They obviously considered the royalties they were giving away to the consultant producers to be worthwhile. The engineer's contribution was eventually rewarded. On later albums he was given a co-production credit and his career made the leap to hyper-space. Talent, patience and paying your dues can pay off.

In fact, a great number of engineers make the leap to producing from having engineered a particularly successful record. Mike Clink produced Guns and Roses' *Appetite For Destruction* after engineering things like Whitesnake for the same label. Brendon O'Brien went on to produce Stone Temple Pilots and Pearl Jam after engineering for Rick Rubin. Hugh Padgham's engineering career included Peter Gabriel's seminal, third solo album. That was the project which gave the world the Phil Collins drum sound. Hugh went on to co-produce Phil Collins, Police, Sting and Genesis. Now he commands production credits of his own.

"Flood developed from engineer to co-mixer to 'recorded by' credit which is always an interesting one," says his manager Ros. "It doesn't really mean anything but implies a better position than just engineer. 'Recorded and mixed by' doesn't actually mean that the person engineered the project. It implies an overseeing, chief engineer kind of position. There could be a dozen engineers on the project. 'Recorded and mixed by' says that you were in charge of the whole recording process but you don't get royalties for that. Some producers do millions and millions of different things and other producers grow with projects. Flood did all of the Depeche Mode albums but started off engineering.

On the second one he was co-producing with the band and on the third one he was producing."

The producer of any hugely successful record immediately becomes massively desirable and, based on the good old principle of supply and demand, wildly expensive, but here's the scenario wherein an engineer might get his first big break. A new artist comes to discuss with his A&R person who he would like to have produce his first record. Inevitably the artist will suggest at least one producer who has a current big hit or a string of hits. Usually, while trying not to flinch visibly, the A&R person will say, "Well, I just spoke to him yesterday and he is not available for the next twelve months at least." If the A&R person is in a semi-honest mood he may say, "No, he's going to cost you at least $150,000 and you don't want to take on that much debt at this point in your career, but how about so and so who engineered the record and has been his right-hand man for the last two years." Well, if you happen to be so and so, that recommendation could be a very painless entrée into a major league production career.

## 3) The Songwriter

Some of the greatest producers and production teams have used their songs as a foot in the door. It may be that the songwriter is not necessarily that interested in production – but enduring a couple of badly produced versions of your beloved songs is generally sufficient to convince you that you could do a better job yourself.

The line between writing and producing has become blurred in recent years for a number of reasons. Writers almost invariably have well-equipped home studios and make very sophisticated demos, but at the same time publishers, artists, producers and A&R people have in recent years been spoiled by the high quality of song demos, and in too many cases can no longer "hear" the voice and piano or voice and guitar demos.

Unless you have a huge reputation, the opportunity to bang out your latest ditty on a piano in the publisher or A&R person's office just does not exist. They not only want to hear a high quality demo but one that is in the style of the artist for whom it is intended. In fact, if you happen to be looking for songs for a less famous artist during the six months after, say, Tina Turner, or Whitney Houston finish their album, the publishers will send you a gaggle of highly produced demos that sound just like Tina or Whitney. These are the songs that have just been released from being "on hold" for the past six, twelve or eighteen months, waiting for one of the coveted ten or twelve places on these mega-artists' guaranteed multi-platinum albums.

The consistently successful songwriter producer is very powerful and usually becomes the All-Singing-All-Dancing type of producer. L.A. & Babyface, Jam and Lewis, Holland, Dozier, Holland, Gamble and Huff, Narada Michael Walden and Walter Afanasieff are good examples.

Collaborating with an artist on their songs is a less hit and miss way of nailing the production job for a number of reasons. You get a chance to build a close relationship with them, you get a low pressure opportunity to prove your production abilities to them and if they enjoy working with you they will go to bat for you with the record company. Also, the artist has a vested interest in the songs you write and produce together going on the album.

Shep Pettibone was able to make the move from being Madonna's remixer to her co-producer on the *Erotica* album by collaborating with her at the writing stage. Obviously, he already had a good working relationship with her because of the remixes he had done for her. Had he simply tried to write songs for her he would have been competing with the entire songwriting population of the free world. Instead he did what he does best: built tracks in the style of his remixes for which she could write the lyrics and melodies. The nature of dance music is such that the production ideas, the parts, the sounds and the song itself are almost inextricably intertwined. Once Pettibone and Madonna had written and demo'd the songs together, not only was there little point in bringing in an outside producer – but they wound up transferring most of the stuff they had recorded on the eight-track demos over to twenty-four-track tape and onto the final record.

Pettibone gives an example of how the process ran: "It took about two or three days to write a song from beginning to end. Still, sometimes even after they were done we'd want to change the flow of the song and ask the song a few questions: Where should the chorus hit? Should it be a double chorus? Sometimes

Madonna would call me in the middle of the 
'Shep, I think the chorus should go like this.' O
verse, fix the bass line.' 'Deeper and Deeper' was
songs she always had a problem with. The middle
wasn't working. We tried different bridges and c ges, but nothing worked. In the end, Madonna wanted the middle of the song to have a flamenco guitar strumming big-time. I didn't like the idea of taking a Philly house song and putting 'Isla Bonita' in the middle of it. But that's what she wanted so that's what she got."

## 4) DJ Producers . . .

. . . are a relatively new phenomenon. The trend started in the early Eighties and is now pretty much a fixture of the club and rap scene, spilling over into R&B/pop with producers such as Nick Martinelli. Usually, however, they specialise in dance or rap records. Their expertise and appeal to record companies stems from being directly plugged into what their audience likes. Very often DJ producers will continue to DJ long after it ceases to be a fiscal necessity, in the knowledge that it is this umbilical connection that keeps them at the cutting edge of club trends. There is a kind of snobbery or resentment that exists towards DJ producers and I am always hearing predictions that this is a trend that will die out. I don't believe so. For the moment the trend may be shifting back to live bands, which favours musician or engineer producers, but there will always be a place for the DJ producer.

Arthur Baker started off working in a Boston record store, went on to spin records at a local club, where he met Tom Silverman of Tommy Boy Records. Baker moved to New York City in 1980, working with one of the early hip-hop artists, Afrika Bambaataa and New Edition. His work as a producer and writer led to remix work with artists such as David Bowie, Mick Jagger and Cyndi Lauper. He now prefers to concentrate on production rather than remixes.

Rick Rubin started producing without any training or background in bands or studios while he was still in college. He had been deejaying at clubs and was fascinated by rap because he saw it was a whole different sound. He says, "Being a fan and understanding what rap was really about, I just tried to capture that on record, and ironically part of the answer was not knowing anything about the technology and what was considered right or wrong in the studio. It was about capturing some really awkward sounds at times. Looking back they're pretty funny-sounding records, but that was what was going on."

Cypress Hill's DJ Muggs has written, produced and mixed tracks for The Beastie Boys, Ice Cube, House Of Pain, Funkdoobiest, Daddy Freddy, YoYo and Mellow Man Ace. He has done remixes for Janet Jackson and U2. His own band's "Black Sunday" went straight to Number One in the *Billboard* charts. DJ Muggs (real name Larry Muggerud) grew up in Queens, New York, and moved to Los Angeles during high school. It was his love of rap music and break-dancing which eventually led to DJ'ing. He started producing his own tracks using a pair of Technics SP1200's while in tenth grade. In the mid-Eighties he formed the "Spanglish" rap group DVX with B-Real and Sen Dog, the three of whom would eventually become Cypress Hill. When DVX broke up less than a year later he joined forces with the rappers 7A3, released an album on Geffen and got a song on the *Colors* soundtrack. When Muggs decided to get back with B-Real and Sen Dog to form Cypress Hill, he sent the early demos to Joe "The Butcher" Nicolo, a young engineer from Philly. He had liked his style when they had worked together on the 7A3 album. Nicolo signed the band to his newly formed Ruffhouse Records and got distribution through Columbia.

Talking about his working relationship with Nicolo, Muggs said, "Joe taught me a lot. He's a hell of an engineer. Now, I go to mix with Joe. When we're mixing songs, he'll add an idea here and there, and he'll ask me if I like it or not. And some things I like and some things I don't. He doesn't mix my records, he engineers my records, and he'll add a few ideas in the mix. Me and Joe have a good vibe together, that's why I stick with him."

DJ producers often work with samples in a montage or collage kind of style. This way of working was pioneered in a purer, more intellectual form by Stockhausen in his *musique concrète* work in the Fifties. The obvious advantage of working with samples is that you are not starting with a "blank sheet of paper". You don't have to build a groove up from nothing and hope that it will work, you simply take a groove from a record that is already proven, add another sample from a different record on top of that and build up a new track from there. Eno says of this, "I admire people like Howie B who turn up with their record collections and they don't bring a single instrument with them. They just patch together other bits of music. This is so intelligent. You get all the cultural resonances of one sound, and then you stick it with all the complexity and cultural resonances of another. I really admire economy more than anything else: elegant ways of making big things happen – which is the opposite of what normally happens in a studio, where you have clumsy ways of making small things happen."

Although Jack Douglas came up through the traditional tape op/assistant way he says, "There's guys out there that just walk into a studio from a club where they're deejaying and they sound phenomenal." He attributes this to the fact that a DJ spends so much time listening to records.

Part-time DJ and record store owner Shep Pettibone capitalised on the Eighties remix craze by rebuilding tracks for dance artists such as Gloria Gaynor, Alisha and Loleatta Holloway. The new wave of British acts such as Pet Shop Boys, Thompson Twins, New Order and Erasure were generating music primed for Pettibone's explosive mixes. Suddenly radio discovered dance music and the remix sound, became "the sound". Janet Jackson, Paula Abdul, MC Hammer, Lionel Richie, Prince, Cyndi Lauper and Madonna had all been re-created for clubs by Shep Pettibone. "By the time I worked on 'Like A Prayer' and 'Express Yourself'," says Pettibone, "it looked as if Madonna liked the remixed versions better than the ones that were on the album. That was great, but producing was still at the top of my wish list." Finally she asked him to write and produce a B-side single for the *Breathless* album. The B-side turned into "Vogue" and became the biggest selling single of 1990. Pettibone had arrived as a producer. Madonna encouraged him to continue writing and a single evolved into the album *Erotica*.

The advantage and disadvantage of working with superstars is that the album is not done when you run out of money, it's done when they are happy with it. "Madonna's attitude was 'Either make the song work, or it's not going on the album. That's that'. Patience was not one of her virtues either and if some sequencing was taking a little time she would say, 'What are you guys doing that's taking so long?' And that was just after the first few minutes," says Pettibone. "We'd tell her to go downstairs and make some popcorn or phone calls so that we could put the song together and she'd do that for about five minutes before screaming, 'Come on guys, I'm getting bored!' I had to keep things moving as fast as possible because it's one of my jobs to keep Madonna from losing interest in what she's doing."

Undoubtedly part of the key to being a good producer is having an instinctive understanding of what a good record really sounds like, and how it works on an emotional level. DJ's are invariably huge fans of their particular area of expertise. They know the history and they have a real feel for what works and what doesn't. Knowing how to get it is a matter of working with the right team and having the intelligence to be able to explain what it is they want.

## 5) Home Studio Hobbyist

This category used to be the domain of the solitary, tech-head. Now it is becoming far more common with the proliferation of inexpensive technology. Often, the home studio hobbyist is also a musician of sorts, so this could be regarded as part of the musician route, but it is possible to be a non-musical, home studio hobbyist. If you don't have musical training or experience, in order to get started from home you will need either an aptitude for technical things or an innate ability to manipulate your friends (in the latter case forget the years of apprenticeship – jump straight into the Merlin style of production).

If you are a natural technical/programmer home studio geek, then you are really treading a modified engineer route without the benefit of the apprenticeship. You're on your own and you'll have to figure it out for yourself. Books, magazines and trial and error will be your main source of information. As applicable to the musician-with-the-home-studio, you may spend ages working out things that are basic to the pro's. Fortunately, in the last fifteen years there have been many books and magazines published that give blow-by-blow accounts of how to record vocals/drums/saxophone and so forth. The upside of the self teaching method is that you will have the opportunity to develop a unique style.

Jack Endino, the Godfather Of Grunge, used a home studio to develop a unique style and to create a place in rock and roll history. He was certainly instrumental in shaping the early Seattle sound, having recorded over eighty albums, one hundred and ten seven inch singles and 300 EPs, from more than two hundred bands, including Soundgarden, Mudhoney, Screaming Trees, Afghan Whigs, L7, Babes In Toyland and, perhaps most famously, Nirvana. He started out in his basement using a TEAC quarter inch four-track machine to record his own band, then around 1983 he started recording other bands such as Soundgarden and Green River for five dollars an hour. He got a track on a popular compilation called *Deep Six* which led to a job engineering in a new local recording studio.

Many of the clients he had in his basement days followed him to the new Reciprocal Studios. "During 85 and 86 there was nobody in Seattle who was good at recording grungy rock bands, and especially for cheap," he says. "It's a small town and when people found out I was making decent-sounding recordings for next to nothing, they beat a path to my door. I was recording frantically – about a single a week. It seemed like everybody was coming to me with or without Sub Pop, with or without a record deal."

Although Jerry Harrison came into producing through the musician route and credits Eno with demystifying the production process for him, he did say, "I think that's a process that's gone on a lot now that people have home studios and home equipment. When I work with bands now, everybody is much, much more familiar with the options one has in the studio. People know about delays, they know about reverbs, 'cause they all have home versions of the more expensive items in the studio. Whereas when I first started making records, the studio was more of a mystery. You went in there and they did what they did. You went out in a room and played and then came in and listened to it. If you went back to the time of The Beatles, the engineers used to wear Lab coats because they considered themselves technicians.

## 6) Finding A New Act

This is not a particularly easy route into the producing game but it can be a great save-your-neck routine when your career is adopting a belly-up posture.

Tony Visconti discovered Marc Bolan. I probably wouldn't have got my first shot at producing if I hadn't become friends with Spandau Ballet well before they were signed. I can't take the credit for getting them signed but being there early and having seen them live, understanding what they were about and being able to build a relationship with them before the feeding frenzy happened, all helped when it came time for them to choose a producer.

Russ Titleman's highly successful career was based on finding an artist. He produced his first album in 1969 by taking a musician friend's band over to another friend, Lenny Waronker, who happened to be at Warner Bros at the time. The musician friend was Lowell George and the band was Little Feat. Lowell and Bill Payne (Little Feat keyboardist) played a couple of songs and Lenny said, "Great. Go talk to Mo (Austin) and let's make a record."

These days deals are not usually done that fast. Clearly, it is not 1969 and most of us don't start out having friends like Lowell George and Lenny Waronker. The principle, however, remains the same. Find a band or artist that you really believe in. Convince a record company that the artist is hot. Somehow establish your own credibility as a producer (be hip and inexpensive) and you might just be in business.

The type of producer who can use this route, especially if it is early in his career, is likely to do well in the music business generally. To be able to find raw talent, sell it to a record company and develop it into a successful act is pretty much what the music business is all about. Those who exhibit those highly sought-after skills usually have the opportunity to rise to the higher echelons of the music business.

Peter Asher is a producer who inhabits the stellar regions of the music business partly because of his production abilities and partly because he was able to discover, sign and develop an artist who became a megastar. He has produced twenty-eight Gold albums, eighteen Platinum and won two Grammy's twenty-one years apart. His introduction to the music business was as a member of the pop duo Peter & Gordon. After nine Top Twenty records he moved into A&R for The Beatles' Apple label. He actually credits Paul Jones, the ex-Manfred Mann lead singer, with giving him his break into production. "I owe him a lot because he was the first person who said he liked my ideas and asked if I would produce his record. A bold step on his part, for which I am grateful."

Right after Asher started working for Apple he made the connection that would secure his place in the Producers' Hall of Fame. Danny Kortchmar, who would also go on to become a successful producer in his own right, had played in Asher's backing band. Kortchmar's childhood friend and partner in a band called The Flying Machine was James Taylor. When The Flying Machine broke up Taylor decided to move to London. Danny Kortchmar had given Taylor Peter Asher's number. The rest of the story is rock'n'roll history: they hooked up, Taylor played a tape for Asher who was knocked out and said, "Listen, it so happens I've just started working for this new label – I'd like to sign you to the label and produce your new record. It all fell into place very easily."

## 7) The Who-The-Hell-Knows-How-They-Got-Started Route

There are producers who don't have a technical or musical background, they weren't DJ's and they haven't worked at a record label. For better or for worse they are usually hustlers. Their ability to do the job depends on them surrounding themselves with talented engineers and musicians. The trade-off for the musicians and engineers who make the record is that the producer pulls in the work. These producers will often claim to have a musical background. Usually they mean they were in a band at school or worked in a record store in the summer vacation.

## OK – So You Want To Be A Record Producer – What Next?

Brian Wilson has called Andy Paley a genius. Paley, who has been a staff producer with both Warner Bros. and Elektra Records, advises young producers to, "Knock on doors. And go where the action is. Don't stay in the middle of nowhere and expect to be discovered, because it's not going to happen. Anybody can sit around and be a tortured artist in a garret someplace but that's not going to get you anywhere. You should go out and knock on doors, show people what you can do where the business is – New York, Nashville, London, L.A. I've met quite a few people who said, 'I'm great, and the world doesn't know it'. Well so what? Where's that gonna get you." He adds, "I used to do that – but I got over the hump and got to work."

Andy Paley's advice is certainly consistent with my experience. I grew up in New Zealand, which is a wonderful place to live but about as far as you can go from anywhere. It's the ultimate small town. I have often wished that I could have learned the things I've learned and done the things I've done from my home town in New Zealand but at the time it was all but impossible. With a population of around three million (in the Seventies), the music business there was very small. The knowledge base was not available to develop the various skills I needed, so I packed my bags. I took private music lessons in Sydney, Australia, went to music school in Boston, USA, and London, England, lived and worked all over Europe and eventually worked my way through New York City and Los Angeles. Everywhere I landed I learnt something. A slightly different attitude here, an alternative technique there, new ways of looking at the same old problems.

Undoubtedly we are entering an era when it will be quite possible for people living in remote places to be able to acquire the knowledge and experience necessary to compete on a world-class level in the music business. Many factors are making this possible. Firstly, digital technology means that a well mastered CD can sound very close to the original masters. So anyone listening to that CD anywhere in the world on good equipment will be getting a very good impression of what the artist, producer and engineer were striving for. I know there is still a lobby out there for vinyl, and at its best it certainly did sound nice (Deutsche Grammophon discs always sounded excellent) but even assuming you could afford a decent (accurate) turntable, you needed to take a degree course to set the thing up properly. Then there was the surface noise, the lousy pressings and the substandard, recycled vinyl that companies would use for pop records, not to mention the degradation after repeated plays and the potential for damage by mishandling. Not only that. If you lived somewhere other than the country of origin, the record would have been remastered by a local mastering engineer who might or might not know what he's doing. Your local version would almost certainly not be the same as the original. CDs are also subject to remastering, but with digital domain copies, discs manufactured worldwide can sound remarkably consistent.

So someone living in the outback of Australia can toss a (mail ordered?) CD in their hi-fi and hear very nearly the same thing that the actual producer heard when he mastered it in London, New York or Los Angeles. Back in the bush, while our hypothetical person is listening to the CD, the chances are they can read an article by the engineer and/or producer about the techniques they used to make the record. Many pro and semi-pro audio magazines are now available worldwide, both in paper and electronically on the world wide web. There are many, many more books about music, the music business, producing, engineering etc. than there were even twenty years ago. In the Eighties there was an explosion of video tutorials and master classes. Add to that the advent of multi-media, the best applications of which (in my opinion) have to date been educational. Engineers of the calibre of Allen Sides are preserving and sharing their knowledge and expertise on CDRom. On his "Allen Sides" Mic Locker' he shares his incredible knowledge of microphones and demonstrates specific uses using his private collection of the best new and old microphones in the world. So you can not only read about the mic's and their applications but you can see, hear and compare them in action in a world-class studio. Many remixers have put out sample CDs of the drum sounds they use, enabling someone in, say, Turkey to have access to the same samples as their favourite artists.

No matter how good you get at what you do, you will still run into the problem that Andy Paley was talking about: how do you let people know what you are capable of. In effect, how do you market yourself? Well, that is still a problem. Highly influential and successful scenes have emerged within the last fifteen years in non-standard music business locations, Grunge being the most obvious. Seattle is not Los Angeles or New York but neither is it the Outer Hebrides or New Guinea. A&R people can pretty easily fly in to Seattle. I don't think it will happen soon, but I do believe that the new communications systems that are currently being put into place will eventually enable some enterprising kid from some really obscure place to launch himself into the world arena without setting foot on a plane. But more of that later,

## Are Qualifications A Help Or A Hindrance?

Very few successful producers actually have any relevant qualifications. And what would a relevant qualification be? A music degree would be handy. An engineering degree from one of the new audio schools or the Tonmeister courses would not go amiss. For that matter, neither would a psychology degree. If producers have educational qualifications, they don't make a lot of noise about them. There are a few famous names who have been given honorary degrees because of their successes in the real world.

In 1960 Columbia Records in New York City ran an actual A&R producers course. Goddard Lieberson, who was the president of the company at the time and was an A&R man himself, took a great personal interest in it. Mike Berniker, who went on to produce Barbra Streisand, Eydie Gorme, Brenda Lee, Perry Como, many jazz artists and Grammy award-winning Broadway shows, was tested for various aptitudes and then given a crash course in how records were made. He says, "It was wonderful, because we not only learned the nuts and bolts of what records are – how they're manufactured and all – but we went into the studio and watched other producers at work, and in effect learned what to avoid, as well as what to do. It was a great training ground."

Speaking of relevant qualifications, Jerry Harrison's education was typically oblique for someone who would subsequently become a producer of note. He took a course at Harvard that could have led into either painting or film making. From there he joined Jonathan Richman's Modern Lovers, taught a little at Harvard, worked for a computer company and was eventually asked to try out for Talking Heads.

Having an opinion is probably one of the most important qualifications for success as a producer. (Although one of the many answers to "How many record producers does it take to change a light bulb?" is "I don't know what do you think.")

Neil Finn of Crowded House said about producer Mitchell Froom, "In some cases he does hardly anything, but he's got a solid opinion all the time. In the studio, when everyone else is wavering, he's good for a consistent opinion." Neil's brother Tim adds, "Even if you don't agree, it's good to have someone who is clear, someone you can bounce ideas off."

Unfortunately, unlike brain surgery and the design of missile guidance systems, when it comes to the record making process, everyone this side of the black stump has an opinion. And they can't wait to give it to you. You can spend months cocooned in Rock'n'Roll Heaven Studios way out in the wilds with a great deal of the technology man has hitherto created, and the best musicians in the solar system. When you emerge blinking into real life, clutching your masterpiece, anyone and everyone will have an opinion.

The reason why a producer gets paid mega-bucks (sometimes) for his opinion and the other guy doesn't is because the producer has "taste" that is proven. It might not necessarily be "good taste" but one that is consistent with a lot of other people's: the people who will go out and buy the record. The skill is in understanding your taste, trusting your instincts and opinions, knowing how to act on them; knowing what action to take to achieve the results you want.

Whether you have a hit or not will depend in the first instance on getting an enthusiastic response from the people in A&R, promotions and marketing. If they don't get excited about your precious work of art then it's highly likely that the only other person who will get to hear it will be your mother. Assuming your baby manages to painfully squeeze its way down the record company birth-canal and arrive in the world alive and undamaged (undamaged is yet another story), in any week of the year it will find itself competing with at least half dozen other, very hungry siblings for the record companies' affections.

The record company expresses its affection, as so many of us do, in monetary terms. This money manifests itself in the amount of promotion and marketing push your record actually gets. Only with the record company's blessing will the reviewers and radio programmers get to pass their opinions on your brainchild. Then, if you're one of the fortunate few and you pass the media frisking, the general public will at last get to vote with their hard-won moolah. And they have their own opinion.

How efficiently and frequently you can translate your opinions into hits or not will determine how long before you either qualify for "Lifestyles Of The Rich And Famous" or need to find a proper job. The means you use, exactly how you translate those ideas, is not necessarily important but it will certainly affect the type of projects you produce.

When it comes to attracting prospective suitors, educational qualifications are not even minutely relevant. Your hair style may even be more significant. It might be that your education enables you to do a better job and that will ultimately be useful to you. But since most people, including those who've actually worked with you, have no idea what you do or how you do it, you will be judged by your results (for results read – how many copies your last three records sold) and a whole host of other superficial factors. Letters after a producer's name have not been proven to be a significant factor in getting work. In fact most successful producers have come up via the practical experience route. This may change over the next few years with more and more engineers coming out of the universities and engineering schools.

Tom Lord-Alge says, "Recording schools can't teach you how to hear, how to mix. They can only teach you how the equipment runs. I learned in the studio, under the pressure. Deal with the people, sit in the chair. You sink or swim. You don't learn until you're put under that pressure, and you learn from someone who is great." He then adds, "Music is hell."

Studio "street qualifications" come from working with great people and seeing how they handle everything. But, there are situations where at least some formal knowledge, if not qualifications, would come in very handy. Alan Moulder says that there are times when he wishes he could read music. "When I'm recording an orchestra for instance and trying to follow the score blindly." But, he adds, "I was lucky in that I got into an area of music that I've always been interested in so I wouldn't say it was too much of a hindrance." He certainly doesn't think having a basic musical training would be a hindrance, but he says, "Having worked in America, I can see that sometimes having a formal engineering training can cause people to get hung up on what is 'good' and 'bad'." Alan tried to get as much technical training as possible when he was assisting. He thinks it can be good to have a more formal training as engineers tend to in America, providing that you use it as a tool not a rule. He adds, "Sometimes it's just better to get it on tape than to worry about the technicalities too much."

Andy Jackson feels that if any qualification would be useful to a producer it would be music qualifications. He says, "You can always farm things out. You can get people in to write dots but it's more direct if the producer can do something that's outside of the ability of the artist like writing a horn arrangement."

You don't learn the people skills in school. The people who seem to go on to do well in the business are the assistants who can come into the studio and be helpful but invisible at the same time. Andy says, "Something that was always put across to me as being very important was to at least not be destructive to the session. In those days as a tape op essentially you were sitting there operating the tape machine, being invisible and helpful at the same time."

It's an interesting combination of qualities. You can have guys who seem to have all the potential in the world, they can be confident, enterprising, quick and smart but they are a pain in the butt to have in the room. My observation is that they are not the ones who go on to be successful. I've had a few assistants who are so aggressively confident that I think "This guy's either going to be a mega producer within three months or he'll be out of the business." Almost invariably they leave the business. One assistant who worked in a studio where I was encamped for a couple of years, exhibited all these qualities. He had natural ability, was comfortable around people and very confident in everything he did. The chief engineer and myself would give him advice and help but generally he seemed to know it all anyway. The one thing we kept mentioning to him was to be extremely careful when lining up the record side of the tape machines, especially when the record pad was at the head of someone's master tape. I even told him stories about famous projects that had been erased by assistants. I came in one morning, the assistant was as white as a sheet. He had erased a master. I breathed a slight sigh of relief when I found out it wasn't my tape. It was, however, a session for a famous artist who had been working on his record for about three years at that point. Subsequently it turned out that the master could pretty much be rebuilt from samples the artist had on disk. In this instance not too much permanent damage had been done. We pointed out that if he'd taken our advice this wouldn't have happened. The long and the short of it was that he stayed on at the studio for another two months. He was never the same again. Eventually he left the studio and dropped out of the music business altogether.

Qualifications are useful if they are tempered with a certain amount of wisdom when it comes to dealing with people. Andy Jackson says he has had situations where he's worked with assistants who've had substantial amounts of knowledge but who are, in a roundabout way, quite confrontational to the main engineer and what he's doing. "That's an appalling situation," he says. "The schools can allow people to come into the studio with more confidence but that may not be such a good thing. It may be more useful to come in somewhat overawed by it all. It makes you mind your P's and Q's more."

## So Exactly How Much Technical Knowledge Do You Need?

Depends what kind of producer you want to be (see Chapter 1). The full range of possibilities are available, ranging from super-tech-head to can't-stop-the-clock-on-your-video-recorder-from-flashing-on-12:00. Your technical ability or lack of it won't affect your ability to make a hit record but it will affect the way you go about making the record. Lack of technical ability will almost certainly make your life in the studio easier. If the computer crashes it's not going to be your problem. If the artist doesn't like the eq on his voice – you can fire the engineer.

George Martin has managed to produce a few hits yet he does not consider himself to be a very technical producer. Talking about the all-important communication with the engineer he says, "You might say that the drum sounds a bit dull or [you'd] like it to be 'snappier'. When it comes to other sounds, like horns and orchestral sessions, then I will be very particular about the kind of sound I want. The engineer has to realise the kind of sound you're looking for, in [terms] of clarity and good 'liquid' sound from the strings."

Surprisingly for someone as technically adept as Steve Albini, even being referred to as an engineer makes him uncomfortable. "I don't have a degree in electrical engineering like some engineers I admire have, and I never had any formal apprenticeship as an engineer. Recording engineering used to be a black art –

you had to know everything involved in building a tape recorder, a loudspeaker, a mixing desk and so on before you could effectively operate them. Only since the Seventies have electronics been user-friendly enough for people who don't know what they're doing to make records. These days, you have people being paid huge sums of money as 'producers' who don't know how to align a tape machine, they couldn't find a burnt resistor on a circuit board or even tell if their monitors are out of phase. Get this – I walked into one of the biggest, most expensive, classy studios in Chicago to mix a tape recorded somewhere else, and their main monitors were 180 degrees out of phase – they'd been living with them that way for weeks and nobody noticed! That really blew my mind."

[Author's note: when speakers are 180 degrees out of phase, if you listen to music while sitting between them at the optimum position for the stereo image, you will feel like your head is turning inside out. In addition to that, most of the low frequencies get cancelled out so the whole thing will sound very thin and trebly. Inconceivable as it is that a major studio could do this I have had a similar experience at a record company. I found an A&R man's system wired out of phase and he had been critiquing mixes and productions with his system in this condition for some time.]

Albini seems to have a healthy sense of humour about the whole business. On a more recent news group posting Albini went on to say, "On every session I've been involved with, I've considered the band to be the actual producer. I've been credited as a producer, but so what. I've been called a 'Gypsy dago creep' too and neither one bothered me."

Maybe the humility is a little overstretched when he said that being referred to as an engineer makes him uncomfortable because he doesn't feel qualified. He goes on to knock himself out of the credits game completely in his final sentence on a "rec.audio.pro" news group posting when he says, "If somebody calls himself a 'producer' who isn't qualified to call himself an 'engineer' then he is a fraud."

If you were searching for an engineer or producer using Steve Albini's criteria, these days you would search long and hard. It would be impossible to put a figure on it but I would guess that well in excess of ninety percent of successful recording and mixing engineers have only a very basic knowledge of the inner workings of studio equipment. We live in an increasingly complex world. Knowing how to build, repair and tune a car will not necessarily make you a world champion racing car driver. However, if you have the potential to be a world champion driver and you take the time to understand the inner workings of the vehicle, I'm sure you could be a lot more help to the support team that does build, maintain and optimise the vehicle. Likewise, in the recording studio the engineer or the producer who has an in-depth knowledge of music and technology is likely to be able to identify and eliminate both creative and technical problems more quickly.

Al Jourgensen and Paul Barker, the production team behind the cutting edge band Ministry, spin-off group The Revolting Cocks and outside projects such as Anthrax, Nine Inch Nails, Mind Bomb, The Jesus & Mary Chain and The Red Hot Chili Peppers (sometimes credited to their pseudonyms Hypo Luxa and Hermes Pan), have an interesting approach to all things technical. According to Jourgensen: "We are knob turners, we are button pushers. We don't know what it's gonna do half the time, but damn it, we're gonna do it. We'll take a day off to slave five compressors together, all overloaded, just to see what will happen. And half the time, the board blows up . . . but so what?" Barker adds "Yeah, we don't know any better, but it takes us places that no one else would go."

Chris Lord-Alge, Grammy-nominated engineer/producer, has a healthy attitude to technology. "Give us the toys, and we will play them. We take the manual and throw it in the garbage and turn the knobs until it blows up."

Classical producers may be somewhat more conservative in their attitude towards equipment but even they don't need much technical knowledge. Grammy award winning Andrew Cornall, Senior Executive Producer at Decca, says he rarely gets involved in decisions about mic preamps or microphones. He adds, "What I want is to hear the timbre of the instrument replicated back in the box [control room]. If it doesn't sound the same then I have a problem because essentially it's these timbral sounds that I am trying to capture. The skill of the crew-especially the engineer on the desk – is by far the most important element."

T Bone Burnett has produced albums by Los Lobos, Elvis

Costello, The Bodeans, Marshall Crenshaw, Bruce Cockburn and Counting Crows, along with albums as an artist in his own right. Obviously this is someone who has rubbed shoulders with his fair share of studio equipment. In spite of that he says, "I know what I want to hear in my music and when I produce other artists. I use everything and I know when it's working, but I don't know what any of it is called or how any of it does what it does. I'm interested in poetry, and all of that equipment is logical. Chesterton said, 'Logic is the natural enemy of poetry. The poet wants to get his head into the heavens, and the logician wants to get the heavens into his head'."

André Fischer says, "I'm technical to the point where there's no engineer who can lie to me, because on one level I know what they know. I can do engineering myself. When I was in Rufus, I'd occasionally find that the engineers were lying to me, and they'd try to give me this technical explanation of why something I wanted to do couldn't be done. So I'd stay after they left and experiment and find out that it could be done."

So it is definitely possible to survive and prosper with virtually no technical knowledge at all. The less technically inclined you are, the more dependent you will be on your engineer for all the engineering and sonic aspects of the production. So you will need to make sure that he or she is not only good at their job but is someone who you can communicate and get along with, since you will spend many hours together.

Bob Ezrin's credits include albums for Pink Floyd, Peter Gabriel, Rod Stewart and Kiss. "I come from a very musical background," he says. "I'm only a tech head in the sense that I've always loved toys. When I was growing up in Toronto, my best friend was my transistor radio. I owned one of the first ones, and I used to listen to all these faraway stations. That's what got me hooked on music and sounds. Over the years I've learned enough to be dangerous, but I couldn't build a circuit if my life depended on it! I just know how things work from having studied it, and if you showed me a schematic, I could only barely read it. But I have an instinctive feeling for technical things, and I have an innate understanding of how things work, if not why."

Different types of records require different skills. Life, radio and MTV would be extremely boring if there was only one type of record being made. I for one am very happy to see the fresher, more spontaneous kinds of recordings the Nineties have brought. The Eighties Lego style production techniques, which homogenised and manicured the artist, are still alive and well. But at least that is no longer perceived to be the only way to make a record.

What a producer really does need to know about technology is how it can best serve the music. Knowing precisely how it all works can cut at least one link out of the creative chain. If a producer doesn't have a clue, then his ability to communicate will be vital. He will have to be able to explain what he is hearing in his head to someone who knows exactly how to get that result.

What makes people go out and buy a record is the emotional impact it has on them. Music can make you happy, sad or reflective. It can become a soundtrack for a particular period in your life. It can stimulate or relax you. Whatever it does, it must do something. What matters from a production point of view is not how the record was made but what it "says" to people or how it touches them and their lives.

Flood is no techno-slug. Technical matters are not a problem for him but he definitely has his priorities. He gives a practical example, "Let's say you have a great part, and you want it to be on your record. You can put it through an amp and go through all the business of doing so and find the sound you want, but by the time you do that you can have easily lost the spark of the moment. I tend to weigh things up like this when recording – what gains priority: sound tinkering, the original idea, or the song itself? First impressions mean a lot for the artist. Essentially, I believe that modern technology is an instrument in the music. I am an advocate for technology as long as it's something that's used rather than something that somebody is used by. It's very easy to become a slave to technology and do something over and over again. Even though you have the ability to try a lot of options with a computer, that doesn't mean that it will be done any better or quicker. It is important that you make sure you use technology to your advantage and don't ever let yourself become used by *it.*"

## How Much Musical Knowledge Do You Need?

The type of producer you will be is going to be defined in large part by your musical knowledge. If you have perfect pitch and a

PhD in music you will most likely be the All-Singing-All-Dancing-King-Of-The-Heap. You don't necessarily need perfect pitch and a PhD to be this producer type, but if you do have those attributes it's highly likely you're going to get frustrated working with bands that don't know where middle C is and can't hold a note to save themselves. Penny to a pound you're going to gravitate towards a very self-contained world where you can possibly even write, arrange and play all the instruments.

Conversely, if you have no musical knowledge you will always be dependent on others for any musical input to the project. You can cope with this by working with bands who are self-contained musically and who either need technical, logistical or philosophical help. Probably the only way you will be able to control specific musical input will be to build a team of musicians, arrangers and composers that you work with on a regular basis.

Marcus Miller, co-producer of many platinum records by Luther Vandross and a phenomenal multi-instrumentalist himself, doesn't think it is absolutely necessary for a producer to have a musical background. "The most important thing is to be able to really hear music and love music. People who love music make the best producers. A lot of times musicians don't make good producers because they're too focused on the mechanics of playing their instruments, and sounds. Those things are important, but the most important thing is the overall music, and I think the best producers don't play any instrument. I think I've gotten very good at listening like a regular person as opposed to listening like a musician. You need to take an overview. The first thing you should hear is the saxophone or the singer, whatever is out front, and how the music supports that. People who don't play instruments really have that naturally. Musicians have to come around full circle to come back to that. I just try to spend a lot of time listening to music, in non-musician situations – in the house, in the car – listening to see what grabs people. When somebody listens to a Luther Vandross record, they're not listening to the bass, at least not at first. They're listening to Luther."

Talking about the amount of musical input he has on a session Steve Lillywhite (Peter Gabriel, Rolling Stones, Big Country and U2) says, "I'm not the kind of person to tell a bunch of Latin players what notes to play, though I get in the right people, the people I know will play what I want to hear."

"When I first became involved in music I couldn't play instruments," says Brian Eno, "but I could manipulate sound with technology – tape recorders in the first place – and then synthesisers and recording studios in general. New technologies have made it easier to cheat. Cheating is the name of the game in a lot of ways now, and is often the name given to new ways of doing things. So it's not really cheating, it's just that we have had a traditional picture of audience/artist, observer/creator, and the new technologies challenge this. They ask us in particular to acknowledge the possibility that someone who rearranges other people's materials is also an artist. I became a musician through cheating for twenty years. I can't play any musical instrument, but what I can do is work with many of the interesting new devices that enable people to put music together. It was called cheating when I started doing it. Now it's what everyone does. It's called using a recording studio."

Eno defines a producer's role as well as anyone I have come across. "What has become interesting is the idea that artists are people who specialise in judgement rather than skill."

## What If You Have Neither Musical Nor Technical Skills?

Not having any specific musical or technical skills will put all the emphasis on your ability to manage people. You will have to communicate your ideas through the musicians, the engineers and programmers. This can work by choosing people who have the right instincts and abilities and who can come close to the results you are looking for – without you having to define precisely every detail that gets recorded. If the project does not go well you will either have to convey to the musicians and/or technical crew what it is that is not right – or change the crew. This can be advantageous. Since you have not been hired for your musical or technical abilities you can be extremely flexible. Providing the budgets will stretch to it, you can change musicians and engineers to suit the situation and needs of the project.

In fact, as a successful production career develops most producers will pull back from direct hands-on involvement to a more managerial style. It helps with the objectivity, improves your status somewhat and claws back five of the ten years that you took off your life when you were putting in seventy-two hour days during your early years in the studio.

When I asked Danny Saber about the musical or technical qualities a producer needs he said, "That's a tough one. For everything I name there's someone producing who doesn't have that. There are no rules." He recounts the story of a very famous producer who was in a panic doing a track for TV. "He kept saying I want it to be sharp, I want it to be sharp. It turned out what he wanted was distortion. He doesn't have a clue [about the specifics and the details] but he turns out excellent records."

Once you start spending time in studios, especially if you are lucky enough to be around a great producer, then you will naturally acquire a certain amount of technical and musical skills by osmosis.

In my first year or so I would hear the producers talking about timing and tuning problems that I simply could not hear. Gradually these subtle nuances became more and more obvious. Eventually working with producers who were apparently unaware of horrible tuning and timing discrepancies started to drive me crazy. "In terms of my early education at home, I guess my parents didn't know how often you were supposed to tune a piano," says Albhy Galuten. "In the studio, while tracking, we tune the piano every day, but in suburban middle America, you maybe tuned the piano every couple of years. I didn't really know what 'in tune' was, and here I was in the studio, never having played guitar, and just took tuning for granted. Jerry Wexler was saying something to Aretha during the session for 'Spanish Harlem' about her pitch being a little flat, and I was thinking, I didn't even hear it.

"Today's technology has made it much easier to hear, so contemporary records are much more in tune and much more in time. The pitch microscope was not so finely tuned back then, and we've learned over the years to look carefully at pitch, make adjustments with harmonizers, look at the meter, use razor blades and delay lines. But around 1970, it was a new world to me – suddenly hearing careful tuning. If you listen to records from that era, many of them are way out of tune. The opening chord comes in, they're singing, the choir comes in and hits that chord, and you go 'Ow!' But back then it sounded normal. To be in this environment with Jerry Wexler, Arif Mardin – their ears were fabulous, well educated and well tuned."

## The Door's Open, The Foot's In, What Next?

I believe that you need to be extremely pro-active. You need to control the shape and direction of your career to the best of your ability. This is not only difficult but also uncommon. The predominant algorithm among producers is that of the wall-flower. You know, the girl (or these days the guy) who sits on the bench, back against the wall at the local dance, waiting to be asked to dance. That's a lot like the way most producers approach their careers. The system works fine when you are in a hot period, not so good when things are cooling off and not at all when you are trying to get started or when your career is being examined for vital signs.

The first project you did you probably had to move hell and high water to get. You might have got involved with the group at an early stage before they were signed and built that all-important relationship with them. Ideally you should pursue your entire career with the vigour and enthusiasm with which you pursued the first project. A good manager can really help out here by planning each move, actively pursuing projects that are suitable for you and not letting you get suckered into vampire projects that are living on your reputation and the successes that built it. A poor manager will tend to take the path of least resistance which may expose you to the risk of enforced early retirement.

Having said that, I would never chase a project when I know that the artist has an established relationship with another producer. It has been done to me, I didn't like it and I subscribe to the what-goes-around-comes-around philosophy.

# 3

## *What's The Job Description?*

*"When two men in business always agree, one of them is unnecessary."* (William Wrigley Jr)

In any human interaction there are at least two points of view. Very often pursuing one or both of those points of view brings you to an unresolvable impasse (an argument). The producers can represent the unspoken third or higher point of view which is 'what would be the best solution for all concerned.'

A great producer sometimes does very little. The producer who knows when to butt in and when to butt out is, in my opinion, the very best kind.

Flood, discussing how you keep the creativity going says, "Some days [that] can mean just sitting there and saying, 'sounds great, just carry on'. Then other days, it's constructing a situation that you hope will spur people on. It might be a really bad idea, but if it gets the ball rolling, then it's a good idea." He's absolutely right: sometimes you need to take a step sideways to get out of a rut or a stagnant way of thinking. It may be that the place you initially step to is all wrong, but all wrong is usually more obvious than not quite right and that can give you the stimulus to find a way, a thing or a technique that you positively do like.

W. Somerset Maugham probably wasn't talking about a record producer when he said, "Like all weak men he laid an exaggerated stress on not changing one's mind," but he could have been describing certain dictatorial and demotivating producers that I have encountered. Just because all eyes are on you as the producer to come up with the next brilliant idea, it doesn't mean that your ego has to be permanently attached to the first thought that comes out. Especially if it should stimulate a better one from someone else.

Some producers do almost everything. In the case of the All-Singing-All-Dancing type, the producer will be the songwriter, orchestrator, engineer, producer and vocal arranger. All the artist has to do is sing the song and occasionally they won't even do that (remember Milli Vanilli). With less experienced singers it's very common for them to copy the producer's guide vocal note for note, inflection by inflection.

Sometimes the producer acts as a stimulant or a catalyst. Bands and artists have a habit of trotting out their clichés (or even worse, someone else's clichés). Quite often they get lazy and settle for the first possibility that comes along. In some cases the first idea is the best, sometimes it's total crap but most frequently it represents a good starting place. Just having someone in the room who asks? "What if we tried this?" can be enough to kick things off. A good producer can be the little bit of grit that irritates and stimulates the artist to create the pearl.

Production can sometimes be about arranging or optimising arrangements. This is about coming up with, and organising, all the bits that will comprise the finished record. Quite often the way the bits are put together on the demo may be a little convoluted. It's not uncommon for an artist to underplay the best parts of a song and overplay the long boring bits. In this case the producer needs to edit and reorganise while treading gingerly through the exploding ego field.

Finding and choosing material can also be a part of the production process. With an artist who doesn't write, this can entail sifting through piles of publishers' demos. Even when the artist is the writer, it may be that the material being put forward for the record is not even the best available. In this case it's necessary for the producer to go through several old demos and bits of songs to find the best material. There have been many occasions when the only hit single off an album was a song that had been buried at the back end of the B-side of a demo cassette, unrecognised and unloved until the producer or A&R person spotted it.

Jerry Harrison of Talking Heads assumes nothing. The first thing he will do at the pre-production stage is to say, "Let's hear everything you have, not just what's been decided on." Then he will listen through to everything on cassette. "Sometimes you'll see that the raw way that they play something sounds better than the way they did it on a demo. A lot of times you'll hear the raw beauty."

You have to be aware of the conditions under which the demos were made. Did the band or a friend of the band produce them? Did their lack of experience create more problems than they solved, such as stilted arrangements, bad sounds, lumpy feels or inappropriate production techniques. A lack of money can push a demo in a weird direction. A band whose main appeal is their rhythm section might have chosen to use a drum machine because they couldn't record live drums in their house. Demos are often the first thing a band does when they get together. A year later when they have done two hundred live shows they will be much tighter. Nothing sharpens up a band's material as much as a full gig sheet.

Sometimes production is about mediating, moderating and protecting the democratic process, other times you need to allow yourself or someone else to be a dictator. "Usually what people are practising is not democracy, but cowardice and good manners," says Eno. "Nobody wants to step on so-and-so's toes, so nobody wants to say anything. The valuable idea of democracy is that if there are five people in the room and one of them feels very strongly about something, you can trust that the strength of their feelings indicates that there is something behind it. My feeling about a good democratic relationship is the notion that it's a shifting leadership. It's not, 'We all lead together all the time', it's 'We all have sufficient trust in one another to believe that if someone feels strongly then we let them lead for that period of time.' And this is what typically happens. Somebody will say, 'No I really think we should do it this way,' and I'll say, 'OK, let's try it, let's see what happens'."

Sometimes you have to protect one person's creativity from another's stupidity. There is a story about a world-famous percussionist and a not-so-world famous producer. Supposedly the producer was not happy with what the percussionist was playing on a particular track, so he hit the talkback button and said 'Could you make it more Cuban'. The percussionist reputedly rose to his full five feet six inches, said 'I am Cuban' and walked out of the studio. So, we know he's a little touchy. Shortly after this happened, I was working with an artist who claimed to be a huge fan of this percussionist. The drummer in particular wanted him to play on their album. I knew the percussionist so I called him. A few days later the guy arrived at the studio with four truck loads of stretched, dead-animal skins and things filled with dried beans. This musician is an incredibly instinctive player. On a previous session for me he had nailed a complex part on the first run-through of a song he'd never heard before. He didn't even look at the chart. Fortunately we were in record. Anyway, back to the session. I ran the tape and our captive Cuban played the most beautiful part. It was perfect, and very exciting. Just over my left shoulder I sensed someone moving toward the console. I looked up in time to catch the drummer making a beeline for the talk-back button. I rugby tackled him (figuratively speaking) and asked him what he was up to. He said that he had a different part in mind, which he sang to me. It was probably the most clichéd bongo part I had ever heard. A Book One, page 1 idea. Sometimes the obvious thing is the right thing, but we could have done this part on a drum machine at much less than triple scale. Fortunately the rest of the band agreed with me and we kept the first take.

The point is you book musicians for what they can do. That's not to say they don't need some guidance or can't be pushed. You can't afford to be intimidated by someone's reputation. The best players can take a lot of direction but you can still disempower even the greatest musicians by not allowing them the space to do what they do best. If a session becomes too much of a struggle then you've either got the wrong guy or you may be getting in the way of the creative flow.

Probably the worst thing that can happen in the studio is for things to descend to the lowest common denominator. To compromise in order to keep everyone happy. Excitement and passion are more likely to produce a great record than conciliation and compromise. Sometimes the producer needs to protect a more vulnerable member of the band while he or she tries out an idea. Creative notions are incredibly fragile. It's very rare that anyone has a fully formed creative thought. More usually the idea starts with vague sensation of something to be reached for, and it's only by actively reaching that the idea can be pulled through. It only takes a single disparaging comment ("It's shit,"

{UK} or "It sucks" {US} seem to be the favourites) from another band member in the early stages of this process to completely shut that door and cut the idea off before it has fully manifested itself. Bands are often riddled with internal politics, jealousies, factions and cliques. Part of the producer's job is to instinctively understand these forces within the band so he can analyse exactly why certain comments are being made. You need to understand whether they represent an honest opinion about the subject in hand or a deeper underlying agenda related to historic events, feuds, long-standing resentments or the fundamental power structure of the band.

Sometimes producing is about defining the parameters, sketching out the boundaries or as Eno puts it "establishing the cultural territory". There are times in a band's career when they are at the centre of what is happening, they instinctively understand who they are, what they represent and how they relate to what is going on around them culturally. Usually this is early on in their career. They have grown up at one with the influences of their generation, they are still carrying the confidence of youth and they are unburdened by an overly wide base of knowledge, so they are able to generate consistent, relevant music of their time. It may be trend-setting, trend-related or trend-following, all three can work. Personally, I would sooner be involved with trend-setters but they are not always the projects that make the money for the record company and they are not hiding around every corner.

Artists are not always focused. The producer in this case needs to direct the artist's attention, and a good way to do that is by limiting their options. Eno tries to do that by asking, "Where are we culturally? What are we trying to be? What books? What films? OK, if this is where we are, then we are not going to do that or that. What are the things that we're not going to do? Let's just get them out of the way and narrow the field a little bit." He adds, "Obviously you don't want to create a situation where you stop all creativity. But you want to create a situation where there is a meaningful amount of attention on something, rather than a small amount of attention on everything."

Andy Jackson thinks that a good producer can liberate the artist, allow them to do what they believe in and break through their inhibitions, fears or preconceptions to fulfil what they potentially could've done anyway. "He's acting as a therapist in some way. He's helping the artist to zero in on what they *really* want to do, rather than what they *imagine* they want to do. To free up their creativity. In that context the producer can say 'OK, you know what you are doing now so go and make the album.' [At that point] he doesn't even have to be there. It's something I have a tremendous amount of respect for."

Sometimes the producer's job is about production in the sense that people use the word most commonly. When someone says that a record has great production it can mean many things: they like the song (even though they didn't mention it), the arrangement feels right to them, the performances are appropriate and exciting, the whole thing sounds really good (clear, punchy, not harsh, not muddy or dull, good highs and lows), you can hear everything (especially the main melodies and lead vocals), everything seems to happen in the right place (the choruses, the little instrumental hooks etc.) or simply that it's exciting.

So how do you make a record sound great, balance it all up so you can hear everything, get everything in the right place and make it exciting as well? The first thing is to make the artist feel comfortable. No artist can perform well unless they are at ease and feel confident in themselves. They should be confident in the people they are working with and feel as though their collaborators have confidence in them.

Understanding the needs of the artist is paramount in production. Knowing when to push them, when to back off a little and when to stop altogether can be the key to getting that extra special performance. As Nashville veteran Barry Becket says, "I wish I had taken Psychology 101 in college instead of making music. It would have helped me out a great deal."

A little preparation can really lubricate the proceedings. An experienced engineer can pre-set the mic levels, EQ, reverbs and foldback (the mix of whatever music the singer will be singing to, either on headphones or speakers) before the singer arrives. If you've worked with the singer before, then you should know what they like to hear in the headphones and what levels they are likely to sing at. If you've never worked with them before, you can take an educated guess based on experience. It's relatively easy to make minor adjustments when the singer shows up.

I've seen singers practically lose their voices (and certainly their patience) while the engineer "gets a sound". There's a bad joke that seems to have travelled round every studio in the world. It's always cracked at the end of a particularly brilliant take. Some bright spark will hit the talkback button and say something like, "OK, we're ready – let's put one down." Sometimes, unfortunately for the performer, the 'bright spark' is not joking. An unrepeatable first take was lost because the engineer was not in record. Your first instinct is to brain the guy. Lack of preparation can also cause unusable takes because levels or compression were not "in the ballpark" before tape was rolled. You don't have to be a genius to get it right first time. You do have to be sensitive to the artist's needs. If you've ever been the victim of poor recording etiquette in the studio as a performer, when you're directing things in the control room you're likely to try harder.

Flood reinforces this. "You've got to make sure that, by experience, you know that even if you haven't heard the person open their mouth, that your mic level and your compressor level and your EQ is going to be OK so that it's not going to distort as soon as they start kicking in the first note they sing." He also points out that if you are always in record, with today's technology, if something's in the wrong place or a bit out of tune, you can fix so many things. "But that human spark – quite often after the first time you go for it – you never get it again."

So, rule number one in the studio should be: record everything. If you don't like the take you can always wipe it or record over it. Bitter experience has shown that you cannot pluck a slice of pure genius back from the ether!

Good solid engineering practices will make sure that the instruments and vocals are recorded well in the first place. It's very difficult to make a great sounding record if the basic instruments are not recorded well. "Fix it in the mix" is a lousy philosophy. A lot of mixers complain about having to "rescue" records that are recorded badly. I always wonder how the producer knew that the recording was finished if he's intending to "fix it in the mix". It takes an immense amount of faith to say, "It sounds like a mess right now but when it's mixed it'll be fine." I like to be able to hear the way the finished record will sound as I go along. The mix is really an enhancement of what is recorded, not a complete re-think (apart from radical dance remixes).

Clever orchestration helps to maintain clarity when you come to do the mix. It ensures that each element of the record occupies its own space in the audio spectrum and does not compete with the other instruments.

An exciting mix entails the use of equalisation, compression, limiting, expansion and gating to optimise the sounds, increase their impact and ensure they occupy their own space in the audio spectrum. (Very simply, equalisation or EQ affects the tone of a sound making it among other things, brighter or duller. Compression, limiting, expansion and gating are generically referred to as dynamic control and they can be used in a number of different ways to affect the shape, the impact, the length or the apparent loudness of a sound or combination of sounds.)

It is also a combination of careful balancing and panning of the instruments and vocals to focus the listener's attention on the most important things, and appropriate use of effects in order to give some front-back perspective, to put certain instruments or voices in relief and to create space between the different components of the mix. (Effects include reverb, delay, chorusing, phasing, flanging, distortion, ambience and combinations of the above.)

Mixing also involves riding (changing levels relative to time and the other instruments) and panning of instruments and vocals in order to improve the dynamic flow of the track to draw attention to different facets of the orchestration at different points in the song, and increase the overall excitement.

There are a handful of producers, George Martin, Phil Spector and Quincy Jones among them, who are as close as producers have gone, so far, to becoming household names. Jimmy Jam of Jam and Lewis says, "After *Thriller* everyone wanted to know, 'What exactly does a producer do?' The producer's not just a guy who simply sits in the studio and spends all the money. The producer can be a writer, an engineer – a self-contained entity. And Quincy's the man who proved that to the world."

One of the most influential and versatile producers who has covered the entire rock & soul spectrum is Tom Dowd. Coming from an engineering background, he had a very wide brief when he was on staff at Atlantic. He actually built and repaired the equipment on which he engineered and produced sessions.

Speaking about a particularly intense and creative period in the Sixties he said, "All of a sudden I was commuting about ten or twelve times a year to Memphis and five or six times a year to Muscle Shoals. I was going into Macon three or four times a year. I was seldom in New York. I'd be on the road; come home; listen to something; do this, that and the other thing; and go back out again. I was wearing different hats on all these missions; sometimes I was needed for updating facilities, or for engineering, suggesting arrangement changes or conducting – you name it. Whatever had to be done, had to be done."

## We Are Not Worthy

Aerosmith's lead guitarist Joe Perry says that every band has a different style and a different relationship with their producer. "Basically the way we work with Bruce Fairbairn, who did *Permanent Vacation, Pump* and *Get A Grip,* is that we will have our songs at a point where we all like them. Then Bruce will come in and listen for the rough spots. As part of the band, you get in the middle of the music, and you need someone with some distance from it. He comes in and listens with fresh ears and works with us to make it the best it can possibly be. If we had one part that we all thought was really smoking, and had something like two months away from it, maybe we would come back to it and see that it needed more. Unfortunately, we never get that luxury, so we get the next best thing: Bruce. Personally, I think that being a producer is such a harrowing experience that I'm glad I don't have to do it to make a living. 'Producer' is like a catch-all title. It's a very important position, but I don't want to get any closer to producing Aerosmith than I am right now. Everybody in the band has strong feelings about it too. I don't think it's wise for us to get to the point where we don't have someone to act as a mediator."

From only a few 'stage-feet' away Steven Tyler has a pretty different perspective on it. He says, "I think it's more difficult to work with a producer. Everybody likes to come in and rework your stuff to validate their punch cards and say that they were part of something. It's like a bunch of people telling you what the sugar cone beneath a big ball of vanilla ice cream tastes like and, oddly enough, it would taste different to you from what everybody else described. Everybody has their own interpretation of things and you've got to decide whether you take a hard-nosed stand and say, 'No way man, this is me and this is the way it stays,' or take chances. That's why we let people into our camp all the time. With each album it gets harder and harder to listen to other people, but every album gets better and better, so a producer is definitely necessary."

Beyond the practical actualities of day-to-day life in the studio and the commercial realities we all face, there can be a deeper inspiration and methodology for the producer. Jim Dickinson summed this up beautifully in his *Production Manifesto* in which he says, "Music has a spirit beyond notes and rhythm. To foster that spirit and to cause it to flourish – to capture it at its peak – is the producer's task." He elaborated on this by saying, "As a producer, I try to remain aware and attuned to the peculiar harmonic properties of the events as they unfold. This is not just musical. I'm talking about how the balance is gonna change in the room constantly during the process, just because of the process itself. It's in the life of the event where you find the soul, and that's what you are trying to capture. This becomes a moral responsibility for the producer. When you talk about records, what is the terminology that is used? This is a good record or this is a bad record. Well, that's basically the way I see it. There are enough bad records that get made, and you know it's your obligation during the process to try to make a good record. I think that in the case of many young bands, who can remain nameless, that the more they compromise, the more they eliminate the very thing that might have gotten them across."

"There are many different ways to produce," says Ros Earls, "The John Leckie type. Those that are surrounded by some sort of cool aura to do guitars. You almost associate them with sounds. People say 'that sounds like a Flood record.' He really hates the idea that people can tell that he produced something. I think that's a credit to [a producer's] attitude but inevitably you contribute something to the sound and it's visible, it's audible. I've never met a really good producer that admits it. Nonetheless it's there.

"If you're Brian Eno you can tell what he brought to *The Joshua Tree* for instance. He invented sounds and turned around a band's career. That's what you look for in a Brian Eno type arrangement, that's why James got him in on their last record. The sounds are what we hear with a producer like that, but there are other things that we don't hear that form the whole really. It was quite frustrating for people working with Trevor Horn. Not in a bad sense. It was always felt that he could be at the end of a phone and tell what needs to happen. That's an extraordinary talent, I think. You've either got it or you haven't. Those that don't have it don't always see the value in it. It's equivalent to someone's name being on a record. You know if you've got Eno on it's going to sound a certain way but you also know that the mere fact that he agreed to collaborate with you is almost enough in itself (because his name's going to be on the record)."

"The vast majority of records are driven by a very fearful thing of not doing something wrong rather than doing something right," says Andy Jackson. "We don't let things go. We're striving for perfection which is actually just avoiding the possibility of someone saying 'Ooh that's weird'. It's true that you can construct an album painstakingly piece by piece or you can till the soil, sow the seed, and pray for rain.' (In some cases it's more like 'light the touch paper and retire to a safe distance' but the principle is the same.) The knack of letting that special thing happen is a difficult to quantify, but a highly desirable, production skill. Andy did an album a few years ago with Tony Visconti. "It was a really quick album," he says. "It only took about two and a half weeks. It was interesting to watch him function. What did he contribute? It mainly seemed that it was just a very easy atmosphere to work in. It seemed that things could happen very easily and quickly. It really struck me at the time."

As I said in Chapter One the producer may also have to decide how and where the record will be recorded, who, if anyone, will help to make it, what technical equipment will be used, how the budget is going to be spent, and who will take care of the administration and paperwork.

Usually, in consultation with the record company and artist, the producer will choose the studio or studios that will be used. This may be one studio for the whole project or different studios for different phases of the recording. It is very common to use one place for the recording or tracking part and a different studio for mixing. There are several reasons for this. If an album stretches out over several months, both the artist and producer want a change of scenery. Budget can be a factor. Mixing rooms usually have large state-of-the-art computerised consoles (a.k.a board or desk) and every piece of outboard signal processing equipment ever made. When you are recording a band or overdubbing you don't need the computerised console or that many channels on the desk, and you'll use only a few pieces of outboard equipment so to have it sitting around doing nothing for several months is a waste of money.

Some producers and their engineers have different preferences for recording than for mixing. In recent years old valve (tube) equipment and the older solid state (but usually with discrete Class A circuitry) has become very popular for recording. Some real audiophiles prefer to record and mix on the older equipment but generally the computerisation, greater number of channels, parametric equalisation, recall or reset and improved ergonomics of the new boards wins out over the older consoles for the mixing.

Often bands like to record in a residential studio. It gets them away from their domestic problems. If they are a young band, it will probably seem like a luxurious experience, they get fed regularly (sometimes they have to slim down again before the tour). The producer has an easier time tracking down the bass player (when he suddenly needs him for an overdub at three in the afternoon) than he would in Los Angeles, London or New York City. A trend that has been gaining momentum over the last ten years or so is to put together a portable studio in a country house. The easy way to do this is to rent a mobile recording facility. The disadvantage is that the producer and engineer spend all day cramped in the back of a truck. So what usually happens is that all the equipment is flight-cased, wheeled in and set up in the most suitable room in the house. The acoustics won't be perfect but the environment is pleasant and there is usually a lot of daylight which for most people makes the whole process more enjoyable. I say most people because I have worked with several artists and engineers who like their recording environment to be dark like a womb, a nightclub or a bordello.

Depending on the type of producer and the kind of artist

involved, there is usually some sort of team to be put together. The most compact situation is the engineer-producer working with a self-contained indie/alternative style band. Usually the only other person needed is the assistant engineer who is mostly supplied by the studio.

If a project is being put together entirely on computer, as most dance records are, the team could be as small as the artist and the producer who between them do all of the engineering, playing and programming. More commonly there will be a separate engineer, assistant engineer, a programmer and maybe some musicians.

When you get into major high end productions involving well established pop artists there will almost certainly be an assistant engineer, engineer, programmer, arranger, possibly the song writer and many musicians, all in addition to the producer. The artist may not be there for the bulk of the recording.

As far as the technical equipment is concerned producers tend to have their favourite ways to work. Some work only on digital equipment, others will not be swayed from the analogue stuff that's been around for over twenty-five years. In the late Seventies and the early Eighties the degree of standardisation in studios hit an all-time high. Most studios had one of about three or four consoles the same with twenty-four-track tape machines, quarter or half inch mastering and monitor speakers. A tape recorded in a top flight studio could be played back in any other high end studio anywhere in the world. Moving from studio to studio and country to country was extremely easy. These days the range of equipment is bewilderingly large. There are several professional digital formats, many semi-pro formats that are finding their way into pro studios in addition to all the standard analogue tape machines. Hard disk editors are proliferating at an alarming rate and compatibility and interchangeability of stored data is less than good. More producers are working out of their own facilities or at least carrying significant pieces of equipment with them so that they have some control over the technical formats they might have to deal with. The sooner manufacturers agree standards for digital equipment the better for everyone including themselves. (Look at the IBM compatible PC. Definitely not as user friendly as a Mac but nonetheless they command 92% of the computer market largely because of the open architecture and the fact that they allowed third parties to manufacture clones. Increased competition kept prices low and compatibility encouraged consumers, third party peripheral manufacturers and software programmers.)

In the Seventies and Eighties it was not uncommon to work on a project with no budgetary constraints, or at least such a large budget that it didn't matter. Those days are gone. Budgeting was always stricter in the USA than in England. The first overage clauses I ever saw were in American contracts (an overage clause is part of the producer contract which basically makes any expenditure over the initial agreed budget the producer's personal expense. It will either be taken out of his advance or future royalties). All-in funds have become much more common. This is where the producer is allocated a fixed amount of money out of which he has to make the record and pay himself. This can work out very well for the producer, particularly where he is self-contained. In R'n'B, Rap and dance music, if the producer is a writer/programmer/musician who owns his own recording facility he can really control the costs. After the initial outlay for his studio has been recouped all he is accounting for is his time, tape, disks and maybe an assistant engineer. An engineer producer working on alternative bands can also do quite well out of an all-in recording budget. They can be pretty sure that they can record and mix the album in, say, five weeks. Their main costs are going to be studio time, tape and some equipment rentals.

When I first started producing, costs were always paid by the record company. The producer was paid a fixed advance in two instalments, one at the beginning and one at the end. The budget would be submitted by the producer before starting the project and agreed by the company. Usually they would want to shave something off the proposed budget. Sometimes the company will tell you up-front how much they want to spend and it's up to you to figure out a way to make the money do everything you, the band, and the company want to do. In many ways I prefer the more traditional, separate recording budget with the bills paid by the company. The upside for the producer is not so good. On an all-in fund, if the producer can control the costs he can walk away with many times more than he would have on a fixed advance.

There are certain disadvantages, though. If costs get out of hand the producer can find himself working for nothing or even paying for the project to get finished. The producer may cut corners to save money. His interests may conflict with the artists. The record company may not be so bothered how you go about making the record as long as you deliver something they like. The artist, however, may want real strings on three tracks. He may want to use a certain studio that is more expensive for part of the project. The producer might be inclined to discourage this because it reduces his profit. On a traditional costs-paid-by-the-company budget the producer may still have to limit spending. The difference is in how it affects the producer/artist relationship. On an all-in fund the artist will be aware that while his spending is being limited, the producer is lining his own pocket.

When the costs are being paid by the company, the producer and the artist are on the same side. They can jointly look at the budget to see whether they can squeeze the extra 'whatever' out of it or go back to the record company and ask for more money. An external budget limitation can increase the bond between producer and artist. An artist may not feel so good about his creative partner imposing limitations that maximise his own profit. This can be aggravated by the fact that an established producer usually lives much higher on the hog than a first-time recording artist. The tens of thousands that the producer is making out of the deal can seem particularly unreasonable to someone who lives on a shoestring, especially when just a few of those thousands could finance the extra overdub.

More bands are coming to realise that the recording budget is ultimately their money. If they spend it, they will have to pay it back out of their royalties. Many artists look at their advances like the guy who hopes to die with his American Express card max'd out. If he actually dies – he won't have to worry about the bill. If, however, he survives the fourteenth of the month, that huge bill has to be paid and within twenty-eight days at that. It's definitely fun to go nuts with the record company's money but I am sure there are a lot of ex-musicians out there who, if they had conserved a little of the good-times, would be having a lot better time than they are right now. Budgets may even get bigger because of overage clauses. No producer wants to get stuck with paying for part of the album. Consequently they pad their initial budget projection.

## Who Will Take Care Of The Administration And Paperwork?

Doing this stuff is like watching paint dry. Not the reason why anyone wants to produce records. You can't even get started on most projects until you have submitted a budget. If you are a delegating type of guy you will have someone else put a budget together. Unless they know your working habits better than you do (this can happen with long-time assistants), you are at least going to have to answer a multiple choice quiz about studios, dates, times, tape, musicians, arrangers and equipment packages. Once you are on the project there are studio bills, phone bills and rental bills to be signed and kept track of. Union forms and rights clearances have to be filled out, signed and submitted. And the budget has to be tracked at all times by comparing the actual expenditure to the original budget allocation. Some producers handle this themselves, some managers will take care of it, others hire production co-ordinators, the rest prefer not to think about it until the record company calls them in because their time (and money) is up.

The only way to avoid paperwork is to cultivate a reputation for being an administrative imbecile and a creative genius. It's a fragile stance that takes some wild, abandoned upkeep but the music business loves to mythologise and protect a helpless prodigy.

## Managing The Session From Day To Day

*a) Pre-production*

Some albums are done completely without pre-production, which allows almost all the creative decisions to be made in the studio and makes the budget extremely hard to pin down. On other records virtually all the vital decisions, and in some cases a large part of the work is done at the pre-production stage. Extensive pre-production makes costing more accurate and often helps to keep the final price of the project down.

John Leckie (Simple Minds, The Human League, XTC, The Fall, Stone Roses) says, "Usually the first decision I make is whether to use a live backing track or a computer and click. The songs will shape themselves after making this fundamental choice. Also, your personal approach to a song may vary slightly or radically from inception to finish. It's an ongoing decision-making process, all the way through to the final mix. You shouldn't decide that a song is going to be of a very specific nature before you begin piecing it together. But when it is good you'll feel it."

If it's going to be a live band recording together in the studio, pre-production is the time when the arrangements are finalised. Then the band rehearses all the songs to the point where they know them inside out. Arranging and rehearsing can be left till you get into the studio, but then instead of going for great takes, you'll be wasting expensive studio time deciding whether the song is better with or without an extra two bars after the chorus. I'd rather work that out at a tenth of the price in a rehearsal room and save my expensive studio time for capturing performances. The same methodology applies if the band members are going to overdub to a click. Pre-production would be the band playing the songs through, figuring out the parts and making sure that everything works together so that there are no horrible surprises in the studio.

However, it's always a good idea to allow for flexibility in the studio. No matter how well prepared you are going in, once you get there and play that first take back on the big monitors your thinking and approach can completely change. Michael McDonald, ex-lead singer with The Doobie Brothers and now a solo artist says, "With the Doobies, no matter how much we rehearsed something out front, the minute we got into the studio, we ripped the thing apart and restructured it totally. That was really the moment that things started to come together." Even when that's the case I still think the increased familiarity that comes through pre-production will make the restructuring process faster.

If the record is going to have outside musicians playing on it, they can either be brought together as a band to rehearse all the arrangements and parts like a self-contained group, or the basic arrangements can be worked out in pre-production and the fine details of the individual parts left until the musicians come into the studio. This approach allows for some spontaneity in the studio.

In the case of a computer-programmed album, not only can the arrangements be worked out in pre-production, but the parts can be played into the computer. Sounds and samples can also be decided on. The only reasons why computer based projects might have to go into a pro studio are either to record the parts onto multi-track, record any live parts such as guitar or vocals or to use a proper mix room with a large mixing console, comprehensive outboard equipment, and studio monitoring. Project studios with modular digital multitracks and the new consumer digital consoles or hard disk based work-stations are fast making it possible to do these projects entirely at home.

"We were in pre-production for seven months," said Rick Rubin of The Red Hot Chili Peppers, "working on the material. Then we recorded the whole album in three or four weeks. So the process of getting the music on to tape is very simple, but getting the music to the point where it's even ready to be recorded is very tough." Referring to bands that like to write in the studio he said, "I'm totally against that. The studio is not a place for writing. It's a place to make magic happen, not to think. I'm a huge fan of pre-production, and that should be done at home or in a rehearsal studio. So with this Chili Peppers-album, I'd say we got the material to the point where if I'd left the project before we recorded, and they'd basically stuck to what we'd worked out over those seven months, I think the resulting album would have been the one I wanted."

Bob Ezrin produced the fourth Julian Lennon album *Help Yourself.* He didn't want to go into the studio until the material was absolutely brilliant, so the pre-production period became really intensive. "In fact it was the most intensive part of the whole project, and it was also the part when we made greatest use of the Akai A-DAM system (the first relatively inexpensive modular digital multitrack). It was during pre-production that I realised we needed to store all of our ideas on some sort of medium that wasn't too noisy, that was going to be relatively faithful, and that would also allow us, if necessary, to later use the demo material in a master recording context.

"We'd take a song, flesh it out on twelve-track, [analogue] do all the overdubs, add all the vocals and harmonies, and then step back and decide if the result was truly interesting. Meaning, are you going to carry on to the next refinement stage of recording, where you sequence out the song in terms of verse and chorus? We recorded several songs on analogue like I described, and then decided that many of the ideas we'd put on tape could be used if only they sounded better – less noisy and less distorted." At that point they switched over to the digital system. "Everything was laid down in a retrievable fashion, so if we recorded a killer guitar riff in a song that wasn't particularly successful, we could still salvage it because we also had SMPTE (synchronisation code)." The pre-production took six months in all but at the end of it they were able to transfer the digital tracks across to the Sony 3348 (48-track professional recorder). Some parts were re-recorded and some of the pre-production demo tracks were kept and used on the actual record.

The modular digital machines are invaluable for this purpose. They can save an immense amount of time and frustration by allowing the producer to use parts of the demos or pre-production work without any serious loss of quality.

Jack Douglas likes to have a good pre-production period of anything from a week to a month depending on the artist. "You have to get the artist ready for the studio, and I don't mean ready like there's not going to be any surprises, like they've learned it like robots. Sometimes I get a band and I have to go the opposite way in that aspect, I have to say, 'Look, let's not lock in so much here'.

"Generally I like the band to know and understand the piece, and, for some reason, drummers usually have to work a little harder at this so they know where the shots are and what has to be emphasised. But for the most part I encourage bands to let go and try things. I always tell them that they're holding back even if they're not. Even if they're at rehearsal playing their absolute best, I will say, 'Well when you get into the studio you can really let go'."

Talking about Aerosmith, Douglas says, "They would come into pre-production with these little guitar riff gems and we would work them into songs while Steven [Tyler] scattered phonetics over them. Then we would take cassettes back to my house and Steve and I would sit there and turn those phonetics into lyrics.

They would always be the right phonetics for the song 'cause they sounded good, so all you had to do was kinda get them to be words and they would automatically fit."

*b) Recording The Live Band*

Any time there is a musician in the studio performing, the intensity level of the session goes up. You have to assume at all times that the current performance may be the best one they are capable of. In which case if you fail to record it well or at all, that performance may be lost forever. "OK now let's take one" is the usual sad studio joke used immediately after a killer performance.

It's bad enough if you forget to record a brilliant guitar overdub but the stakes rise when you have a group of musicians performing together. Suddenly you have multiple possibilities for mistakes, making the perfect performance even more precious. The chemistry that occurs between musicians playing together can create a whole performance which is significantly greater than the sum of the parts. When this chemistry happens, it is often dramatic and unrepeatable. It is a case of death to the producer or engineer who fails to properly record such moments.

"I like live recording, I think you get a better sound than with overdubbing," says George Martin. "It doesn't take longer, it just takes a little more application – but you have to be in a studio that can handle it."

John Leckie says, "I've always believed in recording a live backing track that holds some magical interaction between musicians. This is almost impossible to obtain when doing singular overdubs. So even today I'll start on some songs by getting the bass, drums, a rhythm instrument and the vocal all happening together. I'll choose the take that has this magical interaction or uplift or some spirited feeling that makes the song happen – you just have to feel it. When using a click track and starting with the drums, then bass and so on, you may never have more than one band member in the studio at the same time, and it's quite hard to keep a human essence or organic musical dialogue."

Mitchell Froom, producer of Crowded House, Richard Thompson and Jimmy Scott says, "We don't really do what you call tracking (an American term for laying the basic rhythm tracks to which the vocals and overdubs or 'sweetening' will be added later). We just start working and oftentimes that's the end of the story. You get the sound of the record on the day you're working. We take it as far as we can and sometimes we'll go back to it later. Often it's finished, but you may want a little more perspective, or if the singer isn't in good voice that day we may go back. It seems that the most successful recording is done at the moment. If you have somebody sing on a track, and the engineer is working that sound into the track and everything works together, it's going to be much easier for the person to sing it that moment. Much better than if you do overdubs without considering what the vocal may be. It can be difficult to have someone sing over some foreign sounds, conflicting frequencies and all that. In general, right at the moment people are really into it, they are not paranoid, they are relaxed. If they've sung the song through three or four times through the course of the day they are right there with it. And the same goes for the overdubs. People are into the real feeling of a track, and not coming back to it later, trying to remember. You tend to get the most done in the moment – if you stick with it.

"There's a few ways to approach working on a record. There are parts of a record which may do very well by being orchestrated, and then there's parts that don't. You have to make that decision, whether someone is going after a wild performance, where what they do may change throughout the song or whether it's more planned. Very often it's a combination, and it's not an easy thing to get that feeling of spontaneity but still have it sounding like a record, and not just a thrash.' What he says makes a lot of sense but for various reasons a lot of records are not made this way. Sometimes the budget will dictate that the basic tracks will need to be recorded first. Maybe that's because the studio you needed for tracking was quite expensive, so, to stay within budget, you added the vocals and overdubs later, in a cheaper studio. You need a much larger, more sophisticated facility to record a whole band than you do to record one instrument at a time. Sometimes the tracks will be recorded piecemeal because it suits the producer or engineer. It is much easier to plough on and keep laying tracks once you have all the microphones set up and equalised, than it is to keep chopping and changing, backwards and forwards from band to vocals, to acoustic guitar to horns and so on."

With the advent of larger recording consoles, the current trend is to leave everything set up at all times. This enables you to add, say, a lead vocal or acoustic guitar to any track at a moment's notice. This is a more musical way of working. It short-circuits many of the problems that can happen when you lay all the tracks first and then have, say, a week of guitar overdubs, a week of keyboards and then the vocals. You are more likely to get varied and appropriate sounds and performances doing the overdubs song by song than if you set up to do them instrument by instrument across the whole album. The song-by-song way of working minimises the problem of the singer losing his voice in the middle of doing vocals. There are very few singers who can sing all day, every day, without some negative repercussions on the sound of their voice. Under pressure to deliver vocals, either from nerves or physical overuse, less experienced singers can lose their voices completely. Even if they get through the intense day-in-day-out vocal sessions, the performance and vocal quality may be less than it could have been because of the psychological and physical pressure to perform.

Jack Douglas likes to track with the whole band live as often as he can. He doesn't even worry about too much separation, in fact he goes for a lot of leakage. "I like to hear guitars and bass in the drum track, and on one guitar track I like to hear a little bit of the other leaking in there. I love live vocals. You really get the excitement, and that's important. When you put it all together it just sounds so much bigger." He's not one for absolute perfection but neither does he like a really blatant mistake. Rather than try to patch it with an overdub and have all the leakage disappear he would sooner cut in a piece from another take.

Writing in the studio can be an expensive pastime but when it works the spontaneity and freshness can be unequalled. Daniel Lanois said that U2 is really about performance. "We generally try to get something on tape as a foundation and then add a lot of detail to that. Many studio compositions come about from jam sessions based upon a riff that they had prepared. That tiny riff provides the inspiration to come up with other chords, in a different type of arrangement. What we wind up with is very different from what was originally planned."

*c) Recording An Orchestra Or Big Band*

Recording orchestras is much the same as recording any other group of musicians except that the tolerances are tighter. The microphone techniques are somewhat different and the dynamic range is often much greater than that of a rock group. Orchestral musicians will hold you to the letter of the Union rules so there is not a lot of time for experimentation. A two-minute run-over at the end of the session can cost you a great deal of extra dosh. So the pressure not to screw up is proportionately greater. Preparation is the key. By the time the musicians arrive everything needs to be ready. The microphones must be set up, the chairs and music stands out, the coffee on and the tape ready to roll. There's a lot of responsibility and it can be simultaneously an exhilarating and scary experience.

One of the great engineer/producers, Phil Ramone recalls the first time he engineered a session on his own. "Afterward there were stains on my pants. It was a Neil Sedaka record. I was about 17, and had never balanced a whole rhythm section before. It was like the first time that your Dad says, 'OK son, now you take the wheel.' It was incredibly exciting, and I still get that feeling. Consistently, over the years I have worked with big bands. A few years ago Quincy Jones called and asked, 'Will you do Sinatra with me with a big band?' And I was able to reproduce that experience recently while working with Sinéad O'Connor and a big band. You put your hands on the console, and suddenly you realise, 'Oh, my God. It all depends on me, and if it falls apart it's my ass'."

Another all-time-great engineer/producer is Bruce Swedien. Having been Quincy Jones' right-hand studio person and friend for four decades, he went on to produce tracks for Michael Jackson. Swedien has recorded the greats of the Fifties, Sixties, Seventies, Eighties and is still doing the same in the Nineties. He spoke about recording Count Basie at Universal Studios in Chicago during the Fifties. As was customary at the time the whole band was set up in the eighty foot by sixty foot by thirty foot high room. The singer, Joe Williams, was also in the room but goboed off (gobos are acoustically treated, movable screens usually about eight feet high and four feet wide). At that time there were no second engineers, so Swedien had to set up the room, align the tape machines and everything. He says, "I would never get much of a chance to rehearse and get levels, but by that time I knew the band real well. There was a lot of carrying on and silliness and jokes and everything. Then Basie would raise his hand and say, 'Let's do it.' Dead silence. Absolutely not a sound. It would make your skin crawl. And we would do a take."

*d) Overdubbing Live Musicians*

This usually involves only one musician performing at a time over a pre-recorded backing track. The problem is to get the overdubbed performance to blend with the pre-recorded track. If a band plays together in the studio, even if they can't see each other, they somehow empathically feel the natural dynamic and tempo fluctuations that happen organically. Once a performance is recorded the signals that apparently emanate from a performing musician are not recorded with that performance and it becomes a matter of learning the idiosyncracies of the recorded performance.

Overdubbing has worked fine ever since Les Paul invented the concept. Since the mid-Sixties overdubbing has become the standard way to make records outside of the jazz and classical fields. The process offers many advantages, not least the opportunity for one musician to play all the instruments or for different musicians in different locations and at different times to apparently play together on a record. You can change an arrangement or orchestration if instruments are overdubbed and the engineer's control over the sonic quality of each instrument is much greater. The downside is that the end result can sometimes be a little stiff or sterile.

The band that honed this way of working to perfection was Steely Dan. Walter Becker, who was half of the production team, recently said that it has always amazed him that you could create a tight, live feeling groove entirely by overdubs. "You record all these little bits and pieces, layer upon layer, and then you play it back and it sounds like it happened at the same time. All I can say is to make that really work well, like so many other things, it depends on the choices you make as to what is a good overdub, or what the tracking needs." He also noted that "Back in the

Seventies, our big problem was trying to get the tracks with live musicians to be steadier and more mechanically perfect and so on – whereas now, the big problem is trying to get the machine tracks to be more natural sounding and have more of the feel and variation of tracks played by real musicians." Which leads us neatly to . . .

*e) The Computer-Based Session*

If one single factor would distinguish the computer session from any kind of live performance recordings it would be the lack of adrenalin. Things can always be modified, edited and corrected. The excitement of the performance disappears. Computers generally allow a great deal of procrastination and endless changing of minds. Sometimes this can be a lifesaving thing. Before computers, if the drum sound was not right, the key was wrong or the structure needed modifying, the only thing to do was to start from scratch again. It was very costly to make a mistake. Since computers, the arrangement, the parts and the sounds can stay in a state of flux until everything is printed to multitrack or the computer generated sounds and parts are mixed directly to two-track. Unfortunately the individuals who have difficulty making decisions seem to be the ones who are attracted to making records by computer. These people have great difficulty finishing a record. With everything in a permanent state of flux and no necessity to make a decision, the project can go on for ever.

Walter Afanasieff, producer of Mariah Carey and Michael Bolton, talks about the way the sessions usually run. "I'm a big fan of sequencing technology. We usually programme for a couple of days first, get the arrangement down and then go to tape. Tape is the very last step, though, after the arrangement is exactly as I want it. Because sometimes I'll prepare arrangements for artists and if they decide to change keys . . . well . . . if you're already on tape, you're cooked – no way to transpose without re-recording. I like computers and hard disks, the digital domain. No fuss, no muss, easy to transpose. No analog punch-ins or razor blades."

Annie Lennox's producer, Steve Lipson, tries to avoid getting to the point with technology where you can do so much that you end up doing nothing. Which, he says, is what happened a few years ago with the Synclavier. "We got up our own arses, big time. Trevor [Horn] bought it, and it sat in the room untouched for a while, so I just started fiddling about with it and ended up being the 'Synclavier Operator'. We both got quite excited by its possibilities and ended up investing loads of money in it. Every time an upgrade came out, we got it – but this would mean we'd do another version of a track just because there'd been an upgrade to the synclavier. Hi-hats would take a week – because it could be done. The lesson I learned from that was: *use the gear – don't let the gear use you.*"

Interestingly, happy accidents still happen on a computer session. Lipson tells about one song on an Annie Lennox album . . . "when I'd mucked up in the computer, and one particular instrument was getting every sequence from all the other channels – drum patterns, everything. Whatever was in the sequencer was triggering this one peculiar noise. And it sounded fantastic. These things happen."

*f) The Vocals*

Vocals and drums are often said to be the most difficult instruments to record. In fact, technically, vocals are relatively easy to record. The aspect of vocal recording that seems to cause the most difficulty is capturing the magical performance. A great vocal may well be in-time and in-tune but there are plenty of in-time and in-tune vocals that are less than great shifting oxide every day of the week. Saying a vocal needs to be in-time and in-tune is like saying a car needs four wheels and an engine. Both the backing track and the singer's attitude need to be consistent with the content of the lyrics in order for the final result to be satisfying. Mostly this stuff happens subconsciously, especially when the singer is the writer of the song and has worked on the arrangement as part of the band.

A good production needs to be sensitive to the intention of the song, leaving space for the vocal and supporting it with the right musical attitude. It is a little worrying if you have to drastically modify the singer's interpretation of the song because it indicates a fundamental lack of sensitivity, which can be hard to rectify. Assuming you have the right singer for the job, then getting a good vocal is a matter of creating a comfortable environment for them. This includes setting up a foldback that is both enjoyable and workable. A workable foldback is one that allows the singer to immerse themselves in the atmosphere of the song whilst still being able to hear themselves enough to stay in time and in tune. Very often a novice singer will ask for the foldback to be set up in such a way that it sounds good to them but doesn't help them stay in time or in tune. The best indication that the foldback is unworkable is when a singer who normally sings in time and in tune (when singing live or on scratch vocals) starts having problems.

John Leckie's priority is to make the singer feel comfortable rather than worry about a technically perfect recording. "Some inexperienced singers cannot perform with headphones. So I see nothing wrong in tracking the vocal with an SM58 in the control room with the monitors cranked up. It's easy to freak out about the spill, but you can gate it out later. Sometimes, however, this spill can enhance the rest of the track. It's usually some high-frequency rhythmic thing like a hi-hat that catches the effect on the vocal, and then during the mix this can add a mysterious touch that can work well for the song."

André Fischer, co-founder and member of the band Rufus, producer of great vocalists such as Anita Baker, Brenda Russell, Diane Schuur, Lalah Hathaway and his wife Natalie Cole, won a Grammy for his work on the album *Unforgettable*, a tribute to Natalie's father Nat King Cole. He said that when he works with a vocalist two things he brings to the project as the producer are 'care and protection'. He elaborates, "Basically, most vocalists are scared of being judged before they think it's perfect, but there is no such thing as perfection. What we're doing on a record is creating an illusion; it's not real. It's capturing something that may have been spontaneous, maybe not. To me the truest art form in music is playing live, whether that's recorded or not. If you like to perform and express yourself, the studio should just be another place to play. But a lot of people are intimidated by studios. So my job is to make it conducive and be a catalyst to make things click. The care I give is letting the singers know I'm there to bring the best out of them and be objective, and not make judgements. I never tell a vocalist how to sing. I may make some suggestions: 'You're singing from your nose; you're not singing from your diaphragm; don't sing while sitting on a stool' – commonsense things that don't get into judgements of someone's character or ability. As a producer I might not always get the performance that I want – the discrepancies might come in intonation or in timing or the emotional interpretation of the line – but you have to know how to pull back a little in dealing with that to get what you want in the long run."

The story can be very different when the producer is also the writer of the song and particularly if he is a good singer himself. Often the producer will have sung the demo and when it comes to making the record, he expects the vocalist to sing the melody note for note and inflection for inflection, exactly reproducing the demo. With an inexperienced singer this can work. The singer delivers a vocal that is beyond what they could have come up with on their own. However, I have seen some pretty ugly situations develop where the artist has their own style and wants to give their own interpretation of the melody, the artist is simply not able to reproduce the inflections of the original demo or the producer was so dogmatic about each inflection and vocal styling that the singer is intimidated or offended, and the whole session descends into a major confrontation.

Even the great Jimi Hendrix had to be handled with kid gloves in the studio. Eddie Kramer, who engineered many of his classic records says: "I also knew how to make Jimi feel comfortable in the studio. From the outset, he had strong reservations about his vocal ability – he never really liked the sound of his own voice. To help him overcome this discomfort, I would put partitions all around him when he placed the lead vocal overdubs. Jimi also asked that the lights be dimmed, so they were. After we recorded the track he would poke his head around the screen and ask, 'How was that? Was that OK? Was it all right?' And I would tell him it was fine because, when it came to his singing voice, Jimi needed all the confidence he could get."

"Nine times out of ten, the scratch vocals are better than the real thing because the artist doesn't have the pressure – that 'this is it' rolling round in his or her mind," says Jimmy Jam. "We used to give the artist a tape and say, 'Here's how it goes. Learn it and come back tomorrow.' We never do that anymore. You can catch gold (or platinum as the case may be) while an artist is in the process of learning a song and playing around with addictive new melodies."

He cites Janet Jackson's lead vocal on 'Escapade', one of the biggest singles from the *Rhythm Nation* album, as being a scratch vocal that made it all the way to the actual record.

Speaking from a singer's point of view, Steven Tyler of Aerosmith says "When I record my vocal tracks, I don't like to go in and just throw them down. I like to do them at my own pace, which is pretty quick anyway. I prefer to have six or seven tracks and keep singing the same song with different voices and in different ways. I like after-hours vocals. It's what I did on *Get A Grip* and it's what I did on *Pump.* I go in there after the band leaves – so it's just me and an engineer. That's when I can have the most fun. No-one's listening and there's no pressure. After hours is when I can get closest to a song and its real meaning. The emotions that come out of me then are always in sync with the song."

Many singers are uncomfortable singing in front of a control room full of people. Even if the singer is screened off and can't see into the control room, they might be that much more self-conscious and less likely to take risks. There's probably nothing more disconcerting than being in a darkened studio, exposing yourself vocally, only to hear a bunch of people talking, laughing, or worse, criticising what you just did when the talkback button goes down.

There are those occasions when you are lucky enough to be in the studio with a truly great singer. Barry Beckett tells how, on a session with Joe Cocker, vocal genius turned out to be problem. "He broke into a vocal that was just amazingly good on the first take. I was so totally enthralled that I forgot the structure of the song. At one point he stopped singing and just stood there. The track was going on and I stopped the tape and said, 'Is there something that we can help you with? Is there something wrong?' He said, 'No, this is the instrumental part.' He couldn't punch in. Dylan was the same way. They are among a few who just can't punch in. They would have to do the vocal all the way from the top, good or bad.' He adds, 'I felt stupid as hell. What made matters worse is I only had one remaining track when I got the tape. I was scared to death that we were going to pass up something else. I could have put it into 'input,' and done it all the way from the top, but I might have had something else just as good. He ended up being maybe one percent off what I was hoping for, but it was still good."

Barry Beckett touches on one of the all-time great production dilemmas. When you are working on solos or vocals, very often you get down to the last available track on the multi-track tape. Even if you are working on an unlimited slave system (where you make up work reels with as many available tracks as you might need for overdubs) you can still run out of tracks. It's always possible to make up another slave or work reel, right then and there, but if the creative juices are flowing, by the time you've done that the moment will most likely have passed. Very often at these moments the singer (or soloist) will say, "I can do better than that." You, however, have been listening to this guy all afternoon and you know that the last performance was the best you have heard. You could, as Beckett said, roll the tape in input, which means that you don't record his next performance although the performer will think you are.

These are the potential scenarios:

You don't record the next pass. He reaches deep down inside, somewhere he hasn't been all day, possibly all week and does the vocal of his life. You didn't record it. He's going to know you didn't record it. Very ugly scene ensues.

You don't record the next pass. He doesn't do a great vocal. You breathe a sigh of relief. As you reach for the talkback button to tell him what a clever boy you've been, he says: "That was it. That was the one." Total silence from the control room. You are stuck with the previous take which in his mind is utter crap compared to the one he just did. And he's going to like the one you have on tape even less when he finds out that the one he thought was it is now in magnetic heaven.

You do go into record. You wipe the best vocal of the project or, depending on the artist, the only decent vocal that he did all week. His performance is not quite as good or complete crap. You can't decide whether to shoot yourself, shoot the singer or kick the engineer.

You do go into record. He does the best vocal of the project, You break open the champagne and go to the beach for the rest of the day.

All of this stuff passes through your head in the time it takes the tape to roll back to the beginning of the track. That's about twenty or thirty seconds unless you are recording on a random access system in which case it's no time at all. Clearly if you are a person who has difficulty making decisions, producing may not be for you.

If you are working with a substantial, professional, artist, even if you wiped something irreplaceable they will more than likely say, "No problem, let's just go for another one." After all, everyone makes mistakes. Now . . . if you did it twice, things might not stay quite so chummy.

There is probably no process as personal and individual as vocal recording. Great vocals are done by great singers. There's no studio trickery that will turn an average or bad singer into a great singer. Sure, you can correct a multitude of sins such as tuning and timing but you cannot find a greatness button anywhere in the studio. As obvious as this may seem, it is, nonetheless, a point that more A&R people should bear in mind when they sign acts.

### *g) Which Method Makes A Better Record – Live, Overdubbed Or Computer?*

T Bone Burnett says that he still prefers using real musicians, and he does not like the overuse of computers in music. "It's good for things to speed up and slow down and be out of tune," he says. "Besides being conceptually correct, it's also emotionally true. People even try to program flaws into the music, but it's not the same. Once you program a flaw it's no longer a flaw; it's a program."

Manfred Mann, who nowadays records using a combination of live musicians and computers, said that when records ceased to be played live and started to be built up by overdubbing, a lot of the 'feel' got lost. "If you do live overdubs on a computer track, the musicians are playing to something that is known to be in time. Before computers, if the basic track was not solid you were layering discrepancy on top of discrepancy."

"When musicians physically play together, they get something off each other which you don't get when you're overdubbing. It's a clinical way of doing things," says George Martin. "You can be ultra-efficient, absolutely in tune and dead in time – and if you're not the machine will quantise it for you – but does it make good music? I don't think so. Music is what people do together, that's real good music."

For better or for worse, certain kinds of music would not have come into existence without computers. I was at the forefront of the application of computers to music and I can clearly remember the excitement of being able to program parts that would have been impossible to play, or being able to program all the instruments on a track without having to learn how to play them all. Computers have enabled us to separate technical proficiency from creativity. Nonetheless a bad computer track has very little to commend it. It may be in tune, in time and technically proficient but music is really about the communication of emotions or feelings.

We've all seen bands full of highly proficient musicians who have no ability to communicate. All instruments have varying degrees of expressive capabilities. The human voice is undoubtedly the most expressive instrument, partly because of its immense flexibility, partly because it's directly plugged into our mind and emotions and partly because it has the added dimension of language. The guitar and saxophone have for a large part of this century been the most popular lead instruments because they are immensely responsive and expressive in the hands of a gifted player. Other instruments such as the Hammond organ (which is basically like a set of tuned on/off switches) and the vibraphone are inherently less expressive. Put those instruments in the hands of talented and sensitive musicians such as Jimmy Smith or Gary Burton and they generate emotionally charged and exciting music. A great musician can communicate with two pieces of wood. Computers themselves do not communicate, they are tools just like the Hammond organ, or a paint brush or a pen through which a musician, painter or writer can express themselves. The problem with computers is that they have made it possible for lesser artists to put together 'professional sounding' records. Great musicians and producers will continue to make great records, with or without computers.

In certain sectors of the music fraternity there has been a backlash against new technology. Mostly this has come from the younger musicians and producers who have rediscovered 'live' (in the studio) recording, analogue tape and tube equipment. It's very interesting to listen to the attitude of musicians, engineers and producers who come from the time when you had to do everything live. Miles Davis embraced computers, drum machines and synthesisers in his later years. Rudy Van Gelder, the 'premier' jazz recording engineer of the Fifties and Sixties, loves digital recording.

Art Neville of the ultimate groove band, The Neville Brothers says, "In the past everything was cut right at the time. The musicians were playing all at one time. Now you can put things together in parts and still get the same, and even a better effect. Computers are great – it's a tool, that's all it is – just as long as you don't let it be the whole deal. The computer's nothing without what we're doing."

Herbie Hancock has been recording since he played piano with the groundbreaking Miles Davis groups of the Sixties. He is as well known for his cutting edge use of electronics (check out the album *Future Shock* containing the monster instrumental hit 'Rock-it') as he is for his acoustic piano artistry. There are very few musicians of his calibre at any one time on this planet. Currently he combines both live musicians and sequencers (computers) on his records.

"Overall, we record in a very old-fashioned way," says Jimmy Jam of Jam and Lewis. "We just turn on the tape and go for the gold. That's how you make those wonderful mistakes that give your song the unique touch you're looking for."

Clearly there is no right or wrong way to make records. There is definitely an appropriate way and an inappropriate way to make any specific record. The methodology that the producer employs will have an immense impact on not only the sound of the record but also on the attitude and emotion that will be communicated by it and the way the record will be perceived by the music business and by the public. The sound and attitude of the production needs to match the sound and attitude of the music. It's a gross over-simplification to say that a raw, edgy band shouldn't have slick production and a smooth, romantic ballad might miss the mark if the production was too rough around the edges. Nonetheless the general principle holds that the production should be totally consistent with the style of the artist and the content of the music and lyrics.

Eno says, "As more and more options have become available, and equipment more and more complex, the temptation can arise to forget the possibilities of simplicity. It's a question of balancing external influences and technologies with your own instincts and beliefs."

Many times a producer will be chosen because of the way their previous records sound or because they are known to be good at a certain style of recording. Obviously someone who spends all their time recording bands live in the studio is going to have honed those particular techniques to perfection. At the other end of the spectrum, the producer who likes to make records using computers, samplers and synthesisers will have developed the knowledge and skills to be able to construct a record in that way with great certainty.

## What Are 'They' Going To Expect Of You?

*a) The Artist?*

The artist wants the album of her life. If it reflects their every whim and indulgence, makes them look and sound good then they will love you for ever from the day it's completed. They'll love you slightly longer than forever the day after the A&R man has given it his apparent stamp of approval by saying, "It's a real step forward from the demos (or the last album) and I need to live with it for a couple of weeks." (Interpretation: "I need to play it to everyone in the department and my bosses and if they like it then, and only then, will I come out with a qualified, endorsement."). All previous praise aside, it could become entirely your fault the day it fails to break all chart records. The blame may never be expressed in words but will be characterised by the fact that everyone else who worked on the album from A&R to promotions, marketing, artwork and management will survive. You will be replaced. If it is an indisputable hit you may get an occasional mention, by the artist, in the press as a helpful collaborator but, then again, probably not. The statistical chances of making it to the next album are probably less than even.

As far as the practical aspect of the recording goes, the expectations vary hugely. Alan Moulder believes that bands want someone to be their creative ally, to support what they want to do, try what they want to try and have some creative input.

Albhy Galuten, talking about the different role each member of the production team played during The Bee Gees incredibly productive Miami period says: "Technically, it was produced by Karl Richardson, me and The Bee Gees. The three people who were in the control room all the time were Karl, Barry and myself.

Karl was primarily the engineer, making sure that everything was going well. Barry was the visionary, and I suppose I was the translator. I had an intuitive sense of what Barry was going for. He'd play me a song and I would hire musicians, work out parts, come up with some ideas, work on the arrangements. For many of those records there really was a band working together. It was certainly a collaborative effort with many talented people, but clearly it was the three of us in the studio, all day, every day."

Sometimes bands have a number of disparate influences and don't manage to pull them together into a coherent direction. This is an area where the producer's more objective viewpoint can really help. Michael Hutchence, of the Australian band INXS, talking about their producer Mark Opitz, says: "When we first met him we were scrambling for a style, and we were trying to mix together rock and funk, and he is the first guy to ever put that into some aural context, which was great. It was a revolution for us. The album *Shahooh Shahooh* was fantastic for us, and we made a giant leap forward. Suddenly it was, Ah! We see the light.' He really helped us with that, and he's always been a friend."

Jackson Browne, on working with Don Was (Bonnie Raitt, Was Not Was) says, "It's like taking a recording seminar with one of your heroes before embarking again on a process that you are very familiar with. Part refresher course and part 'Oh, so that's what you do.' He's got great presence in the studio. He's got great instincts, and the standard he brings is something that he puts on the record immediately. I can't say that we agreed about everything we heard or wanted to try, but the process I am familiar with is a long one – it's more writing than anything. You continue to write when you overdub or when you work with someone who's going to solo on your record. What he brings to the process is something that I probably wouldn't even think of, like calling certain players. He made some very cool calls."

Rickie Lee Jones says that her relationship with a producer varies from record to record, and depends on the mood she's in for that piece of work. "The main criterion is that the producer provides a camaraderie, more than technical expertise. I want them to relate to the work, to dig it and help to bring an atmosphere of confidence. In the future, I might like to have a producer like in the old days. You know, I would just walk in and sing, and the producer would do it all. I'm getting tired of doing so much work, but I have the need to control almost every aspect of what I am doing." The different production scenarios she describes here are pretty much at the opposite extremes of the scale of possibilities, but she is totally emphatic when she says: "If a producer always has a phone in his hand at your session, you should fire him."

The producer needs to support the artist. That's not to say he can't disagree with him or try to steer him in a different direction. But, amidst all the anxieties, arguments and discussions that can be part of making a record, the artist needs to feel that the producer has his best interests at heart and that there is a supportive, creative atmosphere within which he can work. Good performances cannot come out of a hostile atmosphere. It would be better to hand the project to someone else if a producer loses respect for the artist.

Bruce Fairbairn (Loverboy, Bon Jovi, Aerosmith, AC/DC) says, "I think I'd be happiest if bands just said, 'We work with Fairbairn because he lets us make our record the way we want to make it.' That's the best advertisement for my work. Basically, I like to be perceived as someone who facilitates the creative process. In a way everything they get from me is something that they've taken from themselves."

When Jack Douglas produced *Double Fantasy* for John Lennon he was sworn to secrecy. Lennon sent him tapes of the songs with him playing guitar or piano, recorded on a little Panasonic machine. Douglas was told to hire musicians and book a studio; if he told anyone who the artist was the project was off. Douglas arranged and wrote out the tunes. The musicians he hired, Tony Levin, Andy Newmark, Earl Slick, Hugh McCracken and George Small, were around the same age as Lennon. Douglas sang the parts at the rehearsals, and the sessions were booked at the Hit Factory in New York. The musicians did not find out till the night before the first session.

As I said earlier the Merlin style producer may have nothing more than a few conversations with the band and still pick up a full production credit. All-Singing- All-Dancing will make the entire record with virtually no input from the artist apart from vocals. Humble Servant will be in the studio at all times with and without the artist but the artist is very much in charge. The collaborator will work more the way Jack Douglas did with John

Lennon. Usually without the secrecy factor. So the specific expectations will vary from situation to situation and from producer to producer.

*b) The Record Company?*

You are their representative on the project. You will be required to read minds, including changing ones, and keep up with trends, including changing ones. The budget is entirely your responsibility, even though you may not have control over the choice of studio or the amount of days the artist simply chooses not to show up. If you're working with a successful artist, how many days will they have to fly out to New York to film an MTV special or Milan to stock up on clothes? How many TV film crews will show up to film them recording their new album? Of course, the singer won't be seen dead singing live on TV (he knows he sings out of tune and has to punch in for every other word). The band's usual MO is to painstakingly piece the album together overdub by overdub. So they decide to mime to a track you prepared earlier. This burns another precious day in the five-star studio of their choosing while you watch your budget rapidly approach overage. You sit up at night re-reading your contract to see whether your 'rottweiler' lawyer beat the record companies' 'pit bull' on that overage liability clause.

The genre of music in which you operate will affect the expectations the company has of the producer. Alan Moulder tends to work with (big selling) indie/alternative type bands. "They want a good sounding record and no problems. They don't really care how you got it," he says. "Some are more involved than others. Some of them are down there a lot and others stay completely away." He understands the importance of giving the company "something they can work with" and says that they like to hear a good progression from what the band's been doing, a good change or at least what they think the band should be doing.

He feels fortunate that A&R departments and managers don't get too creatively involved with the kinds of bands he works with. They give the bands a lot of freedom. "There is less commercial pressure," he says, "because the band is known to go its own way and do its own thing. When I've worked on more commercial projects there have been a lot more problems; a lot more A&R

comment and a lot more pressure but generally not from the management."

*c) The Artist's Manager?*

Some managers are extremely hands-on. They spend a great deal of time with the artist and micro-manage every detail. Others call in once a week from an office located on another continent. Alan Moulder says, "If the manager has a close relationship with the band, then you tend to deal with him and have to deal with him more than if it's someone sitting in an office miles away." He adds, "They all expect you to make things go as smoothly as possible."

Most managers with whom I have come into contact want only success for their artist and a peaceful life. If there is a more difficult job than producing in the music business, it is undoubtedly artist management. On the other hand, of all the slippery characters I have come across in my travels the majority have been managers. Of necessity it is a political job and the support you can expect from the artist's manager will be strictly skin deep. You are a means to an end for the manager. If you keep the artist happy, produce a great album that satisfies the record company and goes on to sell by the bucketload you will have an enthusiastic, albeit temporary, ally. When the time comes around to record the follow-up, expect the manager to be in the frontline with a clutch of alternatives to your faithful self. His artist cannot afford to be held back by growth-inhibiting behaviour patterns such as loyalty. The producer who put his reputation on the line and produced the first gold or platinum album is expendable.

Strong artist management is as important to you as it is to the artist. The artist's management can have a huge influence over the promotion and marketing of the record. Don't expect too much in the way of enduring friendship unless he really likes you, in which case he may well become your manager too.

# 4

## *Will They Still Love You Tomorrow*

*Or, how long can we go on like this?*

### a) What Is Your Working Life Expectancy?

Your working life expectancy can range from producing just one track to masterminding a lifetime of Grammies. If you are talented and successful the question may not be how long will you be asked to continue to produce records but how long will you continue to want to. The answer you come up with relates directly to how much control you have over your destiny and the destiny of the records you produce.

It is extremely frustrating to make good records and watch them disappear for lack of record company commitment. This fact alone has driven a number of successful freelance producers into staff positions at labels. Their motivation is two-fold. Firstly, it is easier to read the record company's commitment to a project from inside the company, thus enabling you to make a more informed judgement about which projects are likely to get the big push. Secondly, you may have slightly more influence over the future of the album if you are on the inside.

Other frustrated freelance record producers start up their own labels, the reality of which is often very different from the principle. If you don't mind flying a desk and a telephone more than a band and a studio, your own label will certainly give you more control. You will still have to deal with the vagaries of distributors who will most likely be one of the major labels anyway.

Some producers can't take it anymore and just get out of the business altogether.

The first couple of years usually weed out the less resilient. If you survive those first few projects, the initial flush of success and the excitement of being the flavour of the month, chances are you will be in it for the long run. A "long run" would be anything over five years.

George Martin recently says: "I don't think I'm as good a producer now as I used to be. I think I suffer fools less and you have to suffer fools gladly to be a good producer. You must be patient, you must have great tact, and you must have that long view. You must know what you want and wait to get it – you can't rush it."

## b) How's Your Health?

The music business attracts more than its fair share of people who treat their physical bits as if they live and (intend to) die by Pete Townshend's credo, before they get old. Rock'n'roll will only make you deaf but nowadays both the sex and the drugs can kill you. Despite the abuse, most wind up facing a more down-to-earth reality; if they'd known they were going to live this long they'd have taken better care of themselves.

For the hands-on record producer, health can be a relevant issue. The hours can be very long for a number of reasons; studio time is expensive and is often sold on a daily (24-hour lockout) basis. If you're trying to stay within budget, the inclination is to take the fullest possible advantage and work in excess of twelve hour days. Fourteen to sixteen hour days are not uncommon. In the dance remix world forty-eight and seventy-two hour days are sometimes the only way to get the job done at all. Residential studios lend themselves to ridiculously long working hours, which is one reason why record companies favour them. In most residentials you're confined by the sheer remoteness of the location. Since you eat, sleep and everything else there, prevailing logic steers you towards the studio all day, *and* after dinner and after the pub if the band is so inclined.

A common residential studio syndrome is that of the "turned around day." On the first day, in the first flush of enthusiasm, you get to bed about two a.m. That becomes three a.m. the second day then four the next etc. Breakfast gets later and later until eventually no-one's up until late afternoon and you're working right through the night until mid-morning again. This can be one of the quicker ways of exposing someone's least desirable personality traits. I've seen more serious arguments break out at four in the morning when everybody's tired than at any other time. Most of us have had the experience of getting carried along on a creative high till six in the morning. More often than not, after one quick listen the next day we scrapped it all and wondered which influence we were under at the time. Unless I'm working with confirmed night owls I instigate a mutually agreed schedule that most accommodates all body clocks concerned. Exceptional circumstances aside, I stick pretty much to that schedule.

If you're in a hot phase, the projects come thick and fast. You hate to turn down anything good. After all, you love the job and you remember how the lean times really were. So the pressure is there to go straight from one project to another. This can be very exhausting. Starting a new album is really not much different from starting a new job: the personalities are all different and the music will be different from the last record. Your role will even be somewhat different unless you're the All-Singing-All-Dancing type. You may even have to fly across multiple time zones to get to the next location. Your utilities may be about to get cut off at home and your personal life may be falling apart because you're never there. Ideally, I take at least a month off between projects just to chill out and do normal things like going to the dentist. According to "scientific" sources the most stressful things in life are getting divorced, changing jobs and moving house. In effect producers face all three prospects about once every other month.

Taking time off to recuperate and to listen to other kinds of music is important to Alan Moulder. "I still do a lot of small bands. Either their first or second record. If I like the band I'll do it and conversely if it's a big band and I don't like it I won't do it. I try to stick with what I like so I can give an honest day's work," he says. "On recording, the band sets the length of the day. Different bands have different burn-out periods. I've worked with some bands where they'll work almost a strict twelve hour day and at midnight even if they are in the middle of a guitar overdub they'll stop. I've done eight-hour days but some of the bands just don't get going until late at night. If you want to record them, you just have to be around until they are ready. Those days can be very long. I prefer a twelve-hour day, and in an ideal world a twelve-hour day and no work on weekends.

When you get to the mix you tend to have more control over the hours and again that is usually a twelve-hour day."

## What Keeps A&R People Coming Right Back To You?

*a) If You're Hot*

Absolutely no problem. If they can run their finger down the *Music Week* or *Billboard* chart and alight one or more times on your moniker, they love you to death. They will keep pushing your name forward to all of their acts (no matter how inappropriate). Until you cease to have a presence in the charts you can rely on their publicly professed friendship and undying loyalty.

Producing is seen from the outside as a "black art". Producers are often selected by someone saying "OK, this guy has had some success, he seems like he might be compatible with the artist (they're both bipeds after all). Let's throw them together in the studio, something good should happen." I don't believe many people in the record business have a clue what the actual process is once producer and band are in the studio.

Steve Albini, in a 1995 news group posting, said, "In the rock music realm, the 'producer' is often chosen by whim, based on whose name has been associated with popular records and sometimes with no regard for the competence of the individual so-chosen. If somebody told me Barney the dinosaur was the 'Producer' on the new Dimbulb Canopy album I'd believe him."

Many of the qualities that induce success in the music business are intangible. They may be related to, but are definitely not directly proportional to talent, hard work, experience, education or track record. At times a hazy pattern, a quasi-formula seems to appear and we all love to quote the quotes such as "you make your own luck" and "the harder I work at it, the luckier I get." Most of us have had the experience of making what we thought was a great record and seeing it fail miserably. Then the next effort, which we privately think is only average, inexplicably goes mega. You did nothing different from the other less successful projects but now success capriciously attaches itself to you and your work. Appreciate it, wallow in it, try to understand it, but no matter what: capitalise on it. Make hay while the sun shines. Use your successes to climb the ladder in terms of the quality of artists you have access to, the suitability of the projects and the financial rewards available. When you are hot, no fee is too high, no royalty too unreasonable. After all, you have the Midas touch and everyone wants you to touch their project.

*b) If You're Not Quite There Yet*

Production careers, like most entertainment jobs, observe the laws of quantum physics. Absolutely nothing, absolutely nothing, absolutely nothing, SOMETHING. You tend not to have gradually increasing good fortune – just endless, arduous, fruitless slog. Then one day you wake up to SUCCESS. I was very fortunate in that the first record I produced was a hit. No slog there. I can, however, draw from the rest of my career as a studio musician and artist. What worked for me was to be out there working with as many interesting people as 24/7 would allow. Obviously you have to be wise about it. I worked for several years in the areas of *avant garde* electronic music and free improvised jazz. I didn't for a moment think that it was going to lead to mega-success and life in the Hollywood Hills. I did it because it interested me. In the end success came, predictably enough, in commercial music through the normal major label route. But, those years in non-commercial and *avant garde* groups paid off in that they gave me an edge, a lead, the drop, an insight, maybe. In my case it was an insight into the use of new technology that got my foot in the door and made me stand out from the crowd. You have to work with music that you like first and foremost. It's good to be realistic about its potential for success. I found a niche for myself that eventually expanded into the mainstream. A niche area of music can create an advantage for you, even if it is not unique. If there are less people chasing the same thing you have a better chance of becoming the expert at it.

To assess a niche, ask yourself why this apparent niche opportunity exists. Is it an unmined vein of gold? (In which case grab it with both hands.) Or is it fringe music that may never join the mainstream? (Almost every trend starts on the fringe and can be spotted months, if not years, in advance. Yesterday's alternative styles are often today's mainstream. But some fringe trends never make the transition. Gogo music has been on the edge for many years but has never made the leap.)

Or is it an old style that has faded into relative and quite permanent obscurity? (Even so it can still present an opportunity. Very few styles completely die out. There are usually one or two artists who can continue to succeed and occasionally an exceptional new act can break with an outdated style of music. The biggest problem you are likely to run into here is within the business itself. Very few A&R executives will align themselves with unhip music. The ones who do often have great success but they do not earn the respect of their peers. The key here is belief – if you find an artist you believe in and you truly love their music, then chances are lots of other people will too.)

A very good example of someone who got started because of their knowledge of what, at the time, was a niche market is Alan Moulder. He says, "I was very, very lucky that I fell into the alternative market in England at the time when hardly anyone else wanted to do it. Slick records were king at the time and alternative or indie records were almost like second-rate music. Other engineers thought they sounded awful and trashy. So I didn't have a lot of competition. A lot of the producers that were doing those records were used to working in cheaper studios with assistants and they came to me because these records are quite difficult to polish up a bit without making them sound slick or smooth. So there weren't a lot of trained engineers who'd come up through the studio system from assistant to house engineer who wanted to make those records. I could co-produce [with bands] and they would only have to pay one person instead of both an engineer and a producer. Combined with the fact that I was not that expensive in the beginning, which helped since those records weren't selling in huge quantities at the time."

*c) If You Were Recently Hot*

This is possibly the most difficult position to be in. You are likely to get offered the second-division projects, the ones that have been turned down by the truly hot, and perhaps more significantly, the projects that are not earmarked for success. Sure, the record company will take success from any artist if it is handed to them on a plate but there are definitely "priority" projects and 'the other kind'. If you happen to be working on "the other kind" you may find the odds of winning the National Lottery are better.

The more of these second division projects you take on, the more failed projects you accumulate, the longer the gap since your last chart showing, the more you attract critical judgements about your success rate and the less recently you appear to have been hot at all.

*d) When The Night's Closing In*

In the music business most artists, musicians and producers struggle for several years to get their first break. Having arrived at the top of the mountain they often assume that the sunlight of success will continue to shine on them for the rest of their lives. As we know, there is only *one way* to go from the top. It should, theoretically, be easier to continue success than it is to create the first break. After all, you have developed all those musical, technical and people skills that enabled you to get there in the first place. The problem is the mountain is not stationary. While Mohammad is sunbathing on top of the supposedly immovable mountain, the mountain is quietly (and sometimes suddenly) eroding beneath him. All kinds of things can happen.

Musical fashions inevitably change and can leave you out in the cold. Many Seventies producers who were used to producing only live musicians were either unable, or perceived to be unable, to cope with the computerised, synthesised Eighties. In the Nineties the trend pendulum has swung back the other way to live bands. A producer who made his name in the Eighties with highly produced computer generated records may find himself, justifiably or not, sidelined.

Technical trends will surely change. If you don't keep up you may find yourself high and dry as an expert in old technology for which there may be much less, or no, demand. Equipment is also becoming much less expensive, to the point that solid studio experience is no longer the exclusive domain of the professional producer. For a few thousand bucks you can put together a home studio that can pretty well match and in some respects exceed the professional facilities of a few years ago. A talented beginner can not only train himself but also produce tracks which he can use as a calling card to get work. These days there are records in the charts that came right out of an enterprising beginner's bedroom studio.

We all get older. Unlike, say, the sciences where age and experience are regarded as positive attributes, for a record producer "over forty" can be unfairly equated to out-of-touch. There are notable examples of producers, such as Quincy Jones, who not only survive musical life beyond forty but actually do their most successful work then. Nevertheless, if you are over forty and the hits are getting thin on the ground, don't expect the same breaks that you got when you were twenty. Your best shot is to find a project that you believe in and use your skill, experience and contacts to get back into the limelight.

You've tackled too many second division projects by now. You haven't had a name check in the *Music Week* or *Billboard* charts for a good few years. At best you are back at square one, looking for a way back in. Unfortunately several of the routes are no longer open to you because you are a known quantity – everyone has preconceived notions about what you can and cannot do – and you are probably a good bit older by now. Ageism is rife in the business, particularly in the UK, and not least from the older executives. They tend to look for young talent, partly out of fear that they are losing touch themselves, partly to save money and partly to appear hip. Youth is apparently contagious – if you hang around it long enough you might catch some. Younger A&R staff can sometimes feel intimidated by older producers. Except if you produced a record that was a big favourite of theirs when they were still at school, then they will jump at the chance to work with you. They will be extremely respectful to the point of being in awe of you – capitalise!!

By now you will need the money more than you did when you started out. You have a trophy wife, kids in private school and a frightening monthly nut to crack. Like a shark you keep swimming or you drown. Unfortunately you can no longer afford the time to develop unsigned projects the way you did when you were starting out.

At this point you may want to consider your options both inside and outside the business. Anyone with a substantial track record as a producer has a lot of transferable skills but it's most likely going to be back to the old entrepreneurial enterprise and having to prove yourself all over again.

My personal experience has led me to believe that there is one thing and one thing only that will guarantee more, high quality, work: CURRENT COMMERCIAL SUCCESS. Danny Saber quite rightly points out that critical acceptance is a factor that can help early on in a career. Nonetheless, he experienced a massive increase in interest once he had a successful record under his belt. He says, "Before I had commercial success I always had to talk them into why they should use me. There were a couple of guys who were really cool and would back me but there was always that doubt. Once you have a hit record you have that to stand on. They still have their doubts because they have their own insecurities. No matter what you did before, it's only going to do them any good if you do good for them." He doesn't think that A&R people pay much attention to what producers actually do. "I think they are more into what looks good on paper. They don't really know. They come in and scratch their balls and try to get out of taking you to dinner. One A&R guy said 'Right so you wrote six songs in four days, so you can write twelve songs in eight days and twenty-four in sixteen days'. They look at it like it's a corporate memo."

*e) What Prevents Them From Coming Back To You?*

It can be as simple as habit. You get on a roll with a couple of A&R men and they keep coming back to you, break that roll and they find someone else. Although they didn't fall out with you or find fault with your work, you don't work with them again for years.

Not being the flavour of the month will immediately eliminate eighty-five percent of your incoming phone calls. If you can't find your name in the top half of at least one current chart, the other fifteen percent may dry up too. Even being difficult to work with or, sin of sins, running over budget, will not create ugly, unwanted spaces in your schedule as quickly as a lack of a name check in at least one trade mag.

Rule number one is that most people don't really know what you do and how you do it; rule number two is success is the primary measure of your ability as a producer. Exceptions to these rules would be if you are very young, considered to be cutting edge hip, extremely inexpensive, managed by the A&R person's producer management company, or someone with a loyal roster of artists who keep requesting you.

Chart positions may be tangible evidence of success but they do not indicate the reasons for it. Often we cannot put our finger on the exact reasons why certain projects are successful and others are not. In the trade press hit projects are dissected like successful military campaigns, utilising the pure 20/20 vision of hindsight. What no-one mentions are the ninety-five percent of all releases that disappear without trace every year despite using very similar marketing, promotion techniques, A&R people and production crews.

The point is that failure is as difficult to attribute to tangible causes as success. Sure, at the qualitative extremes, there are the "truly incredible" and the "really awful" records. In the middle the vast bulk of record releases qualify as OK, not bad or pretty good. The factors that tip the scale from failure to success are intangible, difficult to define and unpredictable. If we could suspend the "Emperor's new clothes" mentality for a second we would see just as many clunkers in the Top Ten as there are in the cut-out bins.

We like, or perhaps need, to sweep our failures under the carpet and in order to slide out from under any responsibility the blame needs to be placed fairly and squarely on someone's shoulders. A&R, marketing, and promotion people all work for the company, the producer is freelance and can be terminated painlessly and at zero cost to artist or company.

Having said all this, it is not only possible to survive multiple failed records, it is absolutely essential. Especially if you intend to produce a lot of début albums. The first time one of your records fails, if you are the least bit sensitive, it really beats you up or knocks you for six depending whether you are American or English.

It's always good to analyse what exactly went wrong, what your level of responsibility was and what you can do to avoid the same problem in the future. Surviving failure comes down to your attitude, your belief in yourself and your relationships within the business. Having just fallen off the horse, you have to get right back on.

Realistically and honestly acknowledging the extent of your responsibility to the artist and label is good. Carrying the can for someone else's failings is bad. Don't catch other people's "hot potatoes". If you know you've made a great record which stiffed, kick the dust off your sandals and move on. Believe me, A&R,

marketing and promotion aren't going to let a failed record blight their careers. Why should you?

*f) How Else Can You Get Work?*

As Alan Moulder succinctly puts it, "Band requests and previous reputation." This is really the best way to get work. If your reputation is big enough that generation after generation of artists keep asking for you, it's quite possible that you could keep working until you got tired of it all and decided to retire to a Pacific island.

*g) What's The Best Way To Handle The Show Reel/Resumé/CV Tap Dance?*

Personally I've always hated sending out CVs and show reels. My best work has come to me by word-of-mouth or personal recommendation. The artist or A&R person will have heard something of mine they liked on the radio or maybe they knew someone I had worked with. Show reels can really be a problem if you're not there to explain the relevance or irrelevance of your previous productions to the one under discussion. I prefer not to take on two similar projects. I like each production to be different from the previous ones. You would think that anyone with half a brain could listen to your previous work and identify the qualitative production factors that would benefit their own project. What seems to happen is that someone gets hung up on the actuality of your show-reel productions (they hate the band or the way the guy sings). They completely miss the point of what you do and decide you're unsuitable. You tend to get stuck in the genre in which you have most recently had success.

Some producers are not the least bit bothered by this. They are interested only in working within a fairly narrow field of music that conforms to their own range of taste. That's fine. If you really like one style of music, provided the market for that type of record never goes completely belly-up you can have a productive, happy career uncomplicated by heavy duty decision making. Personally, I like and listen to, a very wide, constantly changing range of music and I would like my work to reflect that. All I can say is that, from my own experience, it takes a huge amount of personal effort, ingenuity, and constant commitment to escape this kind of typecasting.

"I'm very wary of sending out showreels," says Alan Moulder.

"I try to tailor each showreel to each band. This can be difficult because very often bands come to you for different reasons than you thought."

I've often been surprised when some productions I've done appeal to artists in apparently completely different genres of music. Often the band might have heard something of yours when they were ten, and although they are strictly hard-core now, they still have fond childhood memories of that poppy little ditty you produced way back then.

The scenario I prefer goes like this: my name comes up for the production from whatever source – the band, the band's manager or the A&R person. If I don't survive their preliminary discussions I may never even know I was being considered. If I make it past that initial stage, then either the A&R person or the manager will call to set up a meeting. This first meeting could be with the A&R person, the band or all together.

My objective is to find out whether I can work with the band and whether they can work with me. If we like each other, we're half way there. I like to get right inside their heads, find out what they listen to, what movies they watch, where they hang out, what books they read, what type of people they are, what makes them happy, what upsets them, what the power structure of the group is, who's likely to blow up on me, who's going to be the peacemaker, how their collective and individual sense of humour works (groups often develop their own sense of humour and even their own language).

I also need to know what they think a producer does in general and what I in particular can do for them. In addition, I ask them what kind of record they want to make (it's amazing how many bands are not the least bit unified on this subject). I also want to talk to the A&R person and get his side of the story, find out what he is expecting from me and from the album. It's often truly amazing to behold the difference between the expectations of the A&R department and the band.

At this point they will go away and discuss it amongst themselves and come back with one of three options:

i) "Yes let's do it" – in which case you have to figure out whether you can fit them into your busy schedule. (Whatever they say about having to have the album out by Christmas, they'll start at least three months later than they're telling you now.)

ii) "The band have decided to go with someone else" – in this case it will be the A&R person or manager who calls and irrespective of whose decision it really was they will attribute it to the band.
iii) "No response at all" – this is a music business special. After two weeks of five phone calls a day and Fedex's flying back and forth all over the planet, everybody suddenly forgets how to dial your number. Some people don't have the gonads to pick up the phone and recite option ii). After about three months, when you're in the middle of another project, you suddenly wonder what happened about that such and such a project that everyone was so jazzed about. The very next day you read in the trades that they are working with the guy who produced the other five bands that they sound exactly like. Next week you run into them in a big studio complex in New York City. They're next door laying tracks (three months late remember). You're finishing up some overdubs. Of course you're "real" friendly and so are they. You don't mention the fact that no-one had the courtesy to call you back.

# 5

# *Producer Managers*

## To Have A Manager Or Not To Have A Manager?

If you're in the studio on a project, particularly if you are a hands on producer, life is intensely focused on the record in hand. There is precious little time to pay your gas bill, let alone find and negotiate your next project.

Generally speaking, artists don't love producers who spend the entire project, head tucked under the console, finger in one ear, phone glued to the other, screaming at their lawyer about packaging deductions for their next project. Of course you could leave the room to scream at your lawyer but, depending on the kind of producer you are, (see Chapter One) the session has a nasty habit of coming to a grinding halt when you are out of the room.

This is where managers come in very handy. They can take care of the nuts and bolts of the negotiations, line up the next fifty projects for you, do the budgets, help you find musicians in strange and exotic locations, book the flights and hotels, then summarise it all in a phone call, fax or e-mail.

More than anything a good manager will keep your name in the minds of the A&R people. They may be able to persuade someone to take a creative leap of faith with you based on the manager's more in-depth knowledge of what you do. A&R people have a great deal on their plate and there are a lot of producers out there. If your manager has a good reputation and current roster of producers, an A&R person may even call them for advice. Ros Earls of 140dB has said that she will point them towards a producer she respects but doesn't represent if she doesn't feel she has the right person available for the job. That kind of attitude builds respect in the business and ultimately results in more work for her people.

Danny Saber had a manager from Day One. "Until I had a manager I didn't have anything. The whole thing with managers is timing. If you have a manager that's too far ahead, they won't have time for you. If you've got someone who's too far behind then they're not going to be able to help you. My manager had all cutting edge alternative producers in the same vein that I'm in. When I played her my stuff she was totally blown away, but she could see what direction I needed to go in. Shannon [O'Shea] hooked me up with the Black Grape stuff. They had vision. They were able to put me with the right people and sell me to the A&R people on the back of their more established producers."

## Do They Earn Their Percentage?

*a) Is She Just Fielding Calls Or Is She Out There Pitching For You?*
When you are truly HOT the over-riding temptation for a manager has to be to just field the calls. In actual fact this is when you really need the most active hands-on management.

When you're at the top the only way to go is down. Every project, every deal has to be considered carefully. A couple of bad choices and you find yourself staring down the slippery slope that leads to total obscurity. At a high-point in your career, your manager simply reaching out to catch the calls will still result in a substantial choice of projects, but a high proportion of these projects will be trying to ride on your name and reputation. They need you more than you need them. What you really need at this point is either a project that you believe in with your heart and soul; one that you want to donate your hard-won kudos to, or an artist who's even bigger than you. You've already converted lead into gold, now you need to convert that gold into kryptonite.

How your manager pitches you is a matter of their style. It's vital that you are comfortable with that. One manager will simply field calls while another will be a cold-calling, telemarketing, fool. Good connections can be crucial for a manager. Even with the best connections in the world, if the manager doesn't believe in you enough, is too busy or not really dedicated to your advancement, nothing much is going to happen. You may be better off with a less well connected, more enthusiastic and pro-active manager.

Ros Earls says, "It's important to have a general understanding of what's going on, to be in the general flow, so you know which new bands are coming up, so you know what bands are looking for producers, so that you've got a relationship with A&R men, and so you have constant information.

"You're also seeing the live bands. You're out and about. You present people with the facts; what your guys are up to and when they're available. If you hear about something that's brilliant, that you're absolutely sure that your guy's right for, then that would be the point that you would pitch for a job. My experience is that the pitching and the pushing isn't as important as the general PR that just trickles along on a daily basis. Being in the traffic of people making records and looking for producers."

Recently I've seen a lot more new names producing a record here and there but not sustaining careers the way producers used to. Ros explains this by saying, "There are a lot more producer managers and a lot more people out there [producing]. A lot of bands are co-producing with young people. There is less of a selective process going on. It used to be that certain producer managers were known for certain types of producers. Now, I put up one producer against the whole roster of another manager. For the first five years we were known as being really indie but indie doesn't exist any more . . . it's one big business arena. Everybody's up for everything. It's a very busy business now and a lot of people are settling for second best and not getting the jobs they'd like to get. It's partly a financial thing, partly there's so many people out there and, of course, studios can't afford to keep as many engineers on as they used to. So people that are inappropriate are out in the world competing. If they push hard enough they will get some gigs. There's definitely some undercutting going on but I don't see any point in worrying about that. It's not about how much you cost at the end of the day. As long as you are flexible enough to drop your rates occasionally for a project that you really want to do. You can be flexible about advances and you can prove to people that you're doing something as a trial or as an investment in something new. We're not out of business and we don't undercut people. I'm not interested in what other people can get. There's no one fixed rate. It's whatever you are worth. We have done projects for no advance and higher points. I'd rather not do that because everyone needs to earn a living. I've always thought it was worth getting involved in things that were interesting even if they didn't yield huge dividends immediately."

*b) How Do You Avoid Getting Ripped Off By Your Manager?*

The best insurance you have for not getting ripped off by your manager is to make sure that you are paid directly by the record label. The manager may invoice the record company but the payments can still come directly to the producer. The manager then bills the producer for their commission. If you have a contract with your manager make sure it spells this out. Not all managers will agree to direct payment. It increases their risk of not being paid. If they insist on this and the money goes to them first, make sure your contract with them is water tight and specific about how, when and how much you get paid. Your contract with the record label should be in your name or the name of your company, not in your manager's name. It may be that the payments are sent to your manager's office but your entitlement must be clearly spelt out in your contracts with the label and your manager.

*c) Does He Siphon Off Some Of Your Work To Other Producers In The Stable?*

This can be as costly to you when you are just starting out as it can when you are mega. I had two situations when I first started where already established producers tried to poach projects from me: one before it had taken off (the pre-publicity and expectations for the group were huge) and the other when I had taken the début album to gold on the back of the first three hit singles. This didn't prove to be too much of a problem because we were on a roll and a degree of, shall we say, "functional" loyalty was in place. I may have had bigger problems had these raiders been part of the same management stable. In fact I may never have known what happened had the other producer had more clout than me with the manager. As it happened I ran my own producer management company at the time. It did leave me with a very bad taste in my mouth.

Of course the problem can be even more acute when you hit stellar levels. At this point you are inevitably offered fifteen viable projects for every one that you can actually do. Consequently there are fourteen productions potentially available to other producers. Obviously your manager would like to at least hang on to some of these for his other producers. This may seem OK to you. You can't do a project. Someone else in the organisation can. The record company's happy. The project stays close to home. The record company will come back to your manager because she solved their problem for them. For the management company it's great, producers, "Big Shot" (you) and "Medium Shot" both working and maybe even "Small Fry" got one of the newer bands that had approached you. "Medium Shot" and "Small Fry" are both on projects they wouldn't have got if "Big Shot" hadn't been the bait on the hook. Three commissions instead of one, three chances of a hit instead of one, a possible step up the ladder for "Medium Shot", first rung for "Small Fry".

The only potential downside for you is related to the integrity of your manager. Say you are two months away from finishing your current project when a call comes in to your management company from "Super-cult's" A&R person who just signed them. He thinks you'd be perfect. Your manager says he thinks so too but unfortunately you're in the Mediterranean on a project and won't be back for at least two months. Super-cult have just come off two relatively successful indie albums and want to get started on their first major label album a.s.a.p. They were stretching their budget to afford you because they really love your work. Your manager suggests your stable-mate "Medium Shot", an up-and-coming producer who used to be your engineer. He knows all your moves, is a lot cheaper, has some good solid credits but hasn't hit the big one yet. He's available now so she faxes over his CV and Fedex's a show-reel (which includes a bunch of tracks he engineered with you *not* clearly marked to distinguish between his own productions and the tracks he engineered with you). "Super-cult" call back the following afternoon to say they like the sound of "Medium Shot's" work. If he could fly out to meet them this weekend and the chemistry seems good, could he start in two weeks' time in Colorado? The meeting goes fine, the chemistry is primordial and creation looks set to begin. Cue contract negotiations, enter lawyers stage left.

Where's the problem in all this. You couldn't do it, "Medium Shot" is the perfect second choice. Although "Super-cult" had never heard of him, he worked closely with "Big Shot", knows all his moves, commands a lower advance and royalty and is available now. Perfect.

Well it may work out well for "Super-cult" and it could be the best thing that ever happened for "Medium Shot". In fact when the album tops eight million sales he will have leap-frogged over "Big Shot" and transformed into "Mega-mover". By the end of next year he has his own label deal with "Super-cult's" major record company, goes on to produce "Super-cult's" next eight multi-platinum albums (who by now have dropped the "cult" and are just known as Super) and he is entering the realms of "Unreachable". Apart from a few perfectly natural twinges of envy, what could you have to complain about? You were busy, you couldn't be in two places at once, and we all know that for whatever reason we pass on a project, there's always the possibility of missing the big one.

Let's re-examine that original phone call. When "Super-cult" first called your manager they really wanted you. They were not calling on spec for suggestions or two or three alternatives. The manager with integrity would have immediately called and discussed it with you. You would have been able to tell her that "Super-cult" is your absolute favourite band, you bought both their first two albums on Obscure Records and saw all their early gigs. You'd even drop your price and cancel your holiday, if necessary, to work with them. Your manager could've investigated the possibility of the band waiting for two months to start the project. As it happened the record company's lawyer went on holiday for three weeks, holding up the contract negotiations so they didn't actually get started with 'Medium Shot' for six weeks. If you had started your contract negotiations rolling immediately they would have had to wait only an extra two weeks. There's no guarantee that you would have had the same success with them as "Medium Shot". Even though you're a lot more experienced (and "Medium Shot" learned most of what he knows from you in the first place), successful chemistry is impossible to predict.

Perhaps, fortunately, you never really found out how "Medium Shot" got to produce your favourite band, you assumed they'd called for him in the first place and not you but . . . something about this situation sure didn't hang right. It's not long before you start looking for new management. There was nothing malicious or personal about what your manager did, she was just trying to keep her roster working. Had she bothered to check with you first and found out how strongly you felt about the band, she would never have suggested "Medium Shot" at all but she knew you had plenty of good possibilities lined up and wouldn't be out of work whereas "Medium Shot" was really just getting started. He had a lot of engineering work but his production CV was looking thin. No-one was more surprised than her when what seemed like yet another indie/alternative flavour-of-the-week thing turned into the band of the decade. She'd never really understood that kind of music anyway.

Your next few projects went well; a couple of gold albums, a double platinum and one that should've been if the record company had got it right. You're happy enough but deep inside you wish that you could work on an album that you really loved. Not something that you feel OK about or can do a great job on, but something that you would actually play at home for fun, a record that gets you excited about music the way it did when you were sixteen. Like "Super-cult's" third for instance. It couldn't have happened to a nicer guy than "Medium Shot" (as you used to know him) but sometimes you wonder how he got that break. You put it down to the luck of the draw.

I have had first-hand experience of a manager (in this case also a lawyer) making what proved to be a critical, life-changing decision on my behalf, without consulting me and coming to a conclusion that was diametrically opposed to the one I would have arrived at. He turned down an album that I would've love to have done, not to pass on to another producer in his stable (he was too stupid to realise the artist could be huge) so he let the project go to someone he didn't even know because he wanted me to produce an artist signed to his own label. The record I produced for him did extremely well but I know, given the choice, that I would have picked the other album.

The point here is not to say that all managers are evil. I would say the truly devious manager is very rare. However, I have personally had situations where my rights, needs or ambitions have been compromised in order to line someone else's pocket. Unfortunately, in those situations where your manager's interests and your own are not entirely in sync, you are going to be dependent on their integrity. Be very comfortable with this person before you put your professional life in their hands.

Every producer manager I have spoken to has assured me that not only do they not siphon off work but that the opportunity to do that rarely even comes up. Most artists will have a short list of producers that they are interested in and often they are not with the same management company. Ros Earls of 140dB, who manages Flood among others, says, "Flood is sitting at the top of his tree now but three years ago he wasn't quite there. Flood can't be everywhere at once. He can't do five albums a year. I'd love to clone him. I'd love him to always be able to do U2, Depeche Mode, Polly Harvey and Nine Inch Nails because they are the albums that sell and those are the artists he's most associated with. But he can't. Otherwise he'll never be able to 'dip his toe in' with any new, younger bands. He'd never be able to reinvent himself – which is necessary. So, inevitably, Flood will do half [an album]. He's involving Alan Moulder a lot now. Moulder's getting the gigs that were Flood's. After he'd done 'Some Kind Of Talking' for [Jesus] and Mary Chain he wasn't available, so he recommended Alan Moulder. So what's happened on Nine Inch Nails is he's brought Alan Moulder in to engineer the mixing. Now Alan's got the production gig which is interesting because I don't manage Alan Moulder."

Ros says that she has always found it really difficult to hand projects down to other producers on her roster. She says, "You end up feeling a bit like a door-to-door salesman." In her opinion there may be more than one man for the job but there aren't thirty. What bothers her is that some managers have fifteen people on the roster and they put every single producer up for every single project. Consequently, someone who has twenty years of experience is up against a guy who just got his first production gig.

Record companies do call up and ask for someone who would be suitable for a gig. There's an answer, "Yes, I have somebody and this is who I have in mind, or you could look at it another way, you could consider this other guy that I manage." There's a third answer: "I know who's right for the job and it's XYZ but ABC manages him." I think you have to be free to say that. Not to always try and manipulate things round your roster because you get a name for just filling jobs. Hopefully this attitude makes

A&R people more likely to call in and ask a manager's advice. The more phone calls that come in the more likely you are to find the right work for your producers. Relationships are very important in this business.

Personally, I like to have as much control over my own destiny as possible. I prefer to make my own decisions based on the best information to hand. If your manager does as Ros Earls does and makes you fully aware of all the options, if you then make the wrong choice (as I have) you can at least be philosophical about it.

Obviously, in the story above, if you were "Medium Shot" you'd be extremely happy. The system worked beautifully to your benefit. However, now you've been elevated the pretenders will be hovering round you like vultures. Your money moves up into the big league which makes you vulnerable to the same kind of manoeuvre that you pulled on "Big Shot". Record companies are always looking for ways to save money, and if they think they might be able to get your ideas and techniques and as good a sounding record from your assistant for a lot less money they just might not let their sense of ethics, integrity and fair play get in the way.

## How Do You Define "Best Manager" For You?

Simply, I suppose, the one who gets you exactly the productions you need exactly when you need them. Defining precisely what you need is not so easy. Finding and getting those exact projects can be even more elusive. A high degree of intuition, persuasiveness, creativity and determination are necessary to qualify as a great producer-manager.

I can only say that the best manager is the one who sincerely believes that there is no-one out there who can do what you do as well as you can, and has the ability to convey that to the decision makers who control the projects in which you are interested.

As I said before, when you're hot your manager doesn't really have to do very much to keep you working. That, however, is when they really should be selling you the hardest and trying to move you up into that 'unreachable' international league.

When you're less than hot or when you are first starting out is when the manager's abilities are tested most. Belief is not enough to turn you into a mega-star otherwise most of us would be managed by ourselves, our wives, our girlfriends or our mothers.

Some producers don't rely on their managers to find work at all, they just like them to handle the business side of things. Alan Moulder says, "My manager doesn't get me work, she just discusses money and the terms of the contract, which I find incredibly difficult. I really like the way she represents me."

Like producers, managers tend to come in all shapes and sizes ranging from ex-lawyers to ex-studio managers to ex-record company executives to your basic street fighter (not necessarily in descending order). The perfect, "made in heaven," producer manager would know enough about the job to understand your individual strengths and weaknesses; know what's going on trend-wise (nationally, internationally, musically and technically); be very well connected in the business and be able to get to all the right people; be respected enough to be listened to when he gets there; always have an ear to the ground to find out who's just being signed and who's changing producers for their fifth album; be able to find his way around a contract and know the obvious pitfalls to watch out for; be a tough negotiator; be able to pour oil on troubled waters (contractual, recording, financial or personal) if that should become necessary; have international contacts; treat you with respect; be discreet and hold any potentially sensitive information about you or their other clients in total confidence; and have complete confidence in you and your abilities.

## How Can You Find Such A Person – If They Even Exist?

Unless providence has smiled on you in the most fortuitous of ways the only way I know is to do plenty of research and shop around. Managers, like producers, come in all shapes and sizes and it's probably unlikely you will find someone with all the above ingredients. What makes a producer-manager relationship work is as much about personal chemistry as ability. If you like the manager and the manager likes you, then assuming they have enough of the other ingredients to be able to function and you have talent, drive and determination, the relationship will most likely work.

If you already know A&R people call them and ask them about the managers you are considering. See if they have any suggestions. It's probably not worth looking for a manager too early on. You need to build some sort of reputation or track record on your own, even if it's just on demos or remixes. Be realistic. It's difficult for a manager to convince an artist or an A&R person to trust you with a substantial budget if they haven't heard anything you've done.

## How Do You Persuade Them To Take You On?

I remember a situation in Los Angeles where a producer who had many multi-platinum albums under his belt, but none in the last eight years, was looking for management. Several companies asked him for show reels (which I thought was insulting since if they didn't have most of his records on their shelves they shouldn't be in the business anyway). They all eventually passed on him, if not in so many words, perhaps more disrespectfully by just not calling him back.

He carried on working through his own connections in a low-key way until the inevitable happened and he had another multi-platinum album. Of course this kick-started his career again and the embarrassingly inelegant scramble for his time and attention started once more.

Unfortunately, you can get caught in that same old catch-22 where you can't get representation till you have produced something and you're going to have difficulty producing anything until you get representation. The same applies if you have a recent "gap" in your résumé. You have to be enterprising, lucky, or an excellent salesperson to get your foot in the door.

The reasons why a manager would take you on are numerous: You are on an unbroken run of multi-platinum albums and your last manager retired to Tahiti. You have some sort of reasonably current track record. You have something you can play them that will convince them that you might just have some ability (this only works when you are young, once you've been around or if you are starting at an older age, you will most likely have to prove yourself with actual success first). They are not doing very well themselves and need to flesh out their numbers.

Manager Ros Earls came from a background of managing

world-famous recording studios such as Trident and Sarm in London. She tends to specialise in engineer producers. The talents she looks for in an up-and-comer are particular musical talents, a mature approach to arrangements and someone who responds to bands very well. "There's something indefinable as well that virtually everybody at Trident had." She says, "Mark Stent's gone on, Steve Osborne's gone on, Paul Corkett's gone on, Flood's gone on and on, so has Alan Moulder. All the tea boys turned into engineers. They all had something else. There was the humility thing, but it was more knowing that you had to do your time and get as much information as you can, learn as much as you can as quickly as possible. There is an unquantifiable something that those people all had and I think it was because Flood was there with me in the early days that I was able to spot it. I do know now. There's an undefinable sort of cool as well. You want people to think of you as a creative person but not so much so that you overshadow them. You're a kind of catalyst but it's a very fine line because a lot of producers are very capable as musicians and writers in their own right. But the best producers don't jeopardise the chemistry by selling themselves too much as a creative person and know that instinctively.

"It's not just about the practical elements, it's a lot to do with politics, diplomacy, the balancing of personalities in the studio and generally liaising with the record company. That kind of mature approach from an early stage would be what turns a manager on."

Obviously from the manager's point of view there are only so many hours in the day. The easier it is to find you work and the more hits you can generate, the more money they can make, more quickly. You would feel exactly the same way if you were in their position.

There are a great number of producer management companies around, all with varying styles, abilities and requirements. As important as anything else is the ability to relate to your manager and for them to believe in your particular set of skills.

# 6

## *How Do You Deal With The Artist, The Record Company And The Artist's Manager?*

### What should your relationship with the artist be?

*a) Best Friends?*

*I don't trust him, he's my friend.* (Bertolt Brecht)

I don't personally know of too many cases where a producer and an artist became best friends.

Obviously it helps to be on friendly terms with the artist, and for the duration of the project you may even get quite close, but it is an intense relationship between people whose lifestyles and personality types are often quite different. Generally, once the album is over the artist will go on tour, the producer will move on to his next production and very often they won't meet up again until the next record or when they receive their Grammy award.

Speaking of the bands he works with Jack Douglas says, "It's really important that we get along pretty well, so I like to hang out and socialise with them."

Phil Ramone worked with Billy Joel for over ten years and did three albums with Paul Simon. Of those relationships he said, "You do grow closer personally. Billy's my child's godfather. And Paul Simon and I are still close friends – I named a son after him. But there is a line when you are employed by someone. You keep yourself somewhat at a distance so that they have it clear in their minds that you didn't party the last two nights, because you had work to do, maybe some editing at eight in the morning, that was more important. That's what I consider the proper relationship between an artist and a producer.

"I've always thought a producer's job is to be the objective director of action; you need to know what's going on with an artist because their emotional state may be reflected in their work, in the change of a lyric, for instance. But you get enough intimacy working with them ten and twelve hours a day in the studio. It's not always necessary to spend the weekend with them."

"The personal level comes out of the music anyway," says Quincy Jones, "but if you are closer than that, it gives you an advantage, because you get a chance to know what's underneath the personality. You can comfort that and soothe it and provoke it. You can make the arrangements a musical metaphor for what their personality is about."

The long-term friendships that are made in the line of fire are, unfortunately, somewhat balanced out by the unnecessary difficulties that can be created by self-destructive, over-indulged individuals bent on making what should be an enjoyable, satisfying, creative experience into an island of hell, set in a place that probably looks like paradise.

*b) Able To Fit In?*

Whether this is necessary or not really depends on the type of producer you are. The All-Singing-All-Dancing type has no need to fit in at all. If anything the artist may wish to try to fit in with them. The collaborator probably needs to fit in the most. A lot of the vibe of the session in this case comes from either being like-minded or complementary personality types. Merlin will fit in only in the abstracted way that gurus can appear at home both on the mountain top and on Fifth Avenue.

Alan Moulder says he likes to hang around with the artist and get a personal relationship going. "Fitting in is very important. You want to make him feel as comfortable as possible. Singing in front of someone can be embarrassing. Many singers aren't as extrovert in the studio as they appear on stage. In fact they can be quite vulnerable and insecure about singing one to one. It really helps if they can be comfortable with you. I've made some enduring friendships with people I've worked with. The relationship does change when you finish the record. On tour they may be pleased to see you, but it is a different mindset from the one-to-one relationship of recording."

*c) Willing To Hang After Hours, In Between Albums And Laugh At His Jokes?*

There are superficial similarities here to the best friend relationship but appearances are where it starts and ends. I personally can never cut this gig. It's not fun. In fact it's seriously boring and I don't particularly want to find myself (ever again) in a club at 4a.m. with an artificial grin frozen on my face listening to yet another shaggy dog story.

Why would this even be a possibility? Well, when half the civilised world decides to give its pocket money to an under-educated, demi-talent, that individual's personality may experience an equal and opposite reaction. Ego grows. Legitimate ability to sustain ego shrinks. Result – some very boring tour stories. Of course the majority of artists are extremely nice people.

*d) Somewhat Aloof?*

Not guaranteed to win you the next album but safe in the respect that you are not exposing your inner secrets to the artist. Aloofness reduces the risk of familiarity becoming a breeding ground for contempt.

Being aloof works when the producer is older than the artist and has a more substantial track record. However, if the producer's track record is too much longer than the artist's, then the story telling, ego reinforcing roles can be reversed and the artist might be the one who finds the rigor mortis setting in on his smile.

*e) Professional?*

Speaking about his work with Bob Dylan, Phil Ramone says, "Bob's a very nice man. He's not what you'd call a high-intensity conversationalist, but you don't need that. You have your moments of privacy with somebody and you enjoy them. But my way of working is not to break that code of professionalism and privacy that the artist sets up, whatever that may be. Dylan treats the people he works with in a completely professional manner. Sometimes the doctor-patient thing is vital, so that you keep from getting too close. He shares what he needs to."

*f) How Do You Tell Them Something's Not Working?*
Every producer I have spoken to is agreed about this. George Martin expresses it well: "You do it with tact. It's something I've always done. As a kid in my twenties, I would go up to an orchestra leader and say 'I'd like to do another take, because I think the woodwind were slightly flat.' Generally, if you are right and you do it politely, without throwing your weight around, people actually like you for it. They recognise that you have a good ear and listen to you. And if you build up a reputation over the years and you're successful, eventually people will begin to ask you."

## Where Does Your Responsibility Lie?

*a) To The Artist?*
The short answer to this is that every record producer's responsibility is to show the artist in the best possible light. In reality, it depends very much on the type of artist, the producer's style and the nature of their relationship.

In an ideal world I would always prefer to see the artist be centre stage and in charge of the artistic direction of the recording. This scenario sets the producer's responsibility toward the artist and the artist alone. The producer employs musical, technical and conceptual skills to protect, preserve and realise the artist's vision.

In the same rec.audio.pro news group posting that I mentioned earlier, Steve Albini referred to the necessity for the producer to respect the artist. "This goes beyond merely allowing the band to have a say in their album. It means that the social and artistic fabric of the band is its strength, and its defining characteristic. Take them away (by deconstructing the band with overdubs, click tracks and other Spielbergian techniques or by chopping up their arrangements because they weren't 'right', or by replacing members with session players or sequencers, or by over- accentuating one member as a 'star') and the band loses its identity, and in most cases, its reason to be. The band at hand, no matter how small in stature or weak aesthetically, deserves your respect. This also means you can't lie to them, or misrepresent them to the label or the listening public. Perhaps the guitar player wants his guitar to sound like that."

Albini does say earlier in the same posting that his experience has been almost exclusively with bands who operate as autonomous self-defining entities, not solo performers or dance music acts for whom "production" in the classic sense is an unavoidable necessity.

For a certain type of artist he is absolutely right. The question also needs to be asked "What if the guitar player didn't really want their guitar to sound like that?" Maybe they just didn't have the expertise or the equipment to make it sound better. Maybe they would be grateful for the producer opening up some alternative possibilities for them. A lot of extremely popular records would never have been made if these criteria were engraved in stone. Trevor Horn, Mutt Lange and even George Martin would've had difficulty making most of the records with which they are associated.

All too often, however, the producer is working to conceal serious flaws in the artist's musical, technical or conceptual abilities. The artist's vision may be "I want to be bigger than Madonna." Sadly, their musical and technical skills may be overshadowed by their visionary capabilities.

Some producers prefer this mode of operation because it gives them control. Many pop records are made this way. The producer is in some ways more the artist than the artist. The weak artist enables the producer to, vicariously, realise artistic ambitions that may have been thwarted earlier in their own career.

In practice these producers are worth more than their weight in gold. They are the musical movers and shakers. These are the alchemists, the guys who can take nothing or not very much and turn it into apparently – something. Lead into gold. This type of producer is the genuinely talented All-Singing-All-Dancing-King-Of-The-Heap.

Generally speaking, the closer to "live" a record is the more control the artist will have had. With most so-called alternative bands what you see is what you get. If they can't sing, play or write good songs there aren't many production techniques available to conceal the evidence. (This is currently changing with the increasing acceptance of hard-disk editing systems which allow heavy duty, digital manipulation of live recordings.) With heavily sampled dance-pop records, it's virtually impossible to tell whether the artist can perform or write by listening to the record.

Does it matter? Certainly not to the record company. Sales are sales are sales.

When the artist is strong or already hugely successful, the responsibility is primarily to the artist and they will demand that the focus is on them. With a first time artist or someone not so strong on direction, your responsibility will be to deliver the right record based on a blend of information, starting with the record company brief, taking into account the artist's ideas and utilising your own judgement as to what will work for all concerned.

Talking about producers that will use any means to make the record, Jack Endino says, "I guess there is some value in that sort of sterile sort of produced music, and there must be a market for it, but it's not the way I work. Sometimes I've been asked to play a bass part or something on a record, usually for a very practical reason though, such as there's no bass player, or the bass player had to go home. If you're not technically the best that you can imagine, that's fine – you just have to work with them. I think these days people are valuing bands and respecting them as groups of people who have their own ideas and style of playing. What it all comes down to, and I think this is the most important thing, is you gotta let bands be bands."

Of course if you are the All-Singing-All-Dancing type you are not going to subscribe to this point of view. I think it's healthy for all the different methods and styles of production to co-exist peacefully. There are many ways to make a great record. The Nineties has been a lot kinder to the more artist-oriented projects than the Eighties was. It's always going to be a case of horses for courses, but at least not every record nowadays is highly produced and processed. For the moment you can pay your money and take your choice.

An artist may not be aware that they are stuck in a rut with their attitude towards studio recording techniques. The techniques they are using may be limiting the results they can get. Just as fertilisers and pesticides can produce big, nice looking fruit and vegetables, the organically grown ones, although they may be more difficult and more expensive to grow, nonetheless taste better and have greater nutritional value. Jim Dickinson talked about how he approached the production on Alex Chilton's *Big Star Third.* "I was nailed for indulging Alex on *Big Star Third*, but I think it is important that the artist is enabled to perform with integrity. What I did for Alex was literally remove the yoke of oppressive production that he had been under since the first time he ever uttered a word into a microphone, for good or ill. I tried to show him how to use the studio, rather than be abused by it. And that's what I try to do with any artist who's interested in that. And if they're not interested in that, I try to eliminate the problems that are between them and a successful recording, which is something I learned from Tom Dowd, who is the great problem-solver."

Tony Berg, Producer of Michael Penn, Squeeze, Public Image Ltd and Edie Brickell and The New Bohemians, says, "The producer's dilemma is, who's in charge? I would say that the artist is in charge."

Alan Moulder agrees. "It's their career. The record company and management have other artists. If this one doesn't work out, there'll be others coming along that will. For the artist this is maybe their only crack at it. They may go on to other bands but it may be their only crack at being in this business. My allegiance goes definitely to the band."

As for accommodating artistic idiosyncracies, he says, "If the artist is just slow I'll try to find studios that are really cheap. Even down to doing each individual thing in different studios. I do the drums in one studio that's pretty good, then move to a really small cramped cheap studio to do the guitars and vocals." Even if the artist wants to do something that, in Moulder's opinion, most likely won't work, his approach would be to say, "OK let's try one". The reason he's so flexible he says, "is because I've quite often been proved wrong and if I try [the idea] it covers my backside. I'll allocate a certain amount of time to it, almost demo it, I'll then point out the pitfalls but I get them to choose. If they want to go ahead with it I'll try to make it work. If it's a technical problem but it makes them feel comfortable and I think I'm going to get a good performance out of them then I'll really try to make it work."

*b) To The Record Company?*

In the simplest of terms the producer's responsibility is to make sure that the record company makes money by pulling a hit record out of the hat.

How you perform the sleight of hand is not really an issue. If your style is to call in occasionally from the tennis court (just to see how things are going), unless the artist complains, you'll still get the credit and pick up the kudos since no-one really understands the mechanics of making a hit anyway.

The responsibility for maintaining the artistic direction will fall fairly and squarely on the producer's shoulders. He will have to look to the A&R person in the record company for the initial direction, the brief. After that it's up to the producer to make sure the project stays on track both artistically and financially.

These days the producer's sense of fiscal responsibility towards the record company has been rendered much less necessary by the advent of the overage clause. The overage clause establishes that if the project goes over budget (sometimes it's more than 10% over) the overage will be taken out of the producer's advance and/or royalties. This little kidney punch is guaranteed to deck even the most visionary record producer. There are plenty of variations on the theme, and if you have enough contractual clout you can get the clause deleted altogether – but I can assure you that when it's in you will be painfully aware of it and cannot relax until the last day of production, knowing that you made it on time and on budget.

*c) To Yourself?*

The responsibility you have to yourself is to create the time, space and money to make the best record you can. Every time you make a record you potentially set a series of processes in motion.

Your work will be judged by the record company. If it's judged to be substandard the record may not be released or they may pull you off the project, have it finished by another producer or remixed with additional production (a remix with additional production does not necessarily imply that the producer's work was substandard. A&R departments have become so remix happy these days that the record is not considered complete unless a remixer or three has had a go at it). To be pulled off a project not only has repercussions within the business but unless you have an indomitable spirit and an uncrushable ego it will affect your ability to work no matter how clearly unfair it was.

Your relationship with the band will be tested. I can't think of an instance when a band decided not to use a producer again for spending too much of what is ultimately their money on a record that subsequently became a huge hit. Of course magnetic (and these days digital) heaven is littered with big budget records that didn't sell a single copy and in most instances the producer will, with some justification, be blamed for letting the budget get out of control. So don't think that you can spend your way out of a problem. Unless you are working on a limitless budget there is always a certain amount of pressure to compromise. You need to make sure that you've done your sums up front. Given the abilities, personalities and facilities involved in the project, you need to be confident you will have enough money to deliver the record everyone's expecting.

*d) To The Project*

Unless you are vindictive, lunatic or just plain suicidal I can't think of a situation where you wouldn't want to do the best possible job on every project you take on. I have heard people talk about producers doing albums just for the money, implying that they are interested only in the advance and are not concerned with whether they make any royalties or not from record sales. I don't know anyone who would own up to this and the thinking defies all logic.

You won't get rich off advances but you can from royalties. Every record that gets released with your name under the producer credit becomes your calling card and your passport to future work.

My philosophy has always been to make a record of which I can be personally proud. No producer can guarantee that every record he makes is going to be a hit. Even records that only achieve cult status can be very powerful advertisements for your production abilities. Often successful bands are quite hip in their listening habits and that underground cult band you just produced might well be the thing they listen to all the time in the car. If your work's impressive enough and a band's thinking of changing producers you might well get the call for their next album. On the negative side, if you turn out poorly produced records you could get a practical lesson in how small the international record business really is.

## What About The Drug And Alcohol Connection?

*a) Should You Be Bathroom Buddies?*

My experience is that even the most dissolute artist will be critical of their producer if they feel that his performance is in anyway being diluted by his indulgences. It's OK for the artist to screw up and be screwed up. It's not OK for the producer. You are the stability on the session, you set the pace, you make the running. Of course if you're a megastar whose name alone can guarantee success for the project (this may be a mythical creature like the unicorn) even if you were comatose for most of the album the artist and record company will cut you some slack. We've all heard the apocryphal stories about the rock'n'roll Einsteins who can produce a work of genius in any state of consciousness. Well, maybe once, maybe even occasionally but not consistently and certainly not over a long period of time. Reliable accounts have it that even Charlie Parker was crap when he was blasted. Producing is less about isolated moments of inspiration and more about protracted periods of concentrated, determined, and single minded, focus. Unless you're a nominal name, or a buddy who went to school with the artist, I doubt you can survive constant over-indulgence.

Jefferson Airplane took the matter into their own hands when engineer *extraordinaire* Al Schmitt was producing the band. Referring to LSD he said: "I didn't take it every day [laughs]! Although they did try to spike us every day. I got spiked when we were doing the first Hot Tuna album. I was nailed. The engineer was Allen Zentz, and I thought I was drinking apple juice. I was working in a remote truck, and I had my pad out, ready to go, and all of a sudden the sides of the truck started to breathe. I looked at Allen and said, 'Buddy, you are on your own tonight.' I rarely did any drugs while I was working. Some engineers could smoke joints and keep working, but I couldn't. I didn't drink on the job either, but afterwards we all got into it pretty hot and heavy."

Andy Jackson thinks that generally drugs in the studio are unhelpful. "If nothing else, in terms of efficiency, they make you much slower," he says. "You make more mistakes of judgement. You end up re-doing things, doing crazy hours, which is very counter-productive."

An apparently innocuous practice which triggers the crazy hours syndrome is going to the pub after dinner until 10 or 11p.m. Everybody gets back to the studio fully juiced and ready to roll. Judgement, however, is seriously impaired or suspended. Once everyone goes to the pub, I want to can the session for the day. The likelihood of getting anything fantastic is very slim. Occasionally it works for a certain type of performance. Mostly I have not had good success with post-pub sessions.

I have never met a single producer who has said that an artist performed better because they were using a drug or alcohol on a session. Nonetheless there are producers and artists who don't seem to be able to function, in or out of the studio, without using one drug or another. Andy Jackson thinks this is a wider issue. "You are dealing with someone's entire life. There is an arguable case that marijuana use can be good for inspiration. There's a very clear case that it's not good for work. There's the rub. Making a record is a combination of the two things. Maybe you can divide the two things. The truth of making a record is the ninety-nine percent perspiration thing. There's a degree of inspiration but really that mostly happens at an earlier stage; the writing, arranging and rehearsing. Maybe there's the divide. What qualifies as work and what qualifies as creative? It's, arguably, helpful for one and destructive for the other. It's not a black and white case. It's shades of grey."

*b) Is It OK If It's Outside Of Working Hours?*

It may be OK for the producer to indulge after hours. If you're close friends with the artist, but if your habits translate into diminished performances, your career will eventually diminish too. There are no best friends in hell. Some of the biggest druggies I've had the misfortune to fall over really love to run other people's reputations into the ground. Focusing on their alleged drug use seems to be a popular way to do that. I know of one situation where the producer and the artist had been sniping at each other for several years (through several highly successful albums) about their respective drug abuse and how it was affecting their work. Eventually the producer did get the big push. Interestingly he went on to have more success with other bands – whereas the artist has seemed to be in a "resting phase" ever since.

Tony Visconti talking about this subject said, "I'll be perfectly honest with you, because David [Bowie] is honest about it. I witnessed David taking a lot of drugs around *Young Americans*, and I was no angel myself, though I'd usually limit my drug taking until after the session in a very recreational way. And I must go down on record as saying I haven't taken any drugs at all for about ten years now."

*c) What Do You Do If The Artist Does And You Don't?*

Depending on your relationship with the artist, if it's his sixth album and you're the new kid on the block you could try pontificating. You'll probably get fired. If it's their first album and your fifty-first, you could try the friendly "voice-of-experience" routine wrapped up with a health warning and encompassing the "road-to-success-is-littered-with-the-carcasses-of-talented-people-who-screwed-up" scenario but if their eyes are firmly fixed on Aerosmith, even if they have reformed, your words will surely fall on deaf ears. I'm totally amazed how many artists have a Kurt Cobain/Jim Morrison/Jimi Hendrix/Janis Joplin/James Dean/Elvis Presley fixation (usually all at once). Check the posters in their room: if they have three or more of the above, clear the studio of guns, fast cars, baths, alcohol and drugs. Try to get the album done real quick.

None of this has ever been a problem for Bruce Fairbairn who is known for his work with heavy metal bands, some of whom have excessive lifestyles. He takes a hard line against drugs. "The proof's in the pudding when it comes to drugs and alcohol in the studio. There are bands out there that are smart enough to stay sober and make good music. Those bands are the ones that I've found have the best people in them, are the most successful and are the most genuine, sincere people to work with. All I ask when a band does an album and I'm involved, is to try and do it the right way. It can only help. What they do after they finish the record is their business. But if they feel they can't make a good record unless they're high, I tell them to find somebody else to get high with and make the record with."

*What Do You Do When The Artist Freaks?*

Notice I said when *not* if. It doesn't necessarily happen on every project but it does happen. Second albums are the worst for this.

For the first album they're a bunch of sweet kids who sit humbly at your feet and shyly ask if they can borrow the bus fare to get home (or money to gas up their car/get it out of the car park). By the second album it's "where's the fucking limo/why isn't there any Bollinger/Cristal in the fucking limo" etc. All from the exact same bunch of formerly unassuming kids. Fortunately limos are not the producer's responsibility but the attitude does give a clue as to the philosophical orientation of the group (slightly to the right of self-centred).

This business feeds egos with various permutations of adulation, sex, alcohol, drugs and money. Sooner or later this ego is going to freak. There are, of course, artists who remain completely down to earth and unaffected. You do grow to love those people. It's hard to survive the extremes and excesses of rock'n'roll and it usually takes a few career peaks and valleys to give them some perspective on the whole thing. A studio freak-out can be as mild as throwing headphones across the room because the foldback is not to someone's liking. On the other hand it can be a full blown verbal and/or physical attack. The only solution that has ever worked for me at that point is to walk right out the door. In my personal all time favourite studio incident I wrote out a cheque for the advance I had been paid to date, handed it to the still freaking artist and headed for the hills. I was back at work with a greatly subdued and much more respectful artist within twenty-four hours.

Walking out is, obviously, an absolute last resort and I would never walk out for effect. You need the patience of Job to even get started as a record producer. If someone can annoy me enough to make me give them back their money and walk out the door, at that moment in time I have zero intention of going back. Walk out for effect and there is a serious possibility they will call your bluff. If that happens you have either lost the record or, worse, lost control of the record.

*What Do You Do When The Record Company Freaks?*

One might assume, if one hasn't spent much time in the music business, that the record company would never freak. After all, we're all professionals chasing the same dream, seeking the same objective – a hit record. Orson Wells once said something along the lines of "Hollywood is not, as people think, about sex and money – but power". The music business is not much different. When you get into the higher echelons of the business, egos run as rife as they do among the stars themselves. The difference is that a rampaging star is ultimately going to cause the worst damage to himself. A stampeding executive ego can destroy careers.

When I first started in the music business I thought that the major objective was to have hits and make money. This is largely true but there are a great number of sub-plots and hidden agendas that influence the overall picture. Personal likes and dislikes can be the fuel that rockets an artist to either mega-stardom or oblivion. Obviously talent and the quality of the records are very important factors. A bad singer without good songs is probably not going to make it even with the Managing Director's total support. However, with the head of A&R or MD's (senior vice president and president in the US) good will, the company will hang in for much longer with an artist. They would be inclined to set up co-writing situations with successful song-writers, pull in outside material for the singles, hire the best producers to add some name clout and to cover up the problems. They will be inclined to spend more on promotion and marketing, not to mention artwork and videos. With the will of the company and the co-operation of both artist and management, stars can be created from empty space. Unhappily, a good artist can be lost forever if the goodwill is not there. What sometimes reads as artistic integrity or an unwillingness to be manipulated can be written off as a lack of co-operation by the record company.

I've seen both edits of this video. There are many times when an artist truly does not know what's best for them. The basic talent may be there but the material is not strong, the video concept is all wrong for their market, they won't tour or they insist on touring when there is no point, and they're paranoid and confrontational. All these problems are traceable back to over-inflated ego and lack of experience.

On the other side is the situation in which a talented artist gets pushed through the sausage machine by an uncreative A&R team who think only in terms of "what's happening" right now. They are market led rather than talent led. Chasing the market/trend/fad is a perfectly viable and well established way to achieve success, and for an artist who's not concerned about breaking new ground it may pose no moral dilemma. It creates a clone-like scene but a trend wouldn't be a trend without clones, and sometimes the clones prove to be more enduring than the originators.

The point of all this is that you need the co-operation of the company. By the time the record company does freak out, it is way too late. You need to see the early warning signs, you need to keep the lines of communication open. Generally it is up to the producer to make sure that the company is happy and up to speed with what is going on in the studio. The A&R person usually has more than one project in production at the same time, along with many other company commitments. Often the first time they really get to focus on your project is when you deliver the finished mixes. By then most of the budget has been spent. If the record has gone off the rails or down a different track from what the A&R person had visualised, recovery can be both difficult and expensive. Maybe you or your management can rescue the situation using extreme diplomacy (or clout) but it should never get to this point. The best way to prevent things from falling apart is to communicate with the record company. If all else fails, you can fall back on your relationship with the artist and his management. But, no matter what the artist is saying to you privately, you are the most expendable link in the chain. You will most likely only survive through to the next album if this one sells well and proves your point.

It's also worth remembering that if the record company does freak on you and you can't recover from it, you haven't just smashed some golden eggs you've killed one of the geese that lays them. The question is how many golden geese do you have? (Clue; there are six major labels!) A very personal postscript to this is that I do have a definite limit to the amount of garbage I will take in the name of diplomacy and peacekeeping. There is a point at which I would sooner be off the project, and never work for that particular individual again, than see a record get completely screwed up. As I've said before, much of what producing is about is having an opinion. If I am constantly having to subjugate my opinion to one which I regard as completely off-base, there is absolutely no point in my being there.

Only once in my life have I kicked an A&R man out of the

studio. He was making comments that I regarded as uninformed, irrelevant to the project at hand and totally inane. In short, we clashed on nearly every point and at every level. He saw the group in a completely different light from mine and I began to realise that I was not his first choice producer and that it was the artist who had insisted on hiring me. I realised in retrospect that he had a hidden agenda. He had always intended to get someone else to remix the project, even before we started recording. I later found out that this was his standard MO. So he was nit-picking me to death primarily to provoke a reaction and justify his position.

I don't expect or want to work with that person ever again. He still remixes everything he touches and I still don't like any of the records he makes, so I guess it's best to put it down to a major mis-matching of personalities, styles and musical taste. Since then I've been a lot more careful about vetting situations and making sure that everybody concerned wants me on the project (A&R, management and artist), I can get on with all the players, I'm capable of delivering what they are expecting and they don't have an MO which is at odds with the way I work. (Watch out for A&R men with aspirations to produce. If you hate having your work remixed, check the mix credits on the last few albums the A&R person has been involved with.)

I also make sure that everyone involved is clear about what they want. This was brought home to me in no uncertain terms during a situation where I had been warned about the artist's mental stability by my lawyer, and manager. I later remembered that even the A&R man had a look on his face that is only seen on kamikaze pilots about to embark on their final mission. To make matters worse I agreed to record residentially in a foreign country. I might as well have suggested Alcatraz. I obviously loved this girl's music. I asked her what she wanted and she assured me the full, live band. The next ten days were as close as one could imagine hell to be. We were holed up in a beautiful but significantly non-English speaking country prison. I somehow toughed it through the recording and we took a couple of days off before mixing. The two days turned out to be more akin to the silence between drops in Chinese water torture than a rest. In a spirit of desperation I managed to finagle it so the mixing would be done in a city, I mumbled something about equipment and the rental situation. The city was still non-English speaking but, according to all the horror movies I've seen, a safer place to be than the country if there's a crazy person loose. Nothing in any life I can remember could have prepared me for what was about to happen. Bear in mind that the artist had been present every day, every step of the way so far. Nothing had gone down, on this physical plane, without her knowledge. She let me set up the mix in the morning as is customary and said she would come down to the studio at three in the afternoon. By two-forty-five I was starting to feel better about the whole project, yes she really can sing, I was starting to see that it was worth all the pain she'd put me through. Despite the odds the tracks were sounding great. She walked in, cordial hello's all round – everyone's relaxed and happy. I played the track for her, she sat at the console, I moved to the back of the room (a little trick I learned from old Clint Eastwood and Al Pacino movies – keep your back to the wall). The track sounded great. Often when someone else comes into the room, strangely, you hear things filtered through their attitude. The tape stopped, she hissed in serpent-like tones that I had tried desperately to love "vhere iss da drum machine". About twenty minutes of utterly pointless negotiation ensued. I reminded her of all the discussions we'd had, the fact that she'd been there the whole time and that not only was there not a drum machine on the track but that we hadn't even been graced by the presence of one during the whole recording. Absolutely no luck. I'd finally had enough. I made my one phone call to the A&R person at home. He had also had enough and was, fortunately, sympathetic. I grabbed my stuff and made a run for the border.

*What Do You Do When The Artist's Manager Is A Freak?*

I saw Danny Saber (Black Grape) live through a situation (not with Black Grape I hasten to add) where he was away from home working on a record for a well-known artist. Initially the manager tried to put him in an apartment with mould growing on the walls. Having got somewhat of a negative reaction from Danny they eventually got him a nice place in a nice part of town. All was well. The project went smoothly and Danny's stay was extended. He called the management company not once or twice but three times to remind them to renew the apartment lease.

They didn't make the call until the last day when it was too late. In the middle of recording an album he had to move all his stuff to a hotel. His reaction was "I could have spent this energy on the fucking record instead of moving my shit around town." Now I know Danny and I know there is no way he would let something dumb like this damage his attitude towards the artist or the record. Nonetheless, you have to wonder what planet the manager was on at the time. The hotel was about four times the price of the apartment so the artist got stuck with a much bigger bill. Producers are human. It's unrealistic to expect someone to put in eighteen-hour days, seven-day weeks and then disrupt their life like that without breaking their stride and without affecting their ability to do a good job.

I think it may be a pre-requisite for artists' managers to be freaks. No-one in their right mind would take the job on anyway. As a producer you are bonded to the artist for the duration of the project, as a manager you are fused for five years or more. Anything that goes wrong can be perceived as the manager's fault. It's pretty easy to understand why they can be heavy-handed at times. A manager has to have "clout" with the record company (and street fighters like agents, promoters, merchandisers etc.). For an unknown manager with a "no-count band" this can be achieved only by superhuman acts of willpower and great force of personality. Since they are ultimately held responsible for every mishap and failure along the way, a little crankiness is forgivable. Certifiable as they may be, managers have been known to save the day by going to bat for the album when all on board the good ship "Record Company" have taken to the lifeboats.

# 7

# *Lawyers*

Taking on a music business lawyer is like trying to retrieve your ball from a patch of stinging nettles – you need to reach in there or you won't be able to carry on with your game but you know you are going to get stung.

Ros Earls nailed it when she said, "Lawyers are a necessary evil really. I'd rather not use them and for the most part we take the contract as far as we can. There's only so many things that you expect to see on a contract and you could write the whole thing yourself. You do need to involve a lawyer at some stage because most of the contracts aren't binding unless you have independent legal advice. You can set up a regular deal so that you ask for the same terms as last time but they always try to change things so you have to pay through the nose again, although everybody knows there's only a limited number of things they are going to repair."

No matter how much it hurts, somewhere along the line you will need a good lawyer. As I said before, some producer managers are also lawyers. This can be a convenient arrangement and very economical for the producer. The downside is that it leaves you in a vulnerable position. One of the two times in my career that I have been seriously ripped off was when my lawyer was also acting as my manager. You know the saying "power corrupts, absolute power corrupts absolutely." If somebody has a creative sense of ethics, giving them that kind of power can be bad for your financial well being.

You're safer having an independent attorney who is paid by you. A manager may have a hidden agenda. Your lawyer can give you an objective opinion about legal issues connected with your contract negotiations.

Music-business lawyers see deals and contracts cross their desks all day long. They have a very good idea of what the going rates are. They also know what is standard practice and what is not. This translates to contractual points you can win and points you cannot. You have to have substantial clout as a producer to go against the norm. A good lawyer can actually save you money by advising you on which points you should stand your ground.

Don't, whatever you do, make the mistake that my first band did of using a non-music business lawyer to negotiate a contract. The music business, like most others, has its idiosyncrasies. We spent nearly a year negotiating a contract which in the end was still awful. It could have been done in about two months by a music business lawyer and would have been a much better deal all round.

### a) How Much Will He Cost You?

A lot. But a lot less than if you get ripped off or sign a dumb deal. Different lawyers operate in very different ways. Most will work for an hourly rate. Around £250 ($375–$400) and above per hour is not uncommon. If you have a constant flow of contracts, some firms try to get you on a monthly retainer. I've done this and I didn't like it. The theory is you can get as much advice as you need for a fixed monthly cost. I felt they were trying to do as little as possible for the retainer. It seemed like they wanted to bang out my contracts as quickly as they could and get me off the phone in the shortest possible time. The company invariably has a big name, come-on lawyer, who is one of the partners who you will meet with initially. Once you've agreed to go with the firm on a retainer, all of your contract work will be done by a very junior lawyer. I found it frustrating and at least one of my contracts got royally screwed up. If you opt to pay by the hour, your attorney will talk to you for as long as you like.

There are a lot of multi-producer records being made and albums where you're asked to do one or two tracks before they commit to doing the whole album with you. This has the unfortunate side-effect of creating even more contractual work for the lawyers. It is just as complicated to negotiate a contract for one track as it is for an album. It takes just as long. The producer will usually be paid about ten times the advance for an album as he is for one track. His lawyer's bill will be pretty much the same for a one-track contract as for a ten-track agreement. In the case of a low to mid-price producer this could result in him paying out fifty per cent or more of the single track advance in legal fees.

The only solutions to this are: to negotiate a fixed fee for the contract so you know what percentage of your advance you will be paying out; pay the lawyer based on a percentage of what you make (the downside of this is he's going to want to hold you to this arrangement when you really hit the big bucks); or put them on a monthly retainer. The reservations I have about this are as above. A retainer can be beneficial if you have a constant flow of one, two or three track contracts. The only way to tell is to calculate a rough average of how many hours your lawyer would spend on contracts in a month. Multiply that by his hourly rate and see if you're better off on the monthly retainer. Of course lawyers are not the slowest people in the universe when it comes to finances, so you can bet your boots that if you find you are winning a slight advantage this way it'll be a case of calculators at the ready. He's undoubtedly quicker on the draw than you are and as you read this his secretary just happens to be on the phone to find out when you've got time to come in and discuss their fee arrangements.

## b) How Much Should You Depend On Him?

The least amount possible. Dealing with lawyers gives you some insight into how Daniel might have felt in the lions' den. If the lawyer's feeling particularly hungry he can take a big bite out of your bank account and there's not a whole lot you can do about it. So like Daniel you need to pray that God keeps their mouths shut. Otherwise spend as little time as possible in the den. Not depending too much on your lawyer means spending a lot of time reading contracts and endless faxes referring to clause 13 (i) (ii) and (iii). It's exceedingly boring but, for that matter, so's looking left and right when you cross the road. If you enjoy being financially solvent I would strongly recommend learning a bit about contracts.

## c) How Much Do You Really Need Them?

Sadly, quite a lot. Producing can be an international experience and the laws of each country are somewhat different from each other. Even if you get pretty knowledgeable about the laws in your own country you will, undoubtedly, be in over your head when it comes to another territory. As much as I hate to admit it, a good music business lawyer can ultimately save you a lot of money. Because they are seeing contracts all day long and dealing with all the record companies all of the time, they are in a good position to know about trends and standard conditions in production contracts.

## d) What Happens When They Get It Wrong?

Truthfully, it's your problem. For all the money you've spent on this guy, if he makes a mistake you may never realise it. He could really screw up. Unless you go through your statements very carefully and double check against other agreements you may never know that anything's amiss. Meanwhile your precious royalties will be leaking back into the record company pot.

In one of my earliest contracts, my then lawyer agreed a TV advertising clause that I would never have agreed to in subsequent years. I didn't realise he'd done this (I don't generally spend my Sundays re-reading old contracts) until about eight years later when the group's greatest hits album was TV advertised and went double platinum. I did some calculations and knew pretty much what I was expecting to get. The group's manager even called me and suggested that I might want to think through the tax implications of this huge cheque I would get in about six months. When the cheque showed up it was for less than half the amount my calculations had suggested. I double checked my calculations, they were right, I went to the contract and sure enough, tucked away on page thirty-three, there was this vicious little clause which took away fifty percent of my well-deserved royalties. I called the original lawyer who negotiated the contract. I expressed dismay at the fact that he had allowed me to sign the agreement with this royalty-eating virus in it. I also pointed out that in subsequent contracts I had never had to agree to this pernicious little nasty. His self serving response was that if I wanted to retain (read pay him) again he would take a look at the problem for me.

What an amazing job! They charge you a fortune based on their expertise. Then when it turns out that they weren't such experts they want to charge you again to sort the problem out. You could sue them but what kind of nightmare scenario is that employing one tricky-dicky lawyer to sue another.

## e) What Tricks Do They Get Up To?

As Carol Crabtree of Solar Management said "Music business lawyers are a minefield. They can cost you a fortune by dreaming up ridiculous things to argue over." She cited the example of the lawyer who she caught faxing himself to death (at her expense of course) over the size of the producer's credits and whether they could be seen on the outside of the packaging or not. A legitimate enough subject for discussion. Credits are, after all, an essential part of our livelihood. A missed or wrong credit on a huge hit album can cost you future work. I had a situation where I didn't get paid for a project. I did get my producer credit though. The record turned out to be a huge and influential hit from which I picked up a lot of additional work. This somewhat compensated for the lost income. But to get back to Carol's lawyer who's arguing over credit sizing and positioning. What he omitted to take into account was that the record had been released several months ago so it was a moot point anyway.

I suspect that in the induction lecture at Law School they ask each student to turn to the student next to them, give them a big hug and promise on their Mother's life to drag out every negotiation to the max. The lawyer's code of practice must, I'm sure, require them never to be reasonable or fair with each other even though they both know at the outset what the final result of the negotiation is going to be because they just agreed six identical contracts in the past year.

## f) And That's Just *Your* Lawyer. How Much Damage Can The Other Guy Do?

The way negotiations usually run is that you, your manager or your lawyer will discuss the basic terms such as your advance, royalty percentage (commonly known as points), number of tracks and any other deal breaking points with the A&R person or the business/legal affairs person. They may at that stage send you a deal memo outlining those terms. The record company now sends you their standard producer contract with your basic terms supposedly incorporated. Invariably the original terms you thought you had already agreed will be seriously eroded by the rest of the contract. There may also be a couple of mistakes or misunderstandings in their favour. Basically the first couple of pages will give you what you wanted. The next thirty-two pages will take most of it back again via what are known as deductions and reductions. Your lawyer sends it back to them with the modifications and corrections that you and he want. There will be a bit of to-ing and fro-ing and eventually there will be a red-line or marked-up version of the contract with the amendments underlined. If this is agreeable the final contracts will be sent. Supposedly the final contract should be identical to the red-line or underlined agreement. Mostly this will be the case. But, in two cases I have found alterations to the agreed terms in the final contract. When these alterations were brought to the record company's attention, in both cases business affairs claimed they were typo's or computer mistakes. In both cases the mistakes were significantly in the company's favour. I call it the barrow boy routine. You pay for something with a twenty-pound note he gives you change for ten. If you notice he says "Oh, sorry mate" and gives you the extra ten. If you walk away without noticing he keeps the ten.

I have spoken to prominent lawyers who have had exactly the same experience. Whilst it would be wrong to imply that record companies are unethical, it's obvious that there are some individuals who will try to diminish your terms by any means. The moral of this tale is always check, or have your lawyer check, the signature copies before you sign and return them.

It's not uncommon for the record producer to be in the studio making the record before his contract is complete. This is rarely to the advantage of the producer. Once you set foot in the studio or pre-production room you have, in practice, conceded the rest of the unnegotiated points. Ros Earls says, "I've never had a situation where the producer would pull out of the studio because the contract was not in place. It leaves such a bad taste in any creative kind of situation. What you want to do is to avoid that at all costs. You have to agree things before pre-production starts. So the business politics is not interfering with the other politics and the producer can be the good guy."

My experience is that record company legal departments go slow on the contract. Obviously it kills your negotiating position if you have significant outstanding points and you are already in the studio.

This lawyer business is a love-hate thing. You need them. They need you. I've had some very successful working relationships with lawyers and then again I lost a lot of money to one who went bad. The very best law firms tend to take a long term view when it comes to money. They don't kill you on the small deals, they'll wait until your career develops and then make up the difference.

# 8

# *Difficulties And Pitfalls*

## Studio Nightmares

Bad personality traits can become magnified by the enforced closeness of the studio. Add any amount of drugs and alcohol, sprinkle a little success on top and you have an explosive mixture. Always remember, things are never so bad that they can't get worse.

## Serious Differences Of Opinion

Tony Visconti related a difficult time that he experienced with The Boomtown Rats, "It was a nightmare. It was like a Stephen King novel – it starts out in an innocent little village somewhere. Then there's that little touch of evil that starts to grow . . ." Speaking about Bob Geldof he says, "He's difficult, and he knows it. He's a good performer, a great songwriter, but you have to keep him out of the mixing room. Apparently, he wants everything to sound very sizzley and trebley, so I used to mix a really fizzy top just for him. I used to put this glistening sound on the cymbals, and he loves to hear his sibilance, which was very hard to get on a vinyl record. Then I said, 'Bob, there's a limit. We can't put too much of this on tape.' His drummer told me, 'You think that's bad, he goes home and he takes all the bass off his hi-fi set, and he adds more treble!' It was then I realised I must be dealing with a deaf person!"

Being at real loggerheads with the artist is Andy Jackson's worst nightmare. "Or worse," he says, "different members of the band being at loggerheads with each other." He's never seen a situation where the band has completely broken down. But he has seen disagreements where one person gets pretty upset. "You can usually deal with it," he says. "You just have to take the time and try to make them feel that their concerns are being listened to. Generally, if they feel that they are being listened to they will back down from their stance. If they become very entrenched and you can't find any compromise you have to get them to feel that their opinions are valid."

Bands often have very complex personality interactions going on. A minor issue over a guitar part can turn into a major psychological study of the inter-personal relationships. Childhood stuff can be dug up and thrown along with any other psychological missiles. You know, the "When I was six you did this to me" type of thing.

## The Endless Album

They may not qualify as nightmares but interminable album projects can be mentally, emotionally and physically exhausting. Unless you are seriously into job security and on a daily rate the endless project is a killer. The problem used to be confined to the ultra-rich artists with their own studios. At least you could console yourself with the knowledge that you were working on a record that was definitely chart bound. Now that almost anyone can own a studio of sorts, the problem is becoming epidemic. When the artist owns the studio you're removed from the time pressure. You don't have to finish. Andy Jackson is a veteran of the endless album, he says, "After six months you think 'I want to go into a studio where they have to pay for it, I want to get this damn thing finished'." The discipline imposed by having to pay for studio time can be a good thing and a creative stimulus in itself. Unfortunately it seems like the artists who are most inclined to build their own studios are the ones who have difficulty in making decisions.

## Lack Of Vision

Andy went on to say, "I think a lot of records are made and nobody's sat down beforehand and said 'OK what are we trying to achieve here, what record are we really trying to make.' I remember when I was a house engineer, sometimes you would wonder why you were on the session. You would feel so inappropriate. You were starting to develop a sound that was yours and the project you're working on is just not what you do. Obviously nobody had a clear idea in advance of what they were trying to do. They just said, 'Oh this is a good studio so we'll book it. It comes with an engineer; end of story. Nobody really knew what they were trying to achieve in the first place. You get it, as well, in the actual working practices. Forty-eight tracks crammed full of stuff. Then you attempt to make an arrangement in the mix. It seems like a bizarre way to work to me. Instead of having some vision of what you are trying to make in advance and then make that vision. You've got to deal with the practicalities of making that vision but you don't end up, effectively, just throwing random information at it and hoping that something worthwhile will stick. Obsessive artists are very often the problem. You spend hours and hours and hours dropping in little bits that don't make any difference and probably won't make the mix anyway. It's hopeless. You can't convince them. Their vision has become so microscopic. There is no overall vision. They don't really know what record they are trying to make."

## Panic Stations

### *a) The Singer Can't Sing In Tune/Time*

Nine times out of ten, if a singer who didn't seem to have problems with tuning in a live situation has problems in the studio, it's going to be something to do with his foldback. Number one suggestion is to rework his headphone balance to try to give him more harmonic support. Make sure he can hear enough of himself but not so much that his own voice is drowning out the track. Headphone mixes are a very personal phenomenon. Some singers like them insanely loud, with very little of themselves in the mix, others like to hear a little bit of the track with their voice obliterating everything else. I worked with one singer who wouldn't allow even a smidgen of reverb on their vocal in the final mix. In the studio he couldn't sing without "Phil Spector" style vocal reverb in the headphones. Some singers can survive with almost any mix as long as they have one side of the headphones on and the other side off. Failing all else you can bring her into the control room, turn the monitors up like a live show and she'll probably bag it in one take.

For my sins I was once locked in a residential studio for over a month with a band that had an original sense of time and a singer who couldn't manage more than one syllable out of three in tune. Sadly, the one which was in tune was out of time. I tried every trick that I knew. It was out of the question to hope for whole words to be in tune and whole lines were things I dreamt about at night. Thank God for digital editing. Fortunately I was able to compile (out of an average of twelve takes on each song) the most in-tune set of syllables that she had sung. From there I had to set about tuning each word digitally by hand. It was painstaking but in the end I got the lead vocal part to sound good. Then, she said she wanted to sing the harmony parts. I tactfully suggested that it might be nice to have the contrast of a different singer on the harmony lines.

Certain styles of music are more forgiving. Alan Moulder takes the view that, "With vocals, if the attitude is there, you can stand a certain amount of timing and tuning problems. I'm not averse to a bit of sampling and adjusting with the pitch wheel. Generally I just try to get the best performance I can."

*b) The Band Can't Play In Tune/Time*

What Jerry Harrison says is, "We can work around someone, if someone is not the most proficient guitar player, but if he has a style, we'll work around that. That's what the studio now offers, I can use the studio to help draw out the performances from the people that they maybe can't just do one take after another."

Hopefully you will have figured this out before you get in the studio. Unfortunately, if the demos were made at home on a computer or using a drum machine you have no idea how good the band are until you start working with them. Even if you've seen them live it's still hard to assess how they are going to respond to a studio situation. For a start, you hear things in a great deal more detail. Listening to something on studio monitors is a bit like looking at a poster size enlargement of a photo. You see a lot more than you did even when you were taking the picture. You notice that someone's shoes are dirty, a tie's not straight and the girl has a huge zit on her chin. Same with bands in studios, now there's no audience distracting your attention and you have control of the volume. Alternatively, the band can be intimidated by the studio environment and the pressure of this being their long-awaited opportunity.

So it's the first day in the studio and you find out that the tempos are all over the place.

The first thing to do is apply a bit of analytical thinking. Why are they not playing in time? Is it studio nerves? Is it because the guitarist is rushing and pulling the drummer along with him? Does the drummer change tempo every few bars, does he gradually speed up or slow down or does his time shift dramatically before or after a fill? It's a process of elimination. When I was a studio drummer, I often found that an over-zealous musician on the session would push the tempo. My solution was to discreetly ask the engineer to take that musician out of the headphones. Then I could hold the tempo steady and it was up to the other musician to play to me. This became especially important in the mid-Seventies when playing to click tracks became the norm. If someone else on the session was pushing or pulling, it would sound like World War Three in the headphones. I was desperately trying to stay with the click but the track was trying to roar ahead with the other musicians.

So if the tempo is moving around you can try taking different things out of the drummer's headphones and watch how he responds to that. If the music calls for a very strict tempo, a click may be essential. If someone has never played with a click before, this is guaranteed to freak him out. Never drop that on a drummer for the first time in the studio. If I suspect that it might be necessary to play to a click (because the track has to be sync'd to a computer or because there may be a lot of editing between takes for instance), I would have the drummer practise playing with clicks long before we got to the studio. Fortunately the cycle has turned and click tracks are becoming much less common than they were.

OK, so removing things from the headphones didn't work. You've checked the live demo tapes and found them to be fine. The chances are that you are dealing with a case of red-light-fever. Nothing to do with the studio being in a bad neighbourhood, just the pressure of knowing that this is it. What happens today will be preserved for posterity. Everything the band has dreamed about is coming to fruition and it's scary. In this case it's really a matter of making them feel comfortable, letting them know that they can take risks and if they screw up there is enough time for them to come back to the track and have another crack at it. It is always valuable to record all the run-throughs since they will invariably play better if they don't think they are being recorded. So forget turning the red light on. Press the talk back button and say "Let's run through it to get some levels." Hit 'record' and pray!

Out of tune is less of a problem than it used to be. With modern tuners even someone who's completely tone deaf can get a guitar in tune. I usually record an A440 tone right at the beginning of the project. All the tuners can be referenced to that no matter how many studios, countries or altered states we are in. There are a few tricks with stringing up guitars that prevent them from going out of tune and sometimes the instruments need to be professionally set up so that both ends of the neck play in the same key.

If something does get recorded which you later realise is out of tune with the rest of the track, there are now digital pitch shifters that will change the pitch of an instrument without changing the speed or vice versa. If you record, say, a piano that you later realise is not in tune with itself (i.e. some notes are out of tune with the others) all you can really do is conceal the tunelessness with a heavy harmoniser/chorus/ phase/flange FX or re-do the part with an in-tune piano. This is one of the advantages with computer-controlled midi parts. Should you find that a part that was recorded via midi to a computer is out of tune, you simply have to retrigger an in-tune piano part by running the program again. Any computer generated part currently needs to be referenced to either code, a click track or one of the devices that can analyse the tempo from one or more of the already recorded instruments (these can be less than reliable).

If it proves to be totally impossible to get the band to play in time, thanks again to digital technology it is now possible to quantise (correct the timing of) live audio. There are currently limitations within which this will work. Often it is better to edit parts that are actually in time from another take or from another part of the same take. This can be done either on analogue tape by cutting and splicing the tape, by copying from machine to machine or by using the cut-and-paste function on a random access digital recorder, just as you would cut-and-paste text on any word processor.

Of course nothing to do with technology is as simple as it

sounds, and nothing ever works exactly the way it is supposed to. Sometimes when you have to go through all this stuff you can't help but think that it would have been easier if the musicians just got it right in the first place. Other times you can use this studio trickery to rescue something very special that otherwise would have been unusable because of tuning or timing discrepancies.

Probably one of the most soul-destroying things for a musician is to be replaced by a studio musician. Most band members will be OK with a bit of sampling and digital manipulation or even having their part programmed. But, when another human being comes in to play their part it's generally very uncomfortable. Alan Moulder says, "If the drummer can't play, I'll try tape-edit comping. I wouldn't ever get someone in to replace him unless the band suggested it. I might suggest programming the drums but if they're against it I'll work with what I've got. I try to find what works for them, it may be a time of night or keeping on going back to it. Some people like to keep working on it, punching in until they've got it. Very often it's a matter of working on it in frequent short bursts. The hard part is remaining objective. Once you've gone in with the microscope your perspective is completely lost."

*c) One Of The Musicians Is Screwing Up The Take Every Time*

Tony Brown, President of MCA Records, Nashville, and one of the most successful Country music producers of recent times says, "I've seen one person completely start shutting down a tracking session. The artist needs to be creative and shouldn't have to worry about that problem. It's the producer's responsibility, and how he does it is as important as deciding to do it. You can pull the person out of the room, or have him sit in the control room, but you have to give him a reason. If things start getting weird, then I take him outside to talk. Nine times out of ten, depending on his ego control, he will usually say, 'Have I got time to run an errand?' That means, 'I'm embarrassed. I'm out of here.' I find that great musicians even know when they are not cutting it."

It's even worse when the musician is a permanent member of the band. I had a situation early in my producing career where a band had changed its drummer since they had made the demos that got them the deal. They had a very good reason. As good as the original guy was, he was a complete screw-up as a person. He had just about every problem a musician can have. My problem was I went into the project really excited about the whole thing based on what I had heard on the demos, only to find that the new drummer did not cut it. He didn't have the style, the feel or the timing of the original guy. For me it really goes against the grain to replace somebody on a session. When I was a studio musician, I had often been the drummer brought in to replace a guy in a band. I saw how badly they took it, but more importantly I was aware that, in many cases if the producer had been a little more sensitive, he could have made the guy comfortable and could have got a great performance out of him. Anyway, here I was first day in the studio hoping and praying that a miracle was going to happen and my fears that had developed during pre-production would not come to pass. No such luck, he was more shaky in the studio than he had been in rehearsals. I was faced with no attractive options, I could play the part, I could get another drummer to play the part, do it with drum machine or persevere with this guy. Drum machine was out. It would have destroyed everything the band stood for. Being the supersensitive wimp that I am I chose to stick with this guy. Out of about twenty takes I did thirty-two, two-inch multitrack edits, cutting a bar here and a bar there. I finally got my three-minutes twenty-seconds to make up the song. I did two songs like that and came to the inevitable realisation that for my sanity and the future of the band I would have to have a chat with them. By this time they had realised that something was seriously amiss. The drummer was fired from the band. I hated this situation and I've subsequently tried to avoid it at all costs. The record went on to be a hit and launched a substantial career with a couple of gold albums and multiple hit singles.

Later in my career, with more experience under my belt, I would have dealt with it sooner. It wouldn't have been right to let the band make less of a record than they deserved to. Obviously, when they chose this drummer they didn't have enough time, enough money or enough good players in their home town to choose from. I prefer the band to decide. If a musician is really not up to it but the band decides that they want to make the record with him no matter what, then I think the producer has to decide whether it's possible to make a good enough record with that musician or whether he should bow out of the project gracefully.

In a reverse situation I have made a couple of very successful records with a band that was quite inexperienced but learning fast. We decided to go our separate ways on the third album and even discussed who they might use. They went off and used someone who was very successful and we both thought was good. A day into the first session the new producer decided that the drummer was no good and would have to be replaced. The band later told me about it and I realised that the producer was simply intimidating the drummer with his attitude. He was used to recording either with machines or with studio musicians who have to have callouses on their feelings. Band members, for all their bravado, often have more fragile egos. In fact the last single I did with this band, which had been a world-wide hit, had been a first take. In the end the band decided to bail out on the producer, went with someone else and were able to carry on recording as a group and having hits.

*d) You're Just Cruising Nicely Up To The End Of The Album Right On Budget And The Main Man Decides Half Of It's Crap*

This reaction is usually attributable to "Buyer's Remorse" or "Post Purchase Dissonance". Logic dictates that if someone liked something over a substantial period of time they'll probably come around to liking it again. A break from listening to it over and over again can be invaluable. However, some artists are not that logical. Producer panic at this point in the project will burn whatever budget is left. And, you may go into a dive that you can't pull out of. This may be a good time to bring the A&R person into the debate.

*e) The A&R Person Hates Your Mixes*

Staying calm is the essential factor here. Very early on in my production career I delivered an album that the artist and A&R person had heard right up to the last day in the studio. They had monitored the whole process, from laying the basic tracks to the final overdubs and mixing. Not only had they not said a negative word about anything that was going on, they were very enthusiastic about the ongoing results. So, I delivered the album and started a well deserved break. The very next morning I got a phone call from the A&R person who in a nutshell said that she hated the record. Being of logical disposition, this completely threw me. How, I thought, can you rave about something right up to the day it is completed and then hate it twenty-four hours later? Of course I wasn't experienced enough to have encountered or learned how to deal with "Buyer's Remorse" or "Post Purchase Dissonance" which I explain later. Foolishly, I stood my ground and argued the case, only to completely defeat the purpose. It was about four years before I was able to conduct a low decibel conversation with that particular A&R person. A wiser person than I would have asked for a specific critique. They would have listened sympathetically to the A&R person's gripes and grievances. If I had read between the lines, I would have realised that she was having her metaphorical nuts busted by the artist who was a particularly nasty piece of work. I should have then suggested a three-way meeting (wearing rubber lined disposable kid gloves) to ascertain the precise course of action. Hopefully, in the course of this inquiry I would have been able to defuse the bomb. Instead I actually lit the fuse for them.

This one really blew up in my face and it took me a few years to figure out what I did wrong. In retrospect I realise that there were probably only minor things that were bothering them. If I'd taken the time to hear their comments, hear past their highly charged, critical words and try to interpret what it was they really meant, I could undoubtedly have sorted it all out. It was probably down to a few reverbs, some minor things about the mix. The worst case might have been to re-record a couple of tracks.

Very often, even if the record company is not happy they will tend not to say anything in the studio. This is partly because very few record company decisions are made by one person. The A&R man will come in and say all the right things or at least something like "I'd like to spend some time with the mixes' or "I need to hear the mixes on my own system." Two days later you have an extremely harrowing phone call with her.

There are many reasons why records can be rejected. Andy Jackson says, "I have worked on records where at the end of the day the record company says 'Hmm . . . no, we'll pass on this.' Having spent a hundred grand on it. As much as we despair about it, they are making a commercial decision. They don't want to spend another two-hundred thousand promoting and marketing a record they don't believe in. Unfortunately, in most instances that this happens, it is not because a sound commercial decision was rightly or wrongly taken but because the A&R guy has either left the company or been fired. No-one has any personal mileage in promoting the record. It's not their project. They won't get points on it or a promotion if the album is a big hit."

## What Makes It Seem Like Hard Work?

"The hardest part about being an engineer/producer (because they both fall into the same category) is to be willing to give of yourself to the project," says engineer/producer Bruce Swedien (producer on Michael Jackson's *Dangerous*). "To commit totally to what you are doing. And there are things you have to give up, like free time. But you get out of it what you put into it."

"The hardest thing is the pressure to come up with a strong single," says Steve Lipson. "It makes it easier when you're making a whole album, because your chances of finding and nurturing a single within it are that much greater. You have so much more time and facilities at your disposal, and over time things become clearer."

The anti-social hours would have to be one of the major negatives. I know several producers who insist on working eight hour days, ten to six, eleven to seven or whatever. This makes complete sense. You stay fresh and don't get burned out. Unfortunately most artists do not keep those hours, especially the younger ones who tour. They are used to getting up late and may not feel like singing until at least eight in the evening. Studio days can be as long as eighteen or twenty hours. Working seven days a week is not uncommon. Trying to hang onto a relationship or bring up kids (they get up at seven a.m. no matter what) under these conditions is tough.)

Obviously, it all depends very much on what type of producer you are and what type of artists you usually work with. The All-Singing-All-Dancing type defines his own hours. Merlin drifts in and out as he pleases. The Humble Servant is definitely locked into the artist's working schedule. The Collaborator may be able to influence the hours somewhat but very often the producer will change his working pattern to suit the artist. Since one of the major objectives is to get the best out of the artist, it doesn't pay to have them trying to sing lead vocals at ten a.m. on a Monday morning.

## How Much Loyalty Can You Expect Within The Business?

*a) From The Artist?*

Most of my work has originated from the artist, usually because they've heard one of my records on the radio or in a club, liked it and wanted to work with me. Once or twice I have known an artist long before the subject of production has been discussed. We get a chance to find out about each other which helps if we do work together. Sometimes I have met the artist "cold" on a recommendation. If we hit it off well enough and they like my previous work, we get to make an album together. Where the loyalty comes in is after the first batch of work, could be an album or a couple of tracks. Let's assume what you did together was successful musically, artistically and/or commercially. Does the artist come back to you because you did a good job – or does he use his new-found success, visibility and increased budget to attract another big name producer. Do they go for an even bigger name? Worst of all do they figure that they can get the same results at a tenth of the price by getting your assistant to co-produce the next record?

I doubt that there are many artists who will use a producer again out of loyalty. They may come back because they thought you did a great job and don't want to change the formula (i.e. if you have success don't change a thing – not the studio, the engineer, the assistant – don't even change the ashtrays). They may carry on working with you because it's a comfortable working relationship. Obviously it's easier to use the same producer than it is to change and have to strike up a new relationship. On the other hand there's the first girlfriend syndrome (see below), where you are the first producer an artist has worked with. No matter how good a job you did and no matter how much success you brought to the party, sooner or later they are going to wonder how it would be to work with producer XYZ.

One producer who has engendered a great deal of loyalty from his artists is Tony Visconti. He did nine albums with David Bowie and thirteen with Tyrannosaurus Rex. Asked what he gained from such an extended partnership he says, "Well, obviously there's real team work going on. We were a damn good team. You pick up where you left off, and hopefully it gets better, as long as the artist is making a commitment to improving and going forward, like David used to."

"When the producer or artist makes a change, the work they did together remains," notes Phil Ramone. "The tragedy of it is, the record business demands that you have hits almost every time out. And if a producer has a relationship with someone over a number of years, at some point the time will come where someone, be it the artist or the producer, will say, 'I think I'd better go make a move somewhere else.' Nothing lasts for ever. Every time somebody calls me up and says, 'I'd like to make another album with you,' I'm like, 'Oh! Well great!'"

"I've done two or three records with bands and then thought I don't think they are going to come back to me again because it's time for them to move on," says Alan Moulder. "I try never to expect to be asked back and that way I'm not disappointed. Whilst I'm generally tart for hire if you like, it's the band's career and they have to work with who they think can keep it going. You can't really take it personally." But, he adds, "It can hurt a bit sometimes."

For whatever reason, artists will move on to the next producer. Watching a band go off with another producer can be like watching your girlfriend go off with another guy. Sometimes you're happy (she's his problem now) and sometimes it hurts. Ros Earls says, "Everybody feels that way. If you don't feel like that then I suppose your heart's not really in it. Or the band and yourself were not ideal partners. People present different fronts but to a man everybody finds that the hardest thing. You are invested emotionally not just technically. You've invested huge amounts of time. Some albums take years."

*b) From The A&R Person?*

I never expect an A&R person to put himself or his job on the line for me. A&R is a precarious enough occupation as it is. An A&R person who values work you've done for them is in a very good position to put your name forward for upcoming projects. A loyal A&R person, by offering you a project that's a little bit different, can keep you from getting stuck in a rut. Very often they have the casting vote in a competition for a coveted project.

Do they look out for you very often? Sadly, no. In fact it seems to me that rather than building close working relationships with a small group of producers, most A&R people are either chasing the latest, hottest, most expensive model or trying to find a young engineer who can do the job as cheaply as possible. When I was the flavour-of-the-month I would get the most ludicrous calls for projects. If anyone had looked beyond the fact that I had a current Top Ten hit they could have seen that I was not the best person for the job. Getting good results is partly to do with the correct matching of the producer's creative and technical skills with the artist's needs. It's partly to do with how well the various relationships work. And it's partly to do with the ability of the artist and label to convey to the producer exactly what it is that all parties are expecting. When "Hot Dude" is being hired, the general assumption is that he will figure it out and get it right, after all he's "hot". The fact is that no matter how much you pay someone and no matter how big their last record was, some of their projects will fail. Most record company people just don't notice or don't choose to notice the failed albums that successful producers sweep under the carpet. A multi-platinum album can overshadow a great number of failures.

There are two major labels, for each of whom I have produced only three albums. Each of these six albums had high chart placements, all of them were either gold, platinum or multiplatinum, all made substantial profits, four were début albums that broke the artists. In both cases, when I worked for the labels again, it was at the request of the artist not the label. The gap between projects was often more than five years. So record company – and specifically A&R – loyalty has never been the cornerstone of my career.

When I asked Ros Earls how much loyalty a producer can expect she said without hesitation, "None whatsoever. Once you've made a record you have to try and move on. For a lot of producers it's like leaving their first-born child."

Not being asked to make the next record is one thing, but having the record you have just made changed or taken out of your hands is another. Ros says, "[It's terrible] if the A&R person wants to come in and tamper with their work. It has happened that a new A&R guy has come into the frame and wants to change the tracks that the previous A&R guy absolutely adored. [The producer] felt like he'd reached perfection and for the radio promotion guy to say 'Can't get it on the radio', it's heart-breaking. This is something that nobody I have ever met has accepted – but you have to move on."

*c) Final Word On Loyalty*

When times are tough I've learned not to expect help. In hard times, all the favours I did for other people count for nothing. I have to pull myself up by my own bootstraps. The goodwill I may have generated may be the key to the door at the top of the stairs, but somehow I have to drag myself up those stairs. As far as just getting a call out of the blue – it's never happened.

It's most frustrating to do the first two, career-building records, and then have the artist go off and do the third "mega" album with someone else. You don't reap the financial rewards and it looks as if your earlier records weren't up to scratch. In fact many bands (especially in America) don't hit their stride until the third album. The consolation is that the back catalogue will be, pretty much, guaranteed to sell. If it's an ego boost you need there are always the hard-core fans who prefer the lesser-known early albums. It sure is nice to reap the rewards on the big sellers though.

Jim Dickinson, producer of The Replacements, Ry Cooder and Big Star, says, "In this business, rejection and humiliation are literally a daily occurrence. You can't ask an artist to not be sensitive, but if you take it too personally, it will kill you and your art. I had a coach in high school who told me. 'You've got to remember, Dickinson, they are not doing it to you, they are just doing it.' I apply that to the record business: they are just doing it. It is happening, and it is falling on you and your art, but you can't take it personally."

The bottom line is; aim low to avoid disappointment. Don't expect loyalty from too many sources.

## First Girlfriend Syndrome

This is a very common situation that occurs when you produce a band's début album. I have done several first and second albums and there is an inevitability about the fact that the band will eventually get itchy feet and think about playing the (producer) field. No matter how good you are, no matter how well you get on with the band and no matter how much success you create for them, eventually their thoughts turn to other producers. What would it be like to work with so-and-so who did that amazing record by such and such. Other people's cooking always tastes better than your own, and it is much the same with any creative endeavour.

Most producers I speak to, if they are being open and honest, find it hard – maybe even painful – to watch a band they nurtured go off with another producer. The first producer a band has, the one who introduces them to the mysteries and intricacies of the studio world, the one who breaks them through into the limousine and champagne lifestyle, is really like the high school sweetheart. No matter how much you love her, there are always other pretty girls out there and the grass is always greener. Eventually you screw it up. You may look back and realise that it was a special relationship but for sure you can't ever go back and hope to capture that same, almost naïve trust.

There are several ways to look at it. If the band is not the least bit interested in the nuts and bolts of how the record is made and they manage to strike a successful working relationship with a producer on their début album, then they may very well continue to work with that producer for a very long time. The longer they work together the easier and more comfortable it becomes for them. Each time they go in to make another album the process becomes a little less painful. The only reason for which they would even consider changing would be if something went wrong with the relationship, if sales started to drop off (it's always the producer's fault don't forget) or if the band wants to make a different type of record that is outside the scope of their old faithful. Some bands like to change their sound on every record while others, confident of their identity, prefer to stick to the same formula.

If the artist has self-production aspirations they may immediately want to produce themselves after their first album or two or they may, consciously or subconsciously, decide to go to Producing School. The quickest way to find out how to do anything is to work with the best people in the business. If you want to learn what to do and what not to do, it really makes sense to work with as many good producers as possible.

Mitchell Froom, talking about why Chrissie Hynde stopped working with Chris Thomas after three albums, says, "It's inevitable that after you do three records with somebody, you tend to want to see if you can do it with somebody else, or how it would change the formula. Recording's a constant process of wanting things to be fresh. I think she did it to shake up the formula, to try things differently, that sort of thing. Chrissie Hynde speaks very highly of Chris. I think at that point she just wanted to see what would happen."

If you produce début albums you will almost certainly experience "first girlfriend syndrome".

# 9

## *Success And Money*

### How Much Can You Make?

Potential earnings range from the dirt-eating end of the scale to extreme wealth. Initially the income may not be so great. If you are a complete unknown, you probably won't get a big advance to start with. Until you have a hit or get yourself established in a niche, it may not be enough to live on, unless you live in a mud hut. Prior to producing I was a signed artist who worked as a studio musician on the side. The first project I produced outside my own band was Spandau Ballet's first album. Although the advance was actually quite respectable for an unproven producer, I was still making less than I did working as a studio drummer. However, those albums went gold, launched my producing career and I still earn royalties from them today.

Ros Earls of 140dB uses as a rule of thumb, £50,000 or $75,000 income per 1% royalty rate per million sales at 1995 prices. Royalties are calculated in one of three ways: as a percentage of the retail price of the album, as a percentage of the wholesale price or published price to dealer which is known as PPD, or as a percentage of the record company's receipts.

One % of the retail price of an album that retails for £14.99 amounts to 14.99 pence. This, theoretically, translates to £149,900 per million units. Ros's £50,000 per 1% per million units may be closer to the mark by the time you factor in all the packaging deductions, free goods and the other wild and wonderful ways in which the record company giveth and taketh away.

Producers command anything from no royalty at all to around 3% of retail. Four percent is not uncommon for a very successful producer and above that it's negotiable depending on your leverage.

Using a retail price of £14.99, a 3% producer will make somewhere between £150,000 and £449,700 on a million units. A 4% producer's range will be from £200,000 to £599,600. Whether you are at the top or bottom of the range depends on how well your contract was negotiated and to some extent how good the artist's contract is. When it comes to the way royalties are calculated and the reductions and deductions, the producer rarely gets more favourable terms than the artist.

Some countries and some companies calculate royalties on the wholesale price or PPD (Published Price to Dealer). In this case the percentages are adjusted using a formula so the income works out roughly the same as it would have done on the above retail calculations.

The kind of royalty rate you can command is not simply a function of your reputation and track record but also the stature of the artist you are negotiating with. It may be that generally you are a four point producer but a major world power might ask you to produce their next album for no royalty at all. Now this might not sound like a good deal at all except for the fact that the fee they are prepared to pay exceeds what you could reasonably expect to make from a good royalty on most other projects. Not only that, but the addition of the world power's name to your CV is going to up the ante for future projects and make you a definitely desirable dude.

As Ros Earls says, a good producer can earn millions. "Ideally you want to have several albums that go on selling forever."

## Do Producers Earn Their Percentage?

Producer royalties are almost invariably taken out of the artist's royalty (as is almost everything else) so if the artist will jump for it, generally speaking, the record company will too.

With a solo artist it's not such a big struggle for them to pay a third or sometimes more of their royalty to the record producer. When there are five members in the band sharing, say, a royalty of 14% (before record company reductions and deductions for anything ranging from packaging to record clubs, videos, tour support, independent promotion and TV advertising) must stretch a lot further. If the producer commands a royalty of, say, 4% that leaves each band-member with 2% each. The drummer will be making less than the producer. True, the songwriters will participate in the performance and mechanical copyright income. Bands can also make a fortune from touring and merchandise sales. Nevertheless, that producer royalty can look like a huge bite out of the future pie to a band member.

## So How Do We Justify Our Percentage?

According to Steve Albini we can't. "Paying points to a producer is a standard industry practice, and it's one of the reasons why bands go broke. They have to give a lion's share of their income to other people in the music industry, and everybody ends up making money off them, except them. I think it's criminal for a producer to take a royalty on a record that he produces – especially before the band itself has been recouped.* Royalties are for producers who say people are buying this album because I worked on it, it has my signature sound on it, and so I deserve a cut from every record that's sold. With the points system, the producer has a personal financial stake in making sure the record is commercially successful. The money he makes for himself and his family is more important than the band sounding like itself." (*Record producers are traditionally paid from record one whereas bands have to pay for the recording costs and advances out of their royalties)

Phew. What a bunch of scumbags we all are!

If every band was totally confident of their direction and sound, if they simply wanted (and had the ability) to go into the studio and record their album in a week, then I think Mr Albini might have a point. In fact, many bands are simply not capable of making records that way. For others it is just not the way they want to do it. Part of the vision for many aspiring artists is to sign with a major label, be produced by a well-known producer and make a record that is beyond what they could come up with themselves. There are disadvantages with going down this path but equally there are disadvantages with maintaining your freedom and remaining independent. In a nutshell, signing with a major is a bit like buying a lottery ticket; you have a shot at the big-time. If you win, you win big – if you lose, you're back where you started. Going the independent route is probably more like pumping gas for a living. You get paid and it's steady work with a regular income. You won't live high on the hog but you could keep doing it for the rest of your life. There's always a chance the owner will retire or die and pass the gas station on to you but the odds are slim.

The statistical probability of having a hit record is very low. According to CIN (Chart Information Network who compile the British charts) 12,845 singles were released in the UK in 1995 alone. Only 435 of those records made the Top Forty. This calculates out as a 3.39% success rate. The vast majority of signed artists will fail. Many artists only have one hit. Unless it's an enormous hit, one Top Forty single will not generate a lot of income. In fact, it is generally accepted that only four or five percent of all artists who get signed become profitable. Which means that, something like nineteen out of twenty major-label signings don't earn enough royalties to clear the advances they received from the record company.

Anyone who can shorten those odds is definitely earning their keep.

A successful record producer is, by definition, someone who has had multiple hits. Often with multiple artists. He or she understands (as much as anyone does) the processes involved in making hit records. Many people can (and will) tell you whether a record is likely to be a hit when it's finished. Very few can consistently and regularly take the raw materials and construct one with any degree of certainty.

On a less stellar level a good producer can earn his bed and breakfast just by good organisational and management skills. Groups who produce themselves are notorious for spending years and (sometimes literally) millions attempting to materialise their collective (or not so collective) dreams. The right producer can gently steer the confused, placate the warring and motivate the unmotivated.

Practical organisation of the sessions and musicians can save thousands, tens of thousands and sometimes hundreds of thousands – offsetting part if not all of the producer's advance and royalty.

If there is such a thing as a pure, free market economy in which the laws of supply and demand apply in the strictest sense, it would be in the world of record production. If producers didn't pay for themselves many times over no-one would ever hire them.

Producer advances and royalties can amount to a big chunk out of the artist's income. But, producers do not participate in the future spoils of victory such as merchandise sales, touring, publishing or even future album royalties if he doesn't produce them. His work may have helped put the artist in a position to capitalise on all these things.

Unless the artist is signed to the producer's own production company, the artist usually has no obligation to use the same producer on subsequent albums. Breaking an artist or giving him his first hit is like sending a rocket into space. Most of the energy is expended achieving "escape velocity" in order to overcome the earth's gravitational pull. Once in space it takes only a short burst of the engines to propel the ship through space indefinitely or until you need to change direction. If a producer gives an artist a hit début album, he has not just earned him a nice royalty, but has helped to launch his career and given him a platform from which to launch subsequent albums, tours, sell merchandise or even become TV and movie stars.

Obviously there are others involved in the hit making process but both the record company and the manager have long term contracts that protect them and guarantee them continued income over the next five to ten albums. The record producer, having helped an artist achieve "escape velocity", can be replaced at any time. Another producer or maybe the band, if they go on to produce themselves, will reap the rewards from that initial, often gargantuan, effort that was expended in launching the group.

I'm sure there are producers out there working the system. But, taking into consideration the insecurity of the job, the difficulty of getting started, the travelling, the long hours and the positive consequences great production can have, I don't believe there is any doubt that a good producer earns his keep.

## How Can You Increase Your Chances Of Success?

Is there a direct relationship between ability and success? Or is success purely down to good luck? Andy Jackson thinks there is some connection. "You can be lucky for an album or two but I don't think you can stay lucky. People that stay doing well do so because they are good. If you aren't any good then I don't think you will stay there. It doesn't necessarily mean that just because you are good you will get there either. You've got to be lucky to get there in the first place. If you can be successful and stay successful then you are most likely good. Some people do apparently next to nothing but their contribution is valuable. Other people do everything and there's every possibility in-between."

I don't believe for a second that you can say "if you are good you will make it'. Everyone needs a lucky break. Whether or not you can create your own luck is a deeper issue. (As the saying goes "The harder I work the better my luck gets.") What constitutes "good" in the context of production – as I have indicated throughout this book – is a complex formula. Whatever your specific ducks are they will need to be in a row:

Having an "ear", a "nose", or a "feel" for music that can ultimately appeal to a wide audience.

An instinct for being in the right place at the right time.

Patience and persistence.

Enthusiasm and energy.

Connections and confidence.

Musical, technical and people skills.

Business abilities.

Common sense.

A knack of being able to make diverse situations "work."

An ability to rise above the detail and to keep the ultimate objective in sight at all times.

You can succeed with very few of these qualities. If you happen to be gifted in most or all of these areas I would think it unlikely that you could fail.

## What Is The Secret Of Longevity?

Russ Titleman has probably had one of the most enduring production careers of the last twenty-five years. He started out in a group with Phil Spector while still in high school, wrote songs with Barry Mann and Cynthia Weill, Carol King and Gerry Goffin, played guitar on the internationally successful Sixties pop TV show *Shindig* and worked with Randy Newman, James Taylor, Paul Simon, Chaka Khan, Steve Winwood and Eric Clapton. He also worked in the A&R department at Warner Bros throughout that company's incredibly successful and creative period with Mo Austin and Lenny Waronker. His modest comment on this incredible run of success was that "being in the right place at the right time is part of it."

I would add that you need to be the right person with the right skills in the right place at the right time in order to enjoy that level of success. In Russ Titleman's case he was not only a musician and songwriter who was fortunate enough to go to school with the young Phil Spector but he was able to use his musicianship to unlock the inner doors of the business. On *Shindig* he says: "We played behind Jerry Lee Lewis, Jackie Wilson, on and on. I got to see everybody and play music behind these great artists. I used to hang out at Metric Music with Lenny Waronker (who went on to become president of Warner Bros), go over to Screen Gems where Brian Wilson would be working. I started taking sitar lessons at the Ravi Shankar institute where I met Lowell George (Little Feat)."

This kind of education is incomparable. To be able to observe and work with the great artists of the time is not only inspiring but challenging. For someone with the talent and determination to rise to that challenge, a stellar career like Russ Titleman's may just become a reality.

Ros Earls thinks that the secret of longevity is to restrict your work to projects that you have your heart in. "That's my personal golden rule," she says. "If you look to the money all the time, something's bound to go wrong. It's a negative way to approach any kind of creative project. If you've got your eye on the record you want to make rather than the dollars, the chances are, if you're good enough, you'll make good albums and people will recognise that. Particularly in England. The British attitude is that money is vulgar. If you can be associated with a particular style of music and keep on reinventing yourself that's the most likely way to achieve longevity."

## Winning The Lottery

Sometimes, very occasionally, a producer can find himself in a position where shrewd – or perhaps even crafty – business management, the right act and peculiar circumstances can result in a gigantic payout – or a big pension for life.

The term "production company" seems almost too unspecified to convey any real meaning, but in terms of the record industry it generally indicates a company with whom artists may sign an agreement which guarantees them only *a chance to record* and probably *at their own expense*. The production company will then endeavour to sign an agreement with a record label to release records by the artists signed to them. Thus the artist is not signed directly to the label. Often the artist has signed with a production company only as a last resort. Often the master recordings remain the property of the production company. The head of the production company often has very good connections with the head of A&R of at least one major label.

Production companies can be headed by managers or record producers, and they are in a unique position to profit from these circumstances, in the first instance by playing both ends against the middle. The scenario goes like this: Wizard Productions signs Band A, guaranteeing them a 7.5% royalty on the records they release; Wizard Productions signs a deal with Major Label, which guarantees them a 15% royalty on the records it produces for them; Wizard Productions therefore splits the difference, giving Band A its allotted 7.5% (probably after recording costs) and keeping the other 7.5% for itself; Wizard Productions consists of one man and his secretary; Band A is a five-piece with a manager taking 20% off the top; therefore the individuals in Band A earn a 1.2% (7.5% less 20% divided by five) royalty each, less recording costs, while the producer earns 7.5%, or 6.5 times as much.

This practice is less common today than it once was, and is open to widespread abuse. Artists often realise what is going on and rebel, as was the case of Bruce Springsteen and his first manager/producer Mike Appel. Springsteen had signed to Appel's company Laurel Canyon Ltd., and Appel signed Laurel Canyon to CBS. After two and a half albums Springsteen and Appel fell out over money and production methods. When it came to court Springsteen was eventually free to go with his succeeding manager/producer Jon Landau but not without conceding a substantial payout to Appel who argued, not without justification, that he had discovered Springsteen, nurtured him and supported him before the megabucks beckoned.

But perhaps the biggest lottery win of all landed in the lap of American producer Shel Talmy who in the early Sixties was resident in London and producing many of the bands that followed in the wake of The Beatles. One of them was The Who whom Talmy signed to a six-year production deal in 1965, giving them a 2.5% royalty. He took their records to American Decca who released them in the UK on the Brunswick label, and who doubtless gave Talmy a royalty substantially in excess of 2.5%. The Who's management soon realised how little they were earning and persuaded Talmy to increase their royalty to 4%, but this was probably still far less than Talmy was getting. Worse was to come.

After three singles and one album The Who wanted out – they reckoned they could make better records and still more money without him – but Talmy wouldn't budge. To force Talmy's hand, Who manager Kit Lambert took the group's next single, "Substitute", to Robert Stigwood who put it out on his Reaction label (through Polydor). Talmy sued, and in an out of court settlement was granted a 5% royalty on all The Who's records and singles for the next six years, up to and including *Who's Next* in 1971, all their best selling work. He thus earned considerably more in royalties from The Who's record sales than the individual members of the band did . . . without so much as lifting a finger. Even now, 30 years later, Talmy still collects pro rata royalties on every track The Who recorded up to 1971. He also retains ownership of the master tapes for The Who's first three singles and first album.

This case was exceptional but there are probably other, similar cases around where record producers, having signed the right act at the right time in circumstances that were less than propitious from the act's point of view, are living on Easy Street. It won't make you popular, of course, and I wouldn't recommend this way of doing business myself, but if you've a thick skin and don't mind what people say about you behind your back, it does have certain compensations . . .

# 10

## *What Are The Timeless Ingredients In A Hit Record?*

### a) The Song

T Bone Burnett is pretty clear about this issue. "I'm attracted to good songs and good singers and I don't want to distract too much from that. The way records used to be made is you'd hire an arranger, the first thing you'd write down was the melody line, and then everything would be voiced around the melody. We started going backward with multitrack recording. We'd put down a rhythm track and a hundred overdubs, get two twenty-four-tracks filled in with music and then try to stick the vocal in the middle of all this sound. Jerry Wexler (the legendary Atlantic Records producer) called it 'track-happy'. For me, it's gotta start with the song and the vocal performance."

Rick Rubin is just as emphatic when he says, "I think the most important thing a producer can do is spend time getting the songs into shape before recording. The material is so much more important than the sounds."

L.A.Reid, of the incredibly successful L.A. & Babyface writing and production team says, "The reason we're not that into high tech is because we try to concentrate on great lyrics and awesome grooves. If we spent all our time paying attention to technical tricks, then we'd never get around to the melody, which is the most important aspect of a song. After all, the melody is what we pick up on when we're listening to a song. And isn't that what loving music is all about – being a good listener?"

Producer *extraordinaire* Jerry Wexler was responsible for many of the classic Sixties soul hits on Atlantic Records. Wexler states it very simply, "To me, a record comes down to a singer and a song; other elements must be subordinate."

## b) The Vocal

A great vocal is an undeniable asset to any record. After the song itself, the vocal performance is the next most significant factor that will make people pluck out their credit cards. Greatness in a vocal is very little to do with technical performance or recorded quality; these are the tangibles. A great performance is an intangible that is connected with the interpretation of the emotional content of the song. If you can get the tangibles and the intangibles on tape you're really flying. But focus on the tangibles too much and the intangible will fly right out of the window.

Barry Beckett, of the influential Muscle Shoals Rhythm section, produced an award winning vocal on a Bob Dylan album which he says was cut live. "He had been singing those songs over and over to himself, so he had them down backward and forward. He would just get it on the first pass, which blew me away. I did insist on trying to punch him in on one line, but we couldn't match the voice, so we just let it go. He later won the award for Best Vocal on that song, which was 'Slow Train Coming'. Beckett laughed, saying: "I went up to him later and said, 'I give up'. He just laughed."

"What I do is only as good as the vocal, particularly when I'm doing a remix," says Danny Saber. "If there's a good vocal then it's easy. A good vocal is not necessarily something that's sung really well. It's when the lyric goes with the voice that it's coming out of. When the whole thing clicks then that's special. You can't teach that to anybody, they've either got it or they haven't."

## c) The Arrangement

When it comes to hit singles, after the song and the vocal performance, the arrangement is paramount. It's often assumed that the arrangement is part of the song writing process. Sometimes it is. But, very often the melodies, the chord sequences and the lyrics can all be in place, yet it isn't until the arrangement comes together that the song has that compelling, "I want to hear it again," quality.

"You nurture every song to make it as good as possible, but a single has to be attractive in a more obvious way," says Steve Lipson. "You don't always need a gimmick. The arrangement has to be exactly right, unquestionably. I learned a lot about that from Trevor [Horn]."

Structure is an important part of the arrangement. The structure of a song is the order in which the different sections of the song are played. The rest of the arrangement is to do with what happens within those sections and in what order.

## d) The Performance

"Production should always come secondary to capturing a moment," says Bruce Fairbairn. "None of the songs on *Pump* would have flown if the guys in Aerosmith hadn't played them great initially. Once you have something great on tape then you have a really good solid base to play around with . . . adding the production aspects, mixing in texture and colour to the tracks."

Alan Parsons put it beautifully when he said, "Great records come from great moments – not from great equipment. No amount of knob twiddling can equal someone putting their all into a performance, whether it's a guitar solo, a drum part, even a tambourine part. You can EQ the voice or snare for four hours, but if they finally go out there and hit it properly you have to turn all the EQ off. To me that live thing is to do with the vibe and the confidence from the band all the way through from the beginning. It's got nothing to do with the technology."

There is something incredibly bland about a record that has no life in the performance. Even a completely computer generated record usually has something human about it. Even if it is just the vocal. That unquantifiable quality that you can always perceive as being better from one take to another. You may not be able to put your finger on what it is, but no matter how many times you play it back, even over a period of days, weeks or months, you can still sense that take three has something that take four doesn't.

## e) The Engineering

Bruce Swedien said, "One thing I learned from Bill Putnam (one of the great engineering innovators of the Fifties and Swedien's early mentor) that carries over in my work now is thinking in purely musical terms – as far as recording the instruments – more than in technical terms."

"It's just one of my things, good quality is terribly important to a hit record," says Les Paul. "I don't know how many people have stopped me to ask if it is really all that important, when it's what's in the grooves that sells."

You don't have to look very far to find examples of hit records that don't sound very good. But, it does seem that the really big records, and particularly the timeless, enduring ones, do usually sound excellent. It would be true to say that if a song is not good, the vocal is less than compelling and the arrangement or performance is under par, then the record will not be successful no matter how well engineered it is. Having said that, I have seen songs come to life during production just by being made to sound better. The best example of this is when a record is remixed because the company doesn't particularly like it. Often nothing much changes in the remix except the overall sound quality. Suddenly the whole company is excited about it. If the highs, lows and middle are in balance, the individual sounds are powerful, you can feel the groove and the vocal grabs you, then the record will undoubtedly be a lot more effective than it would have been if the engineering was under par.

In some ways maybe you can't totally differentiate between production, engineering and arrangement, they are so interactive in terms of the way the record sounds. "Even though in some ways they are discreet entities and may be done by different people they are incredibly interactive," says Andy Jackson. "If you look at [something like a] Frankie Goes To Hollywood record those things all worked together as a package. Not a great song but great records and justifiably big hits."

## f) How Important Is The Mix Really?

I remixed a track that looked like it was not going to make it on to an album. We all had serious doubts about the basic song. The remix was so well received that the track became the first single from the album. Andy Jackson thinks that the mix is only important as a potential negative. He says, "You can screw up a great one but very rarely can you take a bad song and mix it into a hit." A mix should optimise the song, the vocal, the performances, the arrangement and the audio engineering. It should make the record current sounding, seem louder, and more exciting.

## g) Timeliness

No matter how perfect the song, the vocal, the playing, the sounds and the mix are, if the record sounds like the last big trend (and especially if the band looks like it too) unless it's one of the bands that spearheaded the trend it's probably not going to work. Then again if it sounds like the trend before last or the one before that . . . who knows?

## h) The Heart

I have always held that there has to be some belief or heart in a record for it to do well. Even the crassest pop ditty has someone behind it who in some way believes in that kind of thing (beyond the money they think they might make). They may know it's not a work of art, but they like the record and they believe in what they are doing. Talking Head's Jerry Harrison says, "I think it's some sort of heart that's the most important thing – really believing in what they're doing. This kind of goes back to what The Modern Lovers (his first band) always stood for, which was this idea that no matter what you were saying, you should really, truly, believe it – nothing should be fatuous in rock'n'roll. I still go along with that. I like people who are a little bit on a mission – things are important to them. It's not just about musicianship, it's about getting an idea across."

T Bone Burnett says, "I couldn't tell you exactly what it is that makes most hit records successful. And I don't think I'm facile enough to sell out. You have to be able to do something you don't mean, and I'm not good enough to do something I don't mean and have it sound like anything. The only reason what I do sounds like anything at all is because I mean it."

"As producer, I felt that my function was to do the best job I could for an artist," says Mitchell Froom, "and if that occasionally meant going along with things and allowing myself to think in slightly conservative ways – thinking that we had to deliver something that somebody commercially had a chance with – then I accepted that. But over the years I found that for me, personally, wherever I'd been more conservative I had failed." By 1991, he says, "the whole thing had come to a point where I felt that I wanted to go down in flames. I didn't want to be someone who would become more and more conservative. I wasn't happy with that at all. So I said, 'I'll go out with a bang and find people who also want to do that'.

"I don't feel any more as if I'm just there to serve the artists as best I can. That's of course still the ultimate aim of my job, but my focus has changed to trying to get to the bottom of what an artist is about and challenging them to be as innovative and adventurous as they dare to be."

"I learned from Quincy Jones," says Bruce Swedien, "to listen to your instincts. That's hard for a lot of people in our business. We have a tendency to cerebralise what we are doing, and it's wrong. Music is organic in the human being. What we are doing must provoke an emotional response, not a cerebral response. There is a big difference between a 'beat' and a 'groove.' I'll go for a groove any day. The beat is repetition, but a groove can have dynamics and be very emotional."

Quincy Jones himself says, "I've done three or four things in my life with artists where I really knew that it wouldn't work, where I got talked into it or pressured. I won't bring up any names, but what that confirmed to me was that you have to love and adore the sound the artist makes and adore the person too – because that's the same sound really, the pain or eccentricity or neurosis or whatever it is, that's where it comes from. Once that happens, you can treat the artist almost like you're an X-ray machine – to go into them emotionally and musically, which is all tied together anyway – I know this sounds abstract – and to feel what is their range and where is their heart, their emotional centre. Then you know what gives them goose bumps; the kind of chord sequences and sonorities and colours or whatever it is that does it. I love to give singers I work for goose bumps all the time."

## i) Are These Rules To Which There Are Exceptions?

There are no hard and fast rules in the music business and even if there were there would be exceptions. There will always, from time to time, be hits that defy explanation. Maybe the song is not particularly good, the record doesn't sound great and the singer can't or doesn't sing. The simple fact is, if you look at the charts, the same basic principles apply today as they did ten, twenty, thirty, even fifty years ago, right back to the very early popular music recordings. The sound of records has changed almost beyond recognition. But, on most very big hits, there is a song with a memorable melody, an interesting lyric, a singer with a distinctive character and well arranged and orchestrated instrumental parts. This is just as true if you look at commercially successful rap or alternative records as it is on 'White Christmas' by Bing Crosby. If anything, perhaps the biggest change over the last sixty or seventy years has been the increasing dominance of vocal recordings. Through the first half of this century instrumental records by artists such as Louis Armstrong, Duke Ellington, Count Basie and Glenn Miller occupied a large chunk of the charts. These days instrumental hit records are only marginally more common than the dinosaur.

# 11

## *Frequently Asked Questions*

### How Much Can You Learn, How Much Is Natural Ability?

Actually a great deal of the job is to do with instinct. Flood said in a recent interview, "So much of what one does has to be based on instinct. From there you use your experience to refine, hone, change and question your original instinct." But we're not talking about the kind of instinct that you're born with. This is the instinct that develops from being around music, musicians and studios your whole life. This, I think, is the reason that DJ's with no musical or technical ability can still become excellent producers. They have listened to many, many records, logged the way people responded to the music and subconsciously programmed their instinct to be able to reproduce those excitement factors in their own records. I played in a lot of Top Forty bands when I was young. I hated it at the time but later when I started to write and produce, I realised that having to learn and play all those hits had instilled in me an instinct for what works and what doesn't. I didn't have to think about how to construct a hit. I just knew. Obviously production values vary from one type of music to another and from one era to another, but since the music you produce will most likely be similar to the music you listen to, the more you listen the more your instinct gets honed.

### How Do You Pick The Right Project?

Jerry Harrison says, "I read a thing where [engineer] Dave Jerden said he really only wants to produce bands that he'd play in. And I kind of feel like that, too. Like Poi Dog Pondering – I love them, and it was great to work with them."

I know I've taken a couple of projects for the wrong reasons and it's never felt good. It's easy if you're a producer with broad musical taste and a good solid musical grounding to look at a project and see right away what needs to be done. You can even do a very good job without really liking the music. I've done it both successfully and unsuccessfully. But, I'm not going to get much satisfaction out of working on an album where I don't have a real love for the music, so it's better if I leave them alone.

## Do Producers Have Their Own Sound?

Some producers definitely do. It's pretty easy to recognise a Jam and Lewis track or Babyface or Quincy Jones. Rick Rubin thinks he has a sound based more on what he doesn't like than what he does. He doesn't like reverb and he likes to capture a performance. He says, "I hate technically slick records that have no sense of emotion or of the artist's performance, and all my records sound like the artist – whether it be The Beastie Boys or LL Cool J or The Cult or Slayer or The Masters Of Reality. I'm not one of those producers who has a stock sound and then adds different personalities on the top as icing." Flood doesn't think he has a sound but his manager Ros Earls says she can recognise the sound of his records right away.

I never wanted to have a sound. The reason why I wanted to be a producer in the first place was to realise the artist's dream. The only way a producer can escape having a sound is to let the artist and the material dictate the engineering and production techniques. To avoid stamping your personality on a record you need to have very broad taste in sounds and musical styles. You either need to be versatile technically and musically or have a diverse range of people to work with. Nonetheless, if you bother to show up at the studio at all, it's going to be impossible for your productions to be one hundred percent transparent. As Rick Rubin said, your dislikes will define your sound as clearly as your likes. Just the kinds of acts that you choose to work with and the material that you pick can be vital sonic clues as to your involvement.

## Should You Get Involved In The Song Writing?

It may be that the very reason why you are producing the act is because you wrote the song. This is very common on R&B and pop projects. The issue of whether to get involved in the writing becomes sticky when you are dealing with a singer-songwriter or a self-contained band. Given that it is the producer's job to make the best possible album for the artist and that the material is the most fundamental element of any record, it would be irresponsible for a producer not to try to improve material that he knew could be better. It makes a difference how you go about it. In the first instance I try to stimulate the band into fixing the problem themselves. I might say "You know, that chord change into the bridge just isn't comfortable," or point out that a particular part of a song is weak and could be improved. Sometimes this will work. The band will rise to the occasion and fix the problem. On other occasions the artist either doesn't agree that there's a problem, doesn't know what to do about it or comes up with an alternative that is no better. At this point you have to make a musical suggestion that they can either use 'as is' or as a jumping-off point to develop a solution of their own. At this point you are involved in the writing. The issue is when do you take credit for it.

"Song writing is not my job," says Bruce Fairbairn. "My job is to help a band create the album they want to make. If I do happen to contribute something writing-wise, unless it's a big, big deal, I'll let it go. If I have an idea and it's going to make for a better song, then it's worth incorporating it. I'm not rewriting choruses for these guys, and I don't take song writing credit. I'm more involved in structuring and arranging the song. You've got to work that way, though. If you bring up an idea and the guys in the band aren't threatened that they're going to lose ten percent of a song over it, they'll be much more inclined to listen to what you have to say. If you start arguing over every chord change, bridge or word, then that's just counter productive to the project."

What Fairbairn says here is exactly right. If you are writing choruses then you probably should take the credit. If it's restructuring or arranging their material, I believe that's part of a producer's job. If you get into altering chord sequences, melodies or lyrics, you have to assess it on a case by case basis. I think the overriding factor, as Bruce Fairbairn says, is that you're much more likely to be able to improve the song if your motivation is not in question.

Speaking about their producer Mitchell Froom, Neil Finn of Crowded House said, "Mitchell is a very musical guy, far more so than many who claim to be producers. He gets involved in arrangements and song structure, makes suggestions for the odd chord change here and there."

Even a producer like Steve Lipson (who made his début as the techno-wiz on the quintessential, Eighties, Trevor Horn productions for groups such as Frankie Goes To Hollywood and Propaganda) says of his production input, "I can write songs, that's how I got started. I'm still one hundred percent involved in arrangements and instrumentation. It varies from song to song, and from artist to artist. With certain artists I'll reconstruct the song completely from head to foot, play it, not play it, change the chords, change the key, whatever it takes."

Song writing proved to be the jet-pack that propelled Shep Pettibone from the top of the remix mountain to the top of the production mountain. He had been working with Madonna on remixes of her records and got the opportunity to produce a B-side. The B-side turned out to be the massive hit 'Vogue' and Pettibone decided to start putting some more tracks together for her. He dropped a cassette of the tracks off to her while she was filming *In A League Of Their Own* in Chicago. She liked all three. This was to be the beginning of his co-production gig on the *Erotica* album. Pettibone wrote the music and Madonna wrote the lyrics. Sometimes he would give her some ideas for lyrics and she would say, "Oh, that's good," or "That sucks." When he did this for the song "Vogue" she very curtly said, "That's what I do." Pettibone adds, "Essentially, her songs are her stories. They're the things she wants to say."

## New Versus Established Artists?

There is no confusion in Walter Becker's mind when he says, "As a producer, I'd like to work with new artists, and with bands who write their own material. Many established artists have it covered in the studio and know how to do it. I'd like to work with people on their first albums, with artists who need someone to help them capture it."

The producer's relationship with an established artist is going to be different from what he would have with a début act. Even for an established producer, working with a musical legend can be intimidating. Barry Beckett produced Dylan's *Slow Train Coming* album. He says, "It took Bob three or four days, while we were cutting, to even trust me. When he finally did, he let me know with a very slight smile, or something like that, to say I was OK. I was pretty nervous when we started."

Most producers will get started by producing new artists. Once you have some success under your belt you have to decide whether you want to increase your odds of having a hit by working with established artists or stay at the sharp end working on début albums. It's commonly held that the major label success rate is around four to five percent. This means that approximately one out of twenty artists signed to a major label will go into profit. Obviously an established artist is already one of the five percent. Their next album has a much greater chance of making money than a new artist's does. They already have a fan base, radio and TV are going to be more receptive and the company wants to capitalise on what it's already developed. It's a hard call. Creatively, it may be more satisfying to work with a new artist who really needs your expertise. Established artists can be more difficult to deal with, they have an identity that they want to maintain and you may have to work within fairly tight constraints. They're often surrounded by yes-men and you'll almost certainly be on their schedule. On the other hand, it can be very exciting to work with someone who you admire and it's nice to know that someone other than the artist's mother is waiting for the record to come out.

## What About The All-Important Credits?

*a) Executive Producer*

The executive producer is usually someone in a position of power who has some overall responsibility for the success of the artist. They may be the manager (Peter Grant was credited as executive producer on every Led Zeppelin album), the A&R person or the president of the record company. The executive producer's role can range from active and highly involved to saying "hi" once on the phone. You won't see this person in the studio on a day-to-day basis but he can be highly instrumental in the selection of the material, producer(s) and mixes.

Executive producers can earn their credit in all sorts of different ways. The music journalist and Omnibus Press editor Chris Charlesworth is now credited as executive producer on virtually all of The Who's back catalogue. "That was because it was my idea to revitalise their back catalogue by adding bonus tracks and a handsome 24-page booklet to every album," he says. "Of course, I've never produced a record in my life by working with an artist in a studio, but if it hadn't been for me these new de-luxe, remastered re-issues of The Who's old albums probably wouldn't exist. I helped choose the bonus tracks, edited the booklet texts and generally looked after the packaging and quality control."

Charlesworth's relationship with The Who goes way back to the days when he wrote about the band extensively for *Melody Maker* magazine in the early Seventies, but in 1993 it was he who approached Pete Townshend, suggesting The Who release a retrospective box set, and he wound up compiling the tracks and generally overseeing the project on The Who's behalf. When *30 Years Of Maximum R&B*, a four-CD Who box, was released, Charlesworth was actually credited as producer, along with Jon Astley (a 'real' producer, and Townshend's brother-in-law, incidentally) who did the studio remastering work, and Bill Curbishley, the band's long-time manager.

*b) Producer*

The producer credit is usually reserved for the individual who is responsible for the creative and practical day to day aspects of making the record. Most of what I have talked about in this book applies to the 'producer' or 'co-producer' role.

*c) Co-producer*

Co-production can indicate a production team of two or more people. Frequently production teams comprise a musician and an engineer, or a song writing team. Co-production can also mean that the producer collaborated with the artist. Increasingly, artists want a co-production credit. This type of joint production credit can be a token gesture to the artist or it can be a full-blown collaborative co-production. It is generally the experienced artist who has made several albums who will want a co-production credit.

*d) Associate Producer*

This credit is much more common in the US than in Europe. Generally it is given to a less experienced or first-time producer who is working under a veteran "name" producer. The veteran may not be in the studio all the time and may be leaning towards the executive producer type of role. The associate producer is very often a musician or songwriter who is trying to get his break into a full production career.

*e) Additional Production By*

This is a very deceptive and potentially unpopular credit. It can mean that the remixer wants to get into production so he added a tambourine to the chorus and claimed an additional production credit. It is often added without the prior knowledge of the producer. It's extremely annoying to pick up an album that you spent months producing and see an additional production credit given to someone who spent a week mixing it and should legitimately be credited as a "mixer" or "remixer". In the case of dance remixes where considerable chunks of the original production have been replaced, "additional production" is warranted. In a situation where everything but the lead vocal was replaced "additional production" is, if anything, an understatement. The "additional production" credit is warranted where a significant amount of material is added to the original production.

*f) Multiple Producer Credits*

There can be multiple producers on any album. This was a trend that took hold in the early Eighties. R&B and pop records are more likely to have multiple producers. Often the producers are the writers of the songs. Most alternative, indie or rock bands have a single producer or co-producer.

*g) Recorded By*

This is really like a chief engineer credit. It usually indicates responsibility for the sonic side of the production but not necessarily total hands-on involvement. Often there will be a studio "house" engineer or even an assistant engineer who does the knob twiddling under the supervision of the chief engineer or producer who will get the "recorded by" credit.

*h) Mixed By*
Traditionally this was a credit given to the engineer who mixed the record irrespective of whether the producer was present or not. Lately the boundaries of what constitutes a "mix" have become blurred. Most commonly 'mixed by' is the credit given to the person or persons who controlled the primary set of mixes.

*i) Remixed By*
Generally indicates that this is not the first commissioned set of mixes. Dance remixes will almost always be credited in this way. Generally the person who does the dance remixes will have replaced a great deal if not all of the original production work. A very common process is for the dance remixer to take just the vocal and build up a completely new track underneath it. They may sample the vocal and just use fragments of it. The track may even be at a completely different tempo. The dance remixer's version is often so far removed from the original (for better or for worse) that it is more like a re-production than a re-mix.

## What Are The Best Moments?

Coaxing a great performance out of a singer, drummer or soloist can be a huge buzz. It's especially gratifying when the performer recognises that something special has happened, that he or she has gone beyond anything they've ever achieved before. You can feel the electricity when a musician plays an off-the-wall but perfect part that transforms a track from the ordinary to the extraordinary. The breathtaking first take vocals or solos. The times when an artist walks in on a mix and can't believe how good they sound.

"Great playing. Great musicians," says Andy Jackson. "When something fabulous happens. Something that moves you. That thing that made us all do this in the first place, that got so fouled and embittered with the years. We stopped listening to music for fun many years ago. Occasionally, you get that spark that you remember, 'This was like when I was fourteen.' It just occasionally happens."

## Why Are There So Few Female Record Producers?

I would love to know the answer to this question. My guess is that it's because there have been fewer female artists and musicians in the studio world in general. From the engineering side it is rare to find a woman who rises beyond the assistant engineer role. I have never been able to account for this, except that maybe women find the hours too socially debilitating, especially in the early years. I have worked with several female assistants and a couple of engineers with excellent results and generally found that having a woman in the studio seemed to keep things somewhat more civilised. Sometimes it gets pretty wild with a bunch of guys locked up together in a studio for months on end. The female presence can be a moderating factor. I can't come up with a single good reason why there are not a great deal more women in studios both engineering and producing.

Surveys by Technet and *EQ* magazine verify the fact that very few women work at the sharp end of record production or engineering. The results showed that women hold mainly administrative and support positions. Less than twenty percent of all technical positions are held by women and less than two percent of those are in "First" or "Lead" positions. Evaluating a list of factors that have led to the scarcity of women in audio production, women themselves cited a lack of prominent role models and a lack of encouragement by primary and secondary educators.

Gender discrimination was regarded as being a lesser or secondary force determining the number of successful women in audio. Perhaps the higher incidence of female artists and all-girl bands since the Eighties will result in some of them going into production.

Gail "Sky" King got into producing through running errands for Arthur Baker. She became an assistant engineer but preferred production and moved towards that via editing and remixing. The production work evolved out of radical remixes where only the original vocal is kept and the track is completely re-created. She got married and had a child. To try to accommodate this change in her lifestyle she built a home studio. She has had some negative experiences which she attributes solely to the fact that she is a woman in a man's world. She says that some men are just not comfortable with women in the studio. She says, "Opportunities are so few and far between that you just can't afford to chuck 'em. So if you get a chance to do this, there can't be any half-stepping. Don't go out there and be all fluff and no substance."

Female engineers who have amassed considerable credits for themselves are Leslie Ann Jones who is a staff engineer at Capitol Records and Susan Rogers who started in the business as a field service technician for MCI and became famous for her work with Prince. Sylvia Massy who has also worked with Prince has gone on to engineer and produce alternative groups such as Tool and Skunk Anansie.

There are, of course, several female artists who either co-produce or produce themselves, Madonna and Kate Bush being obvious examples. Patrice Rushen (who has fired off some blistering jazz-fusion solos behind John McLaughlin and Jean Luc Ponty, wrote and sang the funky pop hit "Forget Me Nots," arranged strings for Prince and MD'd many award shows) would seem like a natural for the producer's chair which she finally occupied alongside partner Charles Mims Jr on an album for Sheena Easton.

## Can You Successfully Genre Hop?

### *a) Advantages And Disadvantages*

Only marketing people think that an individual listens to just one type of music. Very few people are mono-taste-istic. Producers are no exception to this rule. In fact most have much wider taste than the public at large. This is partly because of a general love of music and partly because they are exposed to a wide range of music. In view of this I find it all the more frustrating to be restricted to producing just one type of music. I have genre hopped a great deal in my career. There has been a cost. A&R people have more difficulty placing you with acts. Veteran A&R man Muff Winwood says, "Artists are very often looking for someone whose last four albums sound exactly like they want their next album to sound." OK, fair enough. It's reassuring to be able to listen to someone else's record and say that's how I want my record to sound. If the artist doesn't mind a cookie cutter approach to the production of their record then they probably won't be disappointed. My personal observation is that the biggest, greatest and/or most influential records were not made this way. They were made by single-minded individuals or groups of people pursuing a single vision with creativity and originality, influenced but not dictated to by current trends.

Having a cross-genre track record effectively diminishes the impact of your CV as far as any particular artist is concerned. Artists can be quite limited in their appreciation of other musical styles. If you are discussing work with an alternative artist, your R&B or country hits will probably mean very little to them. They probably won't even have heard of the records you did outside of their genre. Artists and A&R people have difficulty translating production techniques from another genre into what you might be able to do for them. If anything, the most effective way of using a cross-genre track record is to have successfully produced enough different styles of music so the artist can only conclude that you can produce anything. It helps if the artist is also a hybrid. They are more likely to have broad musical taste and be able to hear that your influences match with the various flavours in their own music. Rock and alternative bands are more likely to understand the relevance of R&B and urban productions than vice versa. This may be because rock'n'roll originally came from black American music. The R&B artists don't seem to be able to make meaningful connections between rock or alternative productions and the record they are wanting to make.

I believe if you are capable of putting together a great record at all, then you can probably make a great record in any musical style that you have a genuine passion for because the fundamental rules of production remain pretty constant across the genre lines. Although the details will change, a good producer sees beyond details.

Nonetheless producers do tend to get genre-bound. The All-Singing-All-Dancing producer is more likely to become typecast than another type of producer. They are, by definition, responsible for so much of the character of the record. They are often likely to pin their stylistic colours to the mast.

Of all producers to fall foul of typecasting, the last person you would expect it to happen to would be Phil Ramone. His career has been so long and diverse that you would think his versatility was a given, but when he tried to branch out into country he was thwarted. "You're typecast from day one as a rock producer. I was a big fan of Lyle [Lovett]; we were about to make a record and then the country people got scared that I would take him somewhere else," he says.

*b) Who Has Done It?*

I count myself fortunate in this regard. I started out producing computer generated pop music, went through the pop/alternative of early Spandau Ballet and King, then had success with urban/R&B projects such as Colonel Abrams, New Edition, Melba Moore and Five Star, blue-eyed soul with Living In A Box and back to alternative with Shriekback, XCNN and Rubicon. Along the way were occasional ambient projects such as Virginia Astley and Praise.

Mutt Lange is probably the most successful example of a producer who exhibits diversity in his work. His projects on the heavier end include bands like AC/DC and Def Leppard. He covered a lighter poppier kind of rock with The Cars, ventured into R&B pop with Billy Ocean and did the seemingly impossible by charting a country album by Shania Twain.

*c) Is It A One-Way Street Or Can You Hop Back And Forth?*

The more you genre-hop (successfully) the more likely people are to condone it, consider you for cross-genre projects and those 'stretch' projects where no-one can figure out quite who the producer should be.

## How Do You Deal With . . .

*a) Post-Purchase Dissonance More Commonly Known As 'Buyer's Remorse'?*

This very common syndrome most commonly afflicts artists at the end of a long album project. You've hit the home straight, the last week of recording in the residential studio or maybe you even made it to the mix. As soon as you finish this project you fly to Hawaii for two weeks R'n'R before starting Jim Morrison's long awaited solo album *Voices From The Grave.* Suddenly the current artist comes down with a severe case of "Buyer's Remorse".

The symptoms include an inability to finish the record, characterised by an obsessive need to keep re-recording or remixing tracks. In acute cases the artist will actually start writing new songs for inclusion on the current album in the last few days of mixing, knowing that the record company is expecting delivery by the weekend. Other symptoms are a complete loss of voice the day before commencement of vocal recording, severe toothache/ headache/flu, staying up all night getting completely trashed, disappearing off the face of the earth, having an all-out bust up with their partner and totalling the Harley.

Tony Visconti says: "It's usually that artists get wacky about eighty percent into the album, or even earlier, and then they go absolutely nuts. They think it's going all the wrong way, and then it hits the fan when they try to take control. They usually don't know how to do certain things, so they'll come up with wild guesses and all that. The two Boomtown Rats albums I did sort of went in that direction. Sonically, I'm not very proud of them, because they sort of slipped out of my control."

*b) Post-Partum Depression?*

The album is actually done, delivered, finito. The record company loves it. The artwork is exquisite. The artist is totally depressed. Can't listen to the album/can't stop listening to the album. One minute they love it, the next they want to scrap it and start all over again

The only cure I've ever come up with for post-album blues is to plunge into something else like a holiday, bed, another project, but on no account keep listening to the album. If possible put the DAT away and don't listen to the tracks for as long as possible, two to six weeks should do it. When you come back to it you will be pleasantly surprised. You will not be listening to every move you made on the flying faders or the FX you used and abused – you'll just hear a record the same way everyone else does – aaaah fresh as the morning dew!

## What Happens When The Fat Lady Sings?

*a) How Do You Know When It's Over?*

Five warning signs:

1) The phone 'don't ring no-more'
2) The royalties become more of a trickle than a torrent
3) The outgoings exceed the incomings

4) Your phone calls either don't get returned or don't lead to work
5) The A&R people start to look even younger and less friendly than the cops.

If three or more apply it would be worth checking your investments and considering your options.

Don Gehman said, "Everybody's career has its ups and downs. I had four or five records with John Cougar Mellencamp that were all pretty successful. Then we got to a place where we had basically worked together for ten years and enough was enough. I moved on to other things. I had *Lifes Rich Pageant* (R.E.M.) and enough other things that people were looking at me as a record producer. It was no problem getting work, but getting hit records is difficult. You don't have multi-platinum artists every day." Not long after this interview he produced the record breaking, multi-platinum, award-winning, major-label début album for Hootie And The Blowfish.

Because the industry is so success oriented, as opposed to quality oriented (success = quality in many music business circles), if you hit a flat spot in your career it can be pretty scary. Both the quality and the quantity of the projects you are offered drops dramatically. You not only have less to choose from but less of the projects on offer are any good. Do you take projects that don't excite you just to keep working or do you save yourself for your true-love? I have taken projects on for dubious reasons. I hated myself for it. I find it very hard to work on something I don't really believe in. Every producer I respect seems to feel the same way. Stick to things you like, things you can be proud of whether they are hugely successful or not.

If you really love the job, you've proven yourself to be good at it and you've been sensible with your money through the successful years, things have a habit of turning round eventually. Just when it looks like your career is dead and buried some kid comes along in a hot new band. It turns out that his favourite record was something you produced eight years ago when he was just starting high school and the cycle starts over.

*b) Where Do Old Producers Go?*

Some go into record companies as A&R people. Generally companies that have A&R staff-producers seem to have good success and produce a higher than average number of "great" records. Warner Bros had an incredible run of success with all-time great producers such as Ted Templeman, Lenny Waronker and Russ Titleman on staff. (In the last few years there have been more producers getting staff jobs than I have ever seen before, but it still surprises me that every record company doesn't have at least one successful producer on staff. Even if a staff-producer doesn't actually produce anything for the company, his inside knowledge of recording, mixing, budgeting and dealing with the psychology of it all could save a lot of money and not a few heart/headaches.)

Some start their own producer management companies and who could be in a better position to understand the potential problems than an ex-producer. Studio ownership seems to be popular, especially amongst those who built their own rooms during their "hot years". I know producers who have gone into real estate investment and others who have retired altogether. Most seem to continue to dabble. Some continue their fascination with new technology by inventing, designing or building new gadgets.

*c) Should You Start Making Retirement Plans And When?*

If you haven't already started making retirement plans start today or tomorrow, definitely no later than the following day. This is an insecure business at the best of times. Even if you don't get pushed into early retirement it's highly likely you will hit a flat patch when the phone doesn't ring or the tapes that you get aren't exciting enough to drag your butt back into the studio. The most relevant question then is "How well did you invest your winnings?"

## Why Do People Want To Produce Records?

When I was working as a studio musician I always thought the producer's job was pretty boring. I would come in to lay the basic tracks and then several weeks later they would call me back to overdub percussion. I couldn't help but think about all those hours the producer had spent in the same room listening to the same tracks over and over.

Gradually I noticed that certain producers were getting better results than others out of the same group of musicians. This intrigued me. I saw that the great producers were very good at motivating musicians to squeeze that extra special performance out of them. They also seemed to be better at identifying the good takes. If something was not right they knew what it was and how to fix it. Conversely the lesser producers would miss great performances, not know what was wrong and have no clue how to sort out problems. It is incredibly frustrating for a musician to lay a great rhythm track, only to hear it a few weeks later completely ruined by out of time or inappropriate overdubs that have been piled on top.

In the end it was the bad producers that made me want to produce more than the good ones. Somehow it was always harder to see how the good producer achieved his results. There seemed to be an effortless, instinctive quality to their work. The lesser guys made it all seem like hard work.

Eventually I realised that this was a gross over-simplification based on a musician's-eye view of the production process. In fact some incredibly successful record producers rank high amongst the undecided. The results are definitely considered to justify the means.

What eventually pushed me over the edge was the frustration I experienced as an artist working with producers that I felt were more interested in making their own record than mine. My philosophy as a producer from day one was to make the record that the artist wanted. If I see that the artist's opinion clashes unresolvably with the record company's I turn down the project.

## Why Do People Want To Make Records At All?

Jim Dickinson producer of Ry Cooder, The Rolling Stones, Big Star, The Replacements and G Love & Special Sauce says, "It is the attempt to capture and retain the unretainable moment that I think makes a man seek to record."

The first time I set foot in a recording studio I fell in love with the whole shebang. As a musician I loved the idea of being able to capture special musical moments. As a live performer those moments can only be experienced by one audience at one show. As a composer and arranger it is appealing to be able to perfect and preserve an arrangement on record. As an audiophile, it is amazing to be able to paint a sonic picture using state of the art equipment to scrutinise and optimise each instrument or sound.

## Do You Know When You've Produced A Smash?

I always had a sense or a good feeling, early on, about the records that turned out to be big sellers for me. Sometimes it's from the moment the artist plays you the song on guitar or piano, sometimes it's based on the rough demo. Other times the potential doesn't show until you are in pre-production. I've had tracks blossom during the recording, gradually you realise that you might have a big one on your hands. The really hard thing to predict is just how big something could be. The difference between a record that will top out at a couple of hundred thousand and the one that will sell millions is not always obvious upfront. Then there are the ones that got away. I'm sure every producer has had records that they felt should have gone all the way but for whatever reason didn't.

Don Gehman talked about how you hope every record is great, but that great is not good enough to guarantee success. "There is a huge quotient of luck sitting on top of that, in terms of whether something is successful. Nevertheless, you won't get a shot unless you set out to make great records." Speaking specifically about the phenomenal success of the Hootie and The Blowfish record he said, "There were probably four of us who thought the record had a shot, but nothing like this. We were hoping for a couple of hundred thousand units to start a career. That is all you can really hope for, really. We thought we had songs that could be hits, but the timing was certainly a big part of it. You just never know."

Tom Lord-Alge, co-producer on *Back In The High Life* by Steve Winwood, said, "I had no idea that it would take off like it did. When we were finished, and all the mixes were done, I realised the calibre of the record but had no idea that it would go through the roof."

L.A. & Babyface have produced and written many, many R&B hits but *End Of The Road* by Boyz II Men was particularly significant in that it became the longest running number one pop single in rock history. L.A. Reid says, "While we were recording Boyz II Men's *End Of The Road* at Studio 4 in Philly, Babyface turned to me and said, 'What we have here is a very good song'. But when it was originally being written, I don't think we even tried to ask if it was going to be a big hit or not. Our responsibility as producers and writers is to create quality music, not to worry about how big a song's going to be or what star is going to sing it."

## What Is Demo-Itis?

Most producers have run across this problem. There are many permutations of demo-itis. The most obvious is when the artist, record company or management get so used to listening to the original demo that anything you change in the final production will sound wrong to them. Sometimes they're right. One of the reasons I went into production in the first place was because I had a run of producers who made the masters without seeing my band live and without any serious reference to the demos. At the end of the production we would have a record that sounded much better than the demo but was completely lifeless, the wrong tempo, wrong atmosphere or missing important parts. The best way to deal with demo-itis is not to ignore the original demos but to examine them with a fine tooth comb. Pull out everything of value and use it on the final master and lose everything that is unnecessary or not good.

Knowing how all the interested parties feel about the demo helps to arrive at the right combination of what to keep and what to reject. Maybe the demo is all wrong and what's needed is to take the song and do a complete re-think of the arrangement, orchestration and production. Other times the demo is perfect except for poor recording quality. These are the hardest records to make. When the demo has a beautiful feel and atmosphere to it, making the master can be a fraught experience. I have even been criticised for running too close to the demo in the final production. On one record I started a track from scratch three times. On the first two versions I compared the first day's work to the demo and didn't feel that what I had done was as good. There was no question of using parts from the demo because the recorded quality was too poor. Part of producing is about having the wisdom to know when to change things and when to leave them alone. I would have no qualms about using huge chunks of the demo if it was in the best interest of the record and the artist. "If it ain't broke don't fix it."

Another variation of demo-itis is the attachment to the rough mixes. You finish recording the album at midnight in a residential studio and spend the next three hours running off rough "board" or "monitor" mixes to give to the band and the A&R person. A week later, at great expense, you spend two weeks mixing the album in one of the classic mix rooms in a major metropolis. When you deliver them you find that either the band or the A&R person prefers the roughs. Again, they can be right. The spontaneity and simplicity of the "monitor mixes" can be a positive attribute. (Monitor mixes are so called because, traditionally, recording consoles were divided into two parts, a recording side and a monitoring side. The monitoring side was much smaller and had fewer facilities for effecting the sound. Nowadays most recording and mixing consoles are not built in this split format but in an in-line format where the recording side and the monitoring side are identical. Nonetheless, when a tape label says "rough, monitor or board" mix, it means that it has not been highly worked or processed). On the other hand the negative response to the master mixes can be because the person has been living with the roughs, has played them night and day and just become used to all the idiosyncracies and qualities.

Don Gehman says, "I don't have a problem with certain people coming and listening. In fact I like that. It's a great way to get reactions, so you can see if you are on the mark or not. On the other hand, I don't give anybody copies of anything. I've been very strict. I've always been that way. I don't let people have cassettes of anything, until it is finished. We are basically signing people's lives away, even in the band, to let copies out. I think you're taking your life in your hands. It's a chance for someone to make a judgement in a fixed point in time on something that is still a work in progress. For that reason alone, it's a great way to shoot yourself in the foot. I can't tell you how many managers and A&R guys have come to me over the years and said, 'Man I do this for a living. I know what I am listening for.' I tell them, 'No you don't. You have no idea what you're doing. The only way that this makes sense is if you are here every day. Otherwise, it's going to be something that you lock in time. Further on down the road, when I decide that this is the record, and you still have that older mix, you're going to think that your mix is better. That's because you've got used to it, and you didn't take the time to listen to the new mix and understand where it is going.' If I give that mix out, I risk having a back seat driver or producer that I am going to have to deal with for a long time. Many times, it taints the whole project, if that person is in any postion of power or has played it for people in positions of power."

The flip-side of this situation can be just as damaging. This is where you let out rough mixes to an influential player or to someone who then plays it to a powerful person at the record company. Out of context and, by the time it reaches the third party, unaccompanied by explanation, an unfinished mix or early rough can cause major panic in high places. The next thing you know, you have delegations flying in from Los Angeles to protect their investment and to make sure you haven't completely lost your marbles.

Andy Jackson was involved in an album that came to an early demise. The producer and the artist had not been seeing eye to eye. It got to the point where it was no longer sustainable and the producer stomped off home. In this particular case the producer was trying to make his record rather than the artist's but there was also a great deal of demo-itis going on. Andy says, "The artist had made his demos and as often happens they fall in love with all these little funny wrong notes. They're so buried in it they can't see the big picture. In the end [the artist and producer] couldn't communicate in such a way that they could find solutions to the problem. How it happened was, I was asked if we could take a break, and then I saw the producer going home. That was it, that was the last I heard of it. I don't know if the record ever saw the light of day."

## What Kind Of Person Becomes A Producer?

> *Going to work for a large company is like getting on a train. Are you going sixty miles an hour or is the train going sixty miles an hour and you're just sitting still.* (Paul Getty)

I realised some time back that I have two basic needs in life, autonomy and creativity (maybe they are wants but they sure feel like needs). I can survive extremely adverse conditions if those two qualities are actively present. Stress cannot easily grow in a field of autonomy. Boredom always melts in the fire of creativity. Fortunately I have managed to stay in occupations that supply both the freedom of autonomy and the excitement of creative pursuit. I was first a musician, then an artist and most recently a producer and manager. I would say that anyone who can sustain any kind of producing career is going to have to be independent, self-sufficient, confident in their abilities and sure of their opinions. A helping of patience, some amateur psychology and a dash of streetwise, survival techniques will not go amiss. Babysitting, hand holding and nose-wiping can be called for but personally I try to stay well clear of those projects. Politics can definitely affect what we do but the beauty of being freelance is that you don't depend on one employer for your livelihood. Diplomacy, however, can be a lifesaver. Most producers I know are not, by nature, company men. Even the ones who are on staff at major labels are usually able to carve out their own space within the company, and somehow ride the range with more freedom than the other employees.

Quincy Jones went on staff at Mercury Records in 1961 as an A&R man and had risen to become the first black VP of a major label by 1964 but, despite his success, he had a tough time with the constraints of the nine to five. He said, "I was behind a desk every day. Awful! I had to be in there at nine o'clock, and you had to wear these Italian suits. You had to fill out expense reports and all that kind of stuff. That really made my skin crawl."

One of the most famous producers of all time is George Martin. He started working in the industry in 1950, before the term record producer was even used. If the only artist he had ever produced was The Beatles he would still be a legend. In fact he has a substantial track record of productions with such other artists as The Mahavishnu Orchestra, America, Jimmy Webb, Neil Sedaka, Cheap Trick and Paul McCartney. He says, "The role was something that evolved. Producers come in all shapes and sizes. A good producer has got to really have an understanding of music, and a catholic love for it. Unless you're very specialised, I think that you have to have a very universal approach to music, to have the temperament to like a lot of music. Which fortunately or unfortunately I do! If you're very narrow in your outlook, you're not going to make a good record producer, because you have to be pretty tolerant, too. But in terms of music, it is very important to have an understanding of how music works, although I don't think it's absolutely a pre-requisite that you have a musical education."

## How Do Producers Feel About Remixers?

*The peak of tolerance is most readily achieved by those who are not burdened by conviction.* (Alexander Chase)

Most producers really resent having their work remixed without any discussion or consultation. In order to be an effective and creatively active producer you really need a passion for what you do. To hand your work over to someone else to remix is for most producers the equivalent of going through nine months of a much wanted pregnancy, enthusiastically going to all the classes and reading all the books only to be forced to give the baby away at birth.

Some producers don't want to do the mixing themselves, or don't regard it as one of their strengths. In that case as long as he is able to have some input, such as helping to choose the remixer, discussing the mixes with the remixer or even participating in the mix sessions he is likely to be happy with the outcome.

When a track gets remixed without your input, you breathe a huge sigh of relief if it turns out even reasonably well. Most rock or alternative mixes run pretty close to the original production concept. On the other hand, club remixes use hardly any of the original production ideas. Most producers seem bemused by, but less concerned about, dance mixes. They accept them as a specialist thing designed for a specific purpose. What's really disturbing is to spend months working on a production only to have someone else come along and mix the track with total disregard for the intentions of the producer or artist. Often they don't bother to get the chords right or attempt to be sympathetic to the vocal attitude, timing or melody. They're only concerned with making the track fit a current trend. You're left wondering why the record company doesn't have the remix person produce the track in the first place. They would save an awful lot of money and they wouldn't be putting a producer through unnecessary agony.

Tony Visconti, talking about who makes the decision to have the project remixed, says, "Sometimes it's the artist. They want the benefit of all possible worlds. They keep remixing with people, they might even edit your mix into someone else's mix. Or some A&R person might think it's cool to have someone else mix the album. A lot of times, it's not the best decision to get someone on the outside to remix the album. They don't know why you put a certain track in a certain place, they don't know what level it should be at, and the whole original concept is being placed in the hands of a third party who doesn't know what went into that concept."

It's very frustrating to put in all the little tweaks and idiosyncracies for the artist only to watch them get completely lost at the remix stage. Often the artist is not there and the remixer doesn't have to consider what either the producer or the artist wanted. "They're bypassing the months of blood, sweat and tears that went into making those sounds, and that's what music is about – not technical tricks," says Visconti. "The technical tricks might make the music sound good sometimes, but they don't make the music. We, the musicians and the producer, make the music. In the Seventies the vision of the producers and artists was always respected – you would never tamper with a Led Zeppelin album or an Elton John album or a Queen album. You'd get your balls cut off. The manager would have your guts for garters if you went near it. Now there's no protection from it. If someone told me they got their six-year-old son to remix someone's album I'd believe them. It's lawless."

George Martin says, "This modern tendency for mega mixes, the twelve-inch mix, four-inch mix, 1972 rehash mix and the 1994/95 rap mix is boring. It really is. Leave it as it is. If you want to create new work, create new work."

Part of the problem is that, very occasionally, a remix really works. The right marriage of timing, track and remixer gets pushed into the machine and something inspired plops out the other end. Unfortunately, perfectly good records are subjected to a remix by infinite numbers of hopeful monkeys, in infinite numbers of project studios, in order to achieve this occasional success.

## What's The Remixer's Point Of View?

The Lord-Alge brothers have built awesome reputations as remixers. Chris talked about what they find when the multi-tracks arrive for them to mix. "Sometimes you have to be 'Audio Maid'." Tom adds, "You gotta get in there and clean it up. I get tapes that are recorded well, and I get tapes that aren't. The ones that I find challenging are the ones that are butchered. There are great engineers out there, but unfortunately there are too many bad ones. There are a lot of guys who cannot record live drums." Tom adds, "What I've found in the tapes that I mix is that often the drums sound dull. On vocals, you find a lot of guys who aren't careful enough with the vocal comping and the vocal punching, breaths, words, bad punches all the time." Chris interjects, "The worst thing about mixing, aside from bad-sounding recordings, is getting track sheets that make no sense. They're not notated properly, there are no tempos written down. You'll have four or five vocals, and it's not written what happened or how they did it. No notes. You feel like the engineer didn't care who got the tape next. You have to get their mix to figure out what the hell was done with the vocal."

Arthur Baker says, "I was one of the first to get the 'additional production' credit. On certain records it becomes a category all to itself when you're keeping only the vocal and recutting everything else. It's really a step beyond production, because producers often use the act's arrangement. But when you're working off nothing but the vocal you have to do a lot of arranging. A remixer sometimes does a lot more than the original producer did."

## What Is The "Sophomore Slump?"

This is the American term for the difficult second album. There are a number of reasons why the second album has been the downfall of many a promising career.

The first album is usually written over a long period of time, starting when the band is formed and continuing right up to the time the first album is recorded. If the band is lucky enough to make it to the second album they usually have to write all the songs in hotel rooms, on the road, while they are promoting their first record. Failing that they have to jam it in just a few weeks before the album is scheduled to be recorded.

There is a tendency to try to reproduce the first album. First time out the only objective was to make a great record. Assuming the first record was successful, the pressure will be to repeat the formula, not necessarily from the record company or management but from the band themselves. Songs written under those conditions tend to be inbred reproductions rather than inspired originals.

The opposite and probably even more dangerous option is when bands go out of their way to "prove" their versatility or demonstrate a different side of their talent. This often alienates the very fans that put them in the position to make the second album at all. Not that artists should be frightened to step out and assert their creativity on their second album but at least they should try to draw from the same well of inspiration as they did on the first album.

Muff Winwood, ex-producer and long-time CBS/Sony A&R person says, "The worst problem with second albums is that you just can't tell the artist what to do. They know best and they don't want to listen." He said that sometimes the best commercial decision you can make as a company is to drop the artist if they are in decline after the second album. "They get more and more expensive to maintain at that point, they want to fly to all the gigs instead of riding on the bus, they demand first class hotels and hospitality at the shows even if the sales do not justify it." Most companies do continue to feed out the rope to an artist who has had début success, at least for a couple of records.

Another A&R person referred in particular to an artist who had sold between seven and eight million albums world-wide on her début record. The A&R person still considered her to be an excellent artist but she would not allow any outside opinion to be considered. Her sales by the third album had slumped to below two hundred thousand units. The company concerned kept supporting the artist in spite of the financial realities, because they believed in her basic talent.

# 12

# *Is Classical, Jazz And Country Production Any Different From Rock, Pop And R'n'B?*

## Classical Production

Andrew Cornall is one of the most influential and widely respected classical producers in the world. He won a Grammy for "Best Classical Producer" in 1995 and was nominated again in 1996. He has always worked for Decca and is at the time of writing Senior Executive Producer there and General Manager of the recently revamped classical label Argo.

Speaking about how he got started in the job he said, "Like most people in the record business I fell into it by accident, I don't think anyone ever decides to do classical music production as a career move. I know I didn't."

Well, so far that sounds much like any other form of record production. Most producers I know did not start out in life with ambitions to become a record producer. They usually evolve via the unique set of skills they pick up along the way.

The differences between pop (for lack of a better term) producers and their classical counterparts are probably best explained in Cornall's own words. "All producers are there to get the best out of the artist so that you create the best recording possible. But the fundamental difference between classical and pop is that classical producers are primarily there to get someone else's musical interpretation down on tape and are not part of the creative team to the extent where they are responsible for the orchestra's sound. Classical orchestras and musicians already have their own sound and all the producer should do is capture it. Producers are the bridge between artists, engineers and the technical crew."

For sure the All-Singing, the Collaborator and Merlin are not going to be content without creative input. But, interestingly, if you compare Andrew Cornall's description of the classical producer as somewhat of a "transparent mediator" to Steve Albini's opinion about what effect he thinks the rock producer should have on a band, there is not a whole lot of difference.

Andrew Cornall goes on to say, "The producer runs the session and represents the artist's view to the engineer and vice versa. Our role is to help everyone do the best job they can. I'm not hands on with the equipment – I leave all that to the engineer – so I'm not rushing about moving faders up and down. Of course I discuss what I want with my engineer and will ask for specific things such as more woodwind or advise caution if there is a big 'tutti' coming up. The engineer reacts to me as though I'm the map reader – the navigator who steers everyone through the session. Another fundamental difference between classical and pop producers is where they record. Classical producers are rarely, if ever, studio bound. Usually they are out on location, going to wherever the orchestra is based."

## What's Jazz Production All About?

In some cases producing jazz can be quite similar to producing rock records and in other cases it can be more like a classical role. Traditionally jazz is recorded live and is primarily about capturing the moment. In recent years jazz has diversified. Some projects are done by overdubbing and others even by computer.

Legendary jazz producer Orrin Keepnews has had more than five hundred releases to his name. He prefers live recording for jazz. He says, "I think there are instances in which I will believe in the validity of overdubbing and layering, but I also believe that it can be drastically overused to undercut and do away with the spontaneity that's a very important part of jazz."

Keepnews has started three labels of his own. He thinks that the problem with jazz, and music in general, as it functions in a capitalist system is that it has to be an art and a business at the same time. He went on to say, "That's one of the most anti-creative things imaginable. I believe it is the function of the producer to gain control of the environment so I spent as much of my time and ingenuity as I could working against all those ticking clock situations. Then all I have to worry about is getting product – good, creative, finished music, which of course is what it's all about anyway. The single most important ingredient in creating jazz records is to remove all the unnecessary tensions, while being careful not to remove any of the necessary tensions, and there is a distinction."

In his book *The View From Within* he said that he tries to maintain the attitude, the perspective, that it's the artist's album and not the producer's. "What you need to accomplish more than anything else, is there has to be a very real working partnership between the artist and the producer, which means a recognition on both sides, sometimes implicit and sometimes explicit, that each has his areas of being the decision-maker. I am never going to say to an artist, 'That was the take, I'm not going to let you lift your horn on that tune again,' but I'm not going to let somebody say to me, 'Yeah, that was good enough, let's go on,' if I don't believe it was. If you are able to establish a workable, creative relationship with the artist, you're going to come out pretty good or better. If you're not able to establish this, then neither of you belongs in the studio." Speaking about the technical aspects of jazz production Keepnews said, "My philosophy of sound with jazz is that the sound is only a means to deliver the performance. I don't want extremes of sound. The sound should be as unobtrusive as possible. I don't want a kick drum that calls attention to itself."

The essential ingredients that make a good jazz producer seem pretty similar to that of a rock, pop, R&B or classical producer: a love for and deep understanding of the music, a sense that this is the artist's record not the producer's, an ability to pull together the musical elements such as musicians and arrangements, sufficient knowledge of the technical considerations to be able to hire the right people and communicate with them, enough tact and diplomacy to make the artist feel comfortable, and enough strength of character and personality to be able to keep the session on track.

## Country Producers

Country music producers are a unique breed. They are very often on staff at the record label. The best producers often run the labels yet they remain active in the studio and since they often came up through the ranks of the musicians, they even play on their records from time to time. Most Country records are made in Nashville and that's where the producers live.

The president of MCA Records, Tony Brown, is a good example of the new breed of Nashville producer, as is James Stroud, vice-president of A&R for Giant Records in Nashville. Stroud worked as a studio drummer alongside Brown, and producers-to-be Paul Worley, Keith Stegall and others making gospel records. He remembers, "In the beginning, people like Paul and Tony and me had a hard time getting productions. There was a standard here. The town had gotten to a certain place and was happy selling 150,000 records. Nashville then was a branch town in the music industry. After Eddie Rabbitt went platinum and other records were starting to sell 750,000, it sort of blew the top off. We learned to make Country records with a pop edge."

Stroud cut his production chops on R&B records in LA and Muscle Shoals and was well positioned for the new style of production. His productions included The Bellamy Brothers, Eddie Rabbitt and Dorothy Moore's *Misty Blue* which sold three million units and was nominated for five Grammy's. Now he was a force to be reckoned with in Nashville.

Jimmy Bowen was largely responsible for bringing Country music production techniques up to date. When he first arrived in Nashville, budgets were so low that artists had to cut three or four tracks in every three-hour session. Bowen wanted to spend a day or two on each song, as he was used to doing in New York and Los Angeles. By bringing in recording techniques and sounds from New York and Los Angeles he was able to reach a wider audience than had previously been thought possible with Country music. For his innovation and success he was rewarded with the presidency of most of the major labels in Nashville. He spoke about getting started in Nashville, "Of course, getting in on the ground floor of engineering and producing is difficult any time, any place, but if I were a young man looking to break into the industry now, Nashville would be the place. I'd go around and knock on every door until I got a chance to start my way up the ladder. Engineering and producing is still essentially an apprenticeship process, so if you have to start by custodial engineering and producing a shine on the floors of the studio, then do it. Then, finally, you'll get that first chance to sit down and work at the board and everybody will see if you've got what it takes, or not. It's very much a trial by fire, but that's how it works.

"There are, however, a couple of colleges in Nashville which offer courses in music engineering. From what I've seen of them, they're giving out useful information. We've had a few students in as trainees and have just taken on a couple of graduates in our hirings. That's an opportunity that didn't exist when I was starting. It's not easy to break in, but it's not impossible. As a major record company president, I also think the new project studios are great. I only wish that when I was young we'd had them. When I started, at college, we recorded straight to disk. We had a band, and at night we would go in and use the college studio for a few hours. Anything you learn about working with music, about getting it down properly on tape, can only help you later on. There's still a vast difference, of course, between producing music on a home set-up, regardless of how elaborate, and working in a major studio. I think, though, that it's the difference between flying a Lear jet and a 747 . . . many of the basic principles are the same, but there's a lot more hardware to know and to handle in the jumbo jet."

# 13

# *Technology Rules*

## Has Technology Made Studio Life Easier?

> *"The first rule of any technology used in a business is that automation applied to an efficient operation will magnify the efficiency. The second is that automation applied to an inefficient operation will magnify the inefficiency."* (Bill Gates, *The Road Ahead*)

Computers are totally invaluable in the studio. They have relieved much of the pressures that used to be there. Before the advent of computer controlled mixing consoles, mixing was done manually. This entailed many pairs of (often wilful) hands on the console, moving faders, panpots, effect sends and equalisation knobs from one little grease pencil mark to another, hopefully on cue. The multiple pairs of hands would usually belong to the band. Band members are invariably deaf to their own instrument. The bass player never thinks his bass is loud enough, likewise the guitarist and so on. The exception to this is the singer who strangely, for the rampant ego-maniac that he needs to be, hates the sound of his own voice. Throughout the mix, each musician secretly nudges their own fader up a little. Except the singer who pulls his down. The drummer "gooses" the tom fills a little more on each pass until they leap out of the speakers and strangle someone. What you end up with is a mix that you'd have more luck selling to a karaoke club than commercial radio.

You can get around this by having the drummer ride the guitars, the guitarist the bass, the bass player the drums, I'd better take the vocals and the singer can go hang out with the girl he just met at the pub.

In the days of "steam" mixing the whole process had to be figured out and memorised in one day. If you didn't get it finished that day, by the time you came in the following morning everyone would have forgotten their moves and it often took several hours to get everyone up to speed again to do a perfect take. Only when you had committed the mix to tape could you really sit back and listen to what you had done. So, at four in the morning, you'd turn it up to a hair below painful, lean back in your chair, desperately will the mix to be right and try not to doze off. If you did fall asleep the trick was to wake up as the track ended (the booming silence snaps you out of it), stop the tape and quickly turn to the band saying "What did you think?" If they were studio smart they'd come right back at you with "I dunno, what did you think?" The only dignified response to that was "I need to listen one more time." When you finally made it right through the track in a conscious state there would invariably be at least a couple of things that were still not right. The only two practical options at that point would be to muster up all your self-discipline and will power, send your *girl du jour* (who's been sitting in the lounge area dressed and ready to go out to dinner since 10 p.m.) home in a cab and go for one more take incorporating the new modifications, or live with the mix you have and pray that those little problems you heard don't assume mammoth proportions tomorrow when you play it for the A&R person.

If it turns out that someone can't live with something about that mix, the whole process would have to be repeated from scratch. Unfortunately you might solve one problem and create another. Before the coming of the computerised console it was very difficult to recreate a mix. Say, for instance, the problem with the earlier mix was that the guitars in the choruses were not loud enough. You'd set the mix back up and fixed the guitars but when you compared the new mix to the old one you might find that the vocal sound was not quite as good as before. With a fully computerised console it's relatively easy to set up a mix exactly as it had been even six months or a year before (providing no bright spark has modified the console in the meantime). The computer remembers all the settings, levels and moves you made during the original mix. Some consoles reset themselves, others have to be done manually. Having reset the console it can be a ten minute walk in the park to push those guitars up or fix an EQ.

That's the theory and the theory holds true if you and all involved parties are decisive, in an unmodified state of consciousness and know precisely what you are looking for. The actuality can be frighteningly different. Creative endeavours are not filled with definitive certainties. Creative people are not renowned for being precise and certain. In the manual days of old many decisions were made by default. Maybe the budget was running out or everyone was simply too tired to do another take. The sheer difficulty of setting the mix back up might be sufficient to deter them from going on and on and on. This was not necessarily a bad thing.

Recently I listened to a multi-track tape of "Einstein A GoGo", a track that I had produced with my band Landscape in the late Seventies. I can clearly remember the mixing session for this song. It was long and arduous. We went, pretty much, right through the night and there were hundreds of intricate little moves and changes and much technical jiggerypokery going on. When I put the multi-track on again I simply pushed up all the faders on the console just to see how it all sounded. To my astonishment what I heard was pretty close to the finished record. Now, it had been a hit in the early Eighties, so I'd listened to that record thousands of times as I went around miming to it on dodgy TV shows all over Europe. There is no question in my mind as to how the record sounds. The thing is engraved into my grey-matter. But here was the original multi-track tape unequalised, with no effects and no moving faders, sounding very similar to the mix that we had laboured and sweated over using the state of the art analogue, digital and computer technology of the time.

This experience told me that for all the obvious attractions of new technology we spend large chunks of our studio lives functioning in that twilight zone of diminishing returns. We labour long and hard to improve things in extremely small increments. I'm not saying that it's not worth it. I'm not saying that it doesn't make a difference to the quality of the record or to its chances of success. Some records stand out because of the sheer quality of the production and engineering. But computers and digital technology have been both a blessing and a curse. As

Bill Gates said "If you are efficient the automation will increase your efficiency", but if someone's unable to make a decision then the technology allows them to procrastinate and fuss over details of ever decreasing importance.

I once spent three days perfecting a computer-generated string part for an R&B record. The part was actually all written in pre-production exactly to the artist's specifications and at the time he was happy with it. We got to the studio and just as we were about to print the part to tape, the artist innocently said could we shorten that note a little. Of course having shortened that one, some others to had be shortened also. I mentioned to the artist after about the first six hours that it would be better if I wrote out the parts and hired a real string section. The amount of studio time that we were burning up on this program would more than outweigh the cost of the string section and once they came into the studio the part would be recorded within an hour or so and sound a million percent better anyway. "No!" he said, "it's sounding good and there's only a couple more bits to change." Three days later we had an overworked part that I was no longer convinced about. Probably the only reason we're not still working on the part is that exhaustion finally set in. The artist decided it sounded fine and when it came to the mix, the part was, mercifully, buried somewhere behind the reverb.

What I'm getting at here is that anyone who says that computers make things easier, faster or more efficient has either never actually tried to do anything with one or is trying to sell you one – or owns the studio in which you are working and loves the fact that you just spent a month programming parts that you could've done in three days with real musicians.

Obviously there are projects that need to be done on computers because that's the sound that the artist is looking for. There are bands that have to use computers and drum machines because they can't play well enough to make a record without them. For some projects computers are the only way to go. My observation is that the fewer computers there are in the room the quicker things will get done. What computers have allowed us to do is to keep adjusting, refining and polishing things. We all know, no matter how much you polish a turd it won't get any more attractive. Assuming the project you are working on is worthwhile in the first place, if you have enough objectivity and restraint to know when you have polished, refined and adjusted your work of art enough, then the computer will have been a wonderful, tireless assistant. It's very easy, however, to adjust, refine and polish down to the micro-molecular. You get mesmerised by the process, lose sight of the objective and become a slave of the machine. I see album projects that should last no more than twelve weeks, drag on for five years or more because of this deadly combination of indecisiveness and maximum flexibility. When there are no fixed parameters adjusting, refining and polishing every facet can actually make the gem disappear.

"It's like moving a snare beat in the computer," says John Leckie. "If it's a sample triggered by the snare hit, the dynamic is the same no matter how hard you hit it. So you have to move it because the first hit is a little late and suddenly everything's shifted. Six hours later, you're still fiddling with it. Six hours! This is what goes on . . . Techniques – potentially they hold all the secrets of turning a live performance into a record. But techniques are frequently at the mercy of equipment developments and the promise of progress can readily translate into poor performances and missed opportunities. And sometimes it becomes difficult to distinguish between innovation and indolence, direction and distraction, model and muddle. It's generally accepted that *Sgt Pepper* made a great contribution to recording techniques, but you could also argue that it was the worst thing that happened. It made the recording process abstract. It made the band's performance secondary."

Leckie also thinks that automation has affected the band's involvement in the studio processes. He says, "I'm often surprised nowadays. In the old days bands would be much more involved than they are now, particularly in the mix. It would be four people, hands on the desk – everyone would have their fader to move, or the panpot, or the echo sends. It may be just to do with automation but the band's involvement in the studio process would be a lot more than it is now. I often do records now where the band doesn't even touch the mixer."

## The Revolution Will Be Digitised. Where Is It All Going?

Technology is having, and will continue to have, a huge influence on the job of record production. As in all other areas of life, the new technology will not entirely replace the existing ways of doing things but will slot alongside them. Newspapers and books were not replaced by movies and TV and will not be replaced in the foreseeable future despite electronic media. Nonetheless, the demand for traditional production methods will diminish. As the new technology bites deeper into society and the music business we will see less and less traditional producers of the type who originated the job description in the Fifties, Sixties and Seventies. More and more we will see artists producing themselves.

For the musically challenged, there are sample CDs and pre-recorded MIDI sound files to help them make music by numbers. There could also be music software with wizards and templates. Various software companies have ventured into compositional software with limited success. The level of Artificial Intelligence in computing has either not yet been reached for these techniques to truly work or it hasn't trickled down to a level where it is available to the masses. Sampling techniques were in use at IRCAM in Paris and Stanford University in California for several years before the first commercial sampler, the Australian Fairlight CMI, became available. There were several years of limited availability (due to the price tag). Eventually mass proliferation via the cheaper "knock off's" such as the Emulator, the Ensoniq and the Akai S900 led to the looping and sampling techniques which became the cornerstone of certain styles of record production.

Mass proliferation is an important factor in the success of any new technology. TV was not conceived in order to deliver a daily diet of never-ending chat and game shows. Mass proliferation, economics and supposedly public taste has reduced TV to just that. Once music is digitised or reduced to bits and bytes, we immediately have the potential to manipulate it in a way that was previously not possible. The early days of digital recording (on tape) were more about the market perception of what DDD meant. Less tape hiss and the ability to copy without degradation were the main advantages. The technology (as always) was expensive in the beginning. Consequently it was available only to the most successful artists and producers who were most likely to use it in a traditional way. Initially the only storage medium for digital information was linear reel to reel tape. The recorders were expensive and unless you had two of them the possibilities for manipulating the music were very limited.

ADATs brought digital recording within everybody's reach. Manipulation was still via two machines but at least they were affordable. The inexpensive samplers and their big brothers, the hard disk recorders, were really the beginning of the revolution. Once the ability to manipulate both large chunks and little bites of music came within the economic grasp of anyone who could afford a computer (can you afford not to have a computer) we began to see some extremely creative uses of the new technology.

In an interview in the Seventies I said that the exciting thing about a computer is that it immediately separates the idea from the technique. Unfortunately, a lot of music made on computers is divorced from both the technique and the ideas. But, if someone has an idea in their head they no longer have to spend ten years learning to play an instrument, studying arranging techniques, trying to get Arts Council grants or record company backing just to be able to hear their idea. Perhaps even more importantly, anyone can create a demo to play for other people. So not only is it easier to get feedback on what you create in your mind but the feedback is immediate. After the initial capital outlay the ability to express and preserve your ideas is available, virtually free, twenty-four hours a day.

There are many artists who have record deals and have been successful whom I believe would not have been able to get their foot in the door before computers became platforms for music, performance and recording. So the new technology impacts record production because artists are creating these "works of art" or "works of commerce" in their bedrooms delivering them in digital form to the record companies. The results you can get from a $3000 digital multitrack or Hard Disk recorder and a $400 DAT machine don't sound a whole lot different from records being made on $500,000+ professional studio equipment.

If the artist does a good job technically, there's no point in going into a major recording studio and re-creating everything with a producer who's going to take a chunk of your advance and subsequent royalties. In this situation the only reasons for hiring an outside producer would be either because the artist did not have the technical skills to fully utilise the new consumer digital equipment or is missing certain key creative ingredients.

Project studios reduced recording budgets. You can set up an amazing digital project studio for less than one normal commercial recording budget. The studio is usually situated in a no-rent place like the artist's house. The engineering is often done by the artist and frequently all the instruments are played/programmed by the artist or the members of the band.

So, suddenly, computers and the new microprocessor technology are taking a bite out of the amount of production work available. In keeping with the trend across society, computers are making it possible for people to do things for themselves, things that previously they would've had to pay someone else for or they wouldn't have been able to do at all because of the cost.

## What Does This Mean To The Professional Record Producer?

It means that our own profession will experience the patterns we are beginning to see in society generally: shifting responsibilities and job requirements. Certain jobs disappear altogether. There will be a reduced need for producers who are dependent on the professional studio environment. The trend is swinging towards the more creative producers. Either engineers like Alan Moulder, who collaborate with bands who have a strong idea of what they want, or musicians like Danny Saber, who can collaborate at the writing stage and have an implicit understanding of how sampling and technology interweave with the writing and production process. There will always be a demand for the All-Singing-All-Dancing, Jam and Lewis/Babyface type of producer as long as there are singers who can't write their own hits and don't get involved in the production process. The guru will still have a place because Merlin can function in a project studio environment just as well as a five-star studio.

Paul Saffo, of the Institute for the Future, in Menlo Park, California, identifies a tendency toward "forecasting double vision" in which mass excitement over a coming technology – or for that matter, mass fear – leads people to overestimate its short-term impact. They tend to forget that technology diffuses slowly, and when cold reality fails to conform to overheated expectations, that disappointment can lead us to underestimate impact over the long term. Personal computers are a good case study,

Saffo says, "In 1980 everybody said that by 1983 everybody would have one. Didn't happen. So by 1985–86 people said homes would never have them."

I believe the same thing has happened with both digital technology and the project studio. When digital recorders first became available in the early Eighties, there were all kinds of predictions that analogue would be gone within five to ten years. Here we are fifteen years later and analogue is still the recording medium of choice for a large proportion of artists and producers. At the same time digital is sneaking up on us through the back door. The high end digital machines are still relatively rare animals but go into any project studio, most budget studios, increasing numbers of mid-price rooms and you will find Modular Digital Multi-track machines (such as ADAT's and DA88's) and computer-based hard-disk editors/multi-track recorders (such as Pro-tools and Sadie). Alan Parson's opinion is that, "Eight-track modular digital recorders are probably the most significant thing to happen in the last ten years. I think you will see a lot of major studios shutting down as a result of that technology."

The proliferation of the project studio in the Eighties caused a panic in some quarters. Initially the major studios, particularly in Los Angeles, acted out of fear and tried to have home-based project studios eliminated via the idiosyncracies of the local residential zoning laws. Ironically, governments and corporations all over the world are beginning to encourage the concept of telecommuting, to save on the cost of office space, to reduce motor fuel consumption, to cut down on road congestion and pollution from commuter vehicles, to alleviate the stress on city centres and improve personal life-styles.

Tele-commuting is starting to happen and will definitely affect a significant proportion of the population in the not too distant future. The technology that is making this possible is in a constant state of development. One of these developments is DSVD which stands for Digital Simultaneous Voice Data and is an interim technology which is designed to work with the existing phone system. If both parties have PCs it will be possible to have a conversation and transmit photos or diagrams simultaneously. ISDN stands for Integrated Services Digital Network. It transfers voice and data five to ten times faster than DSVD but requires a special phone line which, disgracefully, is about ten times the cost in Britain than it is in the USA. Cable modems will utilise the existing coaxial cable networks and will have an even greater band width than ISDN. These are all technological steps that can potentially have a sociological impact by reducing the amount of physical travelling we have to do. Unfortunately, the effect these technologies will have is somewhat vulnerable to the myopia of companies like BT who seem as if they would rather make a large profit from a small number of users than they would see mass proliferation. This will affect living standards. Countries that have short sighted or greedy telecommunications suppliers will fall behind in the world market place.

Personally I hate commuting. It's a waste of life. If I can do whatever I have to do by phone, fax or modem I will. I would happily send mixes to the record company or record musicians from another city by ISDN, cable modem or whatever, especially if I could simultaneously tele-conference with them. Or better still, interact with them in a virtual studio so that you have, in effect, visual foldback as well as audio foldback.

Christopher Currell, synclavier programmer with Michael Jackson and owner of a laboratory studio called Audio Cybernetics, has a trademark for Virtual Audio Systems, a three-dimensional system based on the psycho-acoustic research of Dr. Klaus Genuit of Germany and funded by the Japanese. He is also involved in research and development for several electronics companies and works with Technova, the think tank that is owned by the Toyota corporation. Regarding the creation of virtual worlds he says, "Our world is experiencing overpopulation, especially in major cities. It takes forever to drive to work and you can't predict when you will arrive. The results are pollution, frustration, inefficiency. People are tired of this. In the future, you will just walk into your virtual world and go to work. Travelling will be reduced to a minimum, because you can meet your friends in the virtual world and experience them. Of course, people will still like to get together in this reality, but the necessities of jobs and survival will be dealt with easily in a virtual reality. We will be much more efficient, without destroying the environment." One day soon we may be asking "Is it real or is it virtual?'

Of course, it's impossible to predict what the time scale might be on this kind of technology becoming usable enough and inexpensive enough. Saffo notes "You've got to look beyond the common wisdom. The expected future always arrives late and in utterly unexpected ways."

Nonetheless, in time many people will spend a large proportion of their working lives operating out of home-based offices. The commuting century will come to a close. Studios will inevitably go the same way. Just as some people will still prefer to record on analogue tape, some will still want to go to a professional recording studio. Apart from the obvious situations where a large amount of space is required for an orchestra/live band, a great deal of noise is being generated or very expensive, high end equipment is needed, I believe a great deal of future recording will be done at home on computer based recording systems.

Tony Visconti thinks that we may eventually see an end to the record producer role altogether. "It's no longer a great mystery – how to make a record," he says. "There are zillions of books on the subject, whereas when I started twenty-five years ago, there were none whatsoever. Now, the information is available to anyone."

It's certainly true that there seems to be an explosion of new names under the production credits on recent albums. Not only that, more and more artists are producing themselves, partly because they have the knowledge and confidence gained from books and working in either their own home studio or in one of the many inexpensive semi-pro studios that have multiplied exponentially since the mid-Eighties. Andy Warhol's fifteen minutes of fame for everyone is starting to look optimistic. It may well be more like fifteen seconds.

Not only is the status quo under fire from freely available information, greater techno-savvy and a proliferation of inexpensive equipment, but the information dirt-track when it eventually turns into a super-highway will offer unprecedented delivery and distribution systems for anything that can be digitised. Obviously, until we learn to dematerialise and rematerialise anything made of atoms such as clothing, cars and computer hardware, we will still have to travel by road, rail, sea or air. Music, text, video and graphics can be converted into bits and can therefore be distributed electronically through wire, fibre optic or by satellite.

Potentially, this means that the artist could create music (and visuals) in her home studio and collaborate with other e-musicians in a virtual cyber-studio without ever meeting them. Then she could take the finished product and eliminate the whole manufacturing and distribution part of the chain. The artist could then distribute from his home storage system (currently a hard drive) directly to the consumer. In fact the concept of a finished product could disappear for certain artists. In the same way that web-sites are work in progress, it would be possible for an artist to keep adjusting and modifying his music, text, graphics or moving images. So someone who accessed the work in January would hear and see something different than someone accessing in June. When real time 20hz to 20Khz access becomes available, ownership of a hard copy of music or video could become pointless. Consumers will log on and pay for actual use and revisit not only because they liked what they heard and saw but to check on the latest updates. It would certainly cut down on the number of albums I have at home that I bought, listened to once, and filed permanently away on the top shelf.

Under these circumstances we could start to see different sales patterns. I'm sure we've all had the experience of buying the latest album of an artist whose previous album we loved only to be horribly disappointed. If usage was measured rather than outright purchase, sales patterns could change drastically.

Imagine if all the musical works of the world were available at any time on a pay for listen basis. Assuming the per play cost was held at a reasonable level I would listen to a much wider range of music than I already do. I would be more inclined to check out a new album by an unknown artist on a casual recommendation. At least I could listen to a few bars of each track to see whether it interested me. Right now I'd either have to buy the CD or borrow it from someone. I hate borrowing records because I always think I'm going to forget to give them back and I rarely buy an album without having heard some of it on the radio or at someone's house. Too many times I get the record home and find the only track I like is the single. Pay for listen could reduce the possibility of buying a "dog" album. If you liked two tracks on an album you could pay just to listen to those two tracks. For promotion purposes a label might allow consumers one free listen. This could open up the opportunity for new artists to get their music heard by a large number of people. Most people will check something out if they can do it when they want to, for nothing, in their own home.

The benefits to consumers could be free or very cheap previews of new material, pay only for what you listen to or have an alternative lifetime buyout price for records that you want to "own", no bulky atoms (CDs or cassettes) to carry around and the ability to access the bits (music, graphics, video or text) from wherever you are, whenever you want.

The benefits to the artists and producers could be greater creative freedom, and the ability to get something out to a potentially wider audience without being "filtered" through the arbiters of taste at radio and record company.

The benefits to record labels could be the elimination of manufacturing costs and greatly reduced distribution costs.

Labels could theoretically plough this increased profit back into the business. They could offer better advances, better royalty rates and improve their marketing and promotion. If the Internet does turn into the free-for-all that it promises to be, then the battle for the consumer dollar will be fought on the fields of marketing and promotion.

Recent history has shown that when a new technology or format is introduced the record companies use it as an excuse to reduce the artist's and producer's royalties. When CDs first came out, labels wanted to pay only fifty percent royalties in addition to increased packaging deductions. The excuse was increased manufacturing costs. In the beginning they may have had a point. But, instead of an across the board reduction like that, what would have been fairer would have been to pass on any actual increased cost and allow it to decrease naturally as the costs decreased. Today they still try to reduce the royalty from one hundred percent with no justification whatsoever. I fully expect that when the time comes for distribution by wire (or wireless) we will see additional contractual reductions based on the record companies' supposed start-up investment.

## Why Would We Even Need Record Companies Then?

Variety is the spice of life and life would be very boring if everyone made records the same way. There will always be artists who need a bigger canvas and more colours on their palette than they can finance and control from their bedroom computer-based project studio. Not every artist values their artistic freedom so highly. Some would prefer to have a bigger budget and a shot at stardom. They are prepared to trade off a good deal of freedom for help, advice, a large advance and more production and marketing dollars.

The problem with this kind of freedom of distribution and the degree of independence it can bring is that we are already experiencing information overload. Just browsing through the local record store causes my brain to short-circuit. I usually see at least twenty CDs that I would like to check out. Even if I wanted to spend that much money every time I set foot inside a record store, I wouldn't have time to listen to all that music. And, don't forget, this is after 95% of the young hopefuls have been filtered out by A&R departments, radio, TV and MTV programmers. Imagine if you were able to access music directly from the Internet and there was at least twenty, a hundred or a thousand times as much stuff to choose from as there is in your local record store. How could you begin to choose?

One advantage of the Internet is that it is relatively easy to set up preview or audition systems, so at least you can hear the music before you buy it. Just like the old listening booths. (Nowadays listening booths are usually marketing tools for major labels. They pay for their priority artists to be available on the listening posts in major record retailing chains. Any of these marketing techniques tend to bias the charts against the outsider, the newcomer and the unpredictable. Ironically, most major new trends grow out of a movement that was initially regarded as weird, unusual or left of centre.) Virtual agents may soon be able to do the auditioning for you. They will learn about your musical taste from your buying history and go out into the Internet looking for things that might appeal to you.

## Charts

Charts today are primarily marketing tools. There are all kinds of charts, some based on sales, others on airplay. All charts represent a form of feedback which will either serve to reinforce or destroy the initial confidence in a release. Although they can be manipulated by a record company using promotion and marketing techniques, a chart position, or the lack of one, inevitably affects the record company's enthusiasm for a record by creating either a positive or negative feedback loop.

A good showing in a particular chart, whether it be the dance charts, The Hot 100 or radio station, encourages the record company to push more marketing money into the project. Bad figures or, worse, no figures at all, may cause them to abandon their promotion and marketing campaigns unless they are totally committed to breaking that particular record.

Not only will the various charts affect the record company but also the amount of radio play and television exposure a record will get. If stations are playing a record and it does not appear in a chart they will eventually drop it from their play lists even if they previously liked it. Vice versa if a station is not playing a record (assuming it fits their format), seeing it in a major chart or seeing a lot of similar format stations adding the record may well influence the programme director to play it. This obviously reinforces the positive or negative nature of the feedback loop.

The higher up the chart a record goes, the more of a lather the business works up over it. At the moment record companies, radio and TV control the charts. Record company marketing money has a lot of influence on the charts. The Internet could potentially level the playing field a bit. An enterprising artist/computer geek could create, market and distribute entirely from home. The music, of course, would have to be right, the timing perfectly in sync with the development of the Net and the individual(s) would need a multitude of talents.

There are many copyright issues still to be resolved. Obviously you can't allow someone to download an entire album at full bandwidth for a minuscule usage fee. Not only would that person have free use of the music for as long as he liked but currently there is nothing to stop him from making an infinite number of perfect, first generation digital copies.

For whatever reason, the world seems to have latched on to the idea that rock musicians make too much money. Maybe because of this people seem to think it's OK to copy records as many times as they wish. Instead of giving their money to the rightful copyright owner, they'd sooner give it to the blank tape manufacturers (one of whom now owns a major record label).

Take a look at the figures for blank tape sales, then estimate how many of those tapes were used to record talking letters to send home to Aunt Marjorie. If someone invented a machine that would allow you to duplicate a Mercedes Benz for less than half the cost, the duplication machine would be banned before it hit the market place. Counterfeiting money on a colour Xerox is illegal. Somehow the same rules have never applied when it comes to music. Obviously if an artist is highly successful and his personal wealth is in the tens or possibly hundreds of millions, then even if they lose fifty percent of their sales to the various forms of piracy it won't impact their lifestyle.

My concern with piracy is not the effect it has on the super rich. By effectively shifting the wealth from the creators, producers and distributors of the records who are the rightful owners, to the hardware and firmware manufacturers who make the dual cassette decks and blank tapes, we are starving the host and feeding the parasite.

## Will Record Producers Survive The Revolution?

Jazz records are still being made. They represent a smaller proportion of the market than they did in the Thirties, Forties and Fifties. There will in twenty years' time, I'm sure, still be record producers making records in exactly the same way they've been made for the past twenty years. As with jazz, current and past styles of production will continue to be valid alongside newer methods but in order for a producer to survive with any degree of certainty it would be wise for them to broaden their skill base.

To go back to what I said at the beginning, the producer is like the blank cube in Scrabble. He becomes that missing letter, completing the word, whatever the word is that the artist needs to make the winning play. In the future the missing factors may be more than a few engineering, arranging and people skills. In a world where video, graphic and music bits are totally interchangeable, communicated in exactly the same way and through the same channels, the clear dividing line between different disciplines may disappear.

As I said in Chapter One, early recordings were merely captured moments, sonic photographs of events that actually took place. When Les Paul did his first overdubbing or sound-on-sound experiments he took that all important first step, a giant leap away from capturing an event towards artificially synthesising an aural picture. He utilised the recording medium and the studio in a more direct and creative way.

Many artists, engineers and producers have subsequently contributed to the fits and starts development of this process, most notably Phil Spector, The Beach Boys and of course The Beatles and George Martin developing from *Rubber Soul* to *Sgt Pepper.* An artist such as Prince would have been almost unimaginable in the Fifties. It was inconceivable that an artist could have such a spectrum of abilities from composing, to arranging, to performing all or most of the instruments in addition to understanding and controlling the audio production techniques. As with all human endeavour the next generation tends to regard what has already been achieved as the new starting point.

In the same way that recording has become an art form in itself – multi-media could well become an all-in-one conceptualisation for a new type of artist. The past decade has seen the rise in prominence of the movie soundtrack. Movie music is no longer primarily for dramatic reinforcement of the visual action. A carefully put together soundtrack becomes a powerful marketing tool for both the movie and the featured music artists. Video clips feature footage from the movie intercut with the artist's performance. The right soundtrack helps target a specific audience demographic for the movie. The right movie can launch music careers and boost already successful ones. MTV welds music and visuals together in the mind of the viewer. The lines are getting blurred between music and visuals.

It is no accident that Avid, the creators of one of the premier video hard disk editing systems, bought Digidesign, the creators of one of the leading audio hard disk editors. With both audio and video on random access disks it's possible to manipulate visual bits and audio bits together. This allows complete interchangeability in the prioritisation of the music or the visuals. With a little push from less expensive, more widely available technology, we will see some interesting hybrid projects in the very near future. In the not too distant future I believe we will see the emergence of some young, computer literate audio-visual artists who will produce full-blown multimedia works out of their own bedroom-based audio-visual project studio.

Albhy Galuten has moved on from producing and has been concentrating on developing the enhanced CD format which will carry not only full bandwidth, uncompressed audio but also text, graphics, photos and video. He spoke in a recent interview about where he sees things going with the new technology. "As a producer, I learned to listen with my guts and solve problems with my mind. You do a lot of left-right brain shifting. Producers may be well-suited for these new media forms. Artists are usually visceral, and computer people tend to be quite analytical. The ability to make viscerally engaging multimedia 'objects' is going to require the ability to shift back and forth, to communicate. To me it's no different from trying to use a tape loop on a Bee Gees record, or two twenty-four tracks instead of one. Technical innovations can be very stimulating, and I enjoy hanging around at that intersection, working with artists and programmers."

Inevitably, producers will emerge who are equipped to respond to these trends but not everyone will have to deal with multimedia. In the same way that film, television and video have not replaced books, there will always be a need for pure audio. The great thing about music and radio is that you can enjoy it while you are doing other things like driving, working, even reading. Anything with both audio and visual content demands a great deal if not all of your attention. Undoubtedly multi-media with all its ramifications and implications will offer a window of opportunity for the producer with cross-discipline skills or at least enough savvy to be able to put together and manage a team of people with both the technical and creative skills in computing, video, graphics, text and music.

# 14

# *The Final Cut*

Phil Ramone, after a lifetime of working with the legends of the music business, is still not resting on his laurels. "I've always been worried that somebody is going to do it better. There is a competitive side to making great music and finding ways for it to slot better, to sound better, to be heard in a different way than ever before. I'll be honest with you, when you start a new record there is no cushion under your ass."

This kind of attitude is all the more remarkable when you consider all the technological changes that someone like Ramone has had to deal with in the last thirty years. Not only has he dealt with them but he has been in the forefront of the implementation of many of them. He embraced digital audio very early on, picked up on the advantages of the low priced modular digital multi-track machines, and was one of the first people to utilise ISDN to record artists in remote locations.

John Leckie says, "Just be into the music and try not to worry so much about technology. Do whatever it takes, but you have to enjoy the music you're recording. Never stop looking for different kinds of music to work with – there's a tremendous amount of it out there."

Jack Douglas feels that the trick to working with an artist is to let him realise that you're on his side. "I like to work with new artists and new artists have always been suspicious of people that are on the other side of the glass. They feel that in some way or other we're out to get their music and do something to change it. I want to convince an artist that all I want to do is take his music and help him get it on the record so that it is, in fact, what he wanted to begin with. New artists especially get very insecure about their own stuff. If I can keep an artist's confidence up in the early part of building a record, that record is going to work."

There are a handful of producers who get mentioned again and again as influences and sources of inspiration to other producers. A partial list would include George Martin, Quincy Jones, Phil Ramone, Jerry Wexler, Arif Mardin and Tom Dowd. Phil Spector had a relatively short career but in that time he established the idea that the independent record producer could be a creative force in his or her own right. He had such a powerful creative identity that people often refer to the hits he produced as "Phil Spector records" rather than by the names of the artists.

The greatest of the all-time great producers, Quincy Jones, says, "Our whole life is about the blank page: 'What are we going to do, because right now we have nothing!' Ideas are the sustenance of creative life. What's always amazed me is how one person will take the first idea that comes or the second surge of inspiration and say, 'Fine'. Another person will say, 'That's not it yet.' They get to the twenty-seventh layer before they say, 'That's it.' How do you know that?

"I'm the twenty-seventh through the fortieth. I don't know how, but somehow you know, you just say, 'That's it.' But that's a very important decision in creativity.

"I guess the trick is to dream real big. But if you do that, you have to get off of your ass and execute real big! That's the killer. I think our higher power likes our dreams to be very specific. Don't just say, 'Oh God, I wish I was happy.' Give me a break, man! It doesn't have to be like a machine, but I think when you start dreaming and visualising, you've got to be very specific or it won't happen."

Clearly there is no such thing as the average record producer. All you can say about a person who does this successfully for a living is that he or she is "someone who gets the job done and gets it done well", whatever "done well" means. There's zero job security – you're as good as your last couple of projects. Previous and recent success is the most sought-after qualification. Experience is vital but not valued. Good connections are essential – you'll never see an ad for a record producer. Job satisfaction is extremely high. When you finally think you've got it all pinned down, reality intervenes to explain that the only constant is change.